HOW COULD THIS HAPPEN

HOW COULD THIS HAPPEN

EXPLAINING THE HOLOCAUST

DAN McMILLAN

BASIC BOOKS
A Member of the Perseus Books Group
New York

Books published by Basic Books are available at special discounts for bulk purchases in the United States by corporations, institutions, and other organizations. For more information, please contact the Special Markets Department at the Perseus Books Group, 2300 Chestnut Street, Suite 200, Philadelphia, PA 19103, or call (800) 810-4145, ext. 5000, or e-mail special.markets@perseusbooks.com.

Designed by Jack Lenzo

Library of Congress Cataloging-in-Publication Data
McMillan, Dan, Ph.D.
How could this happen : explaining the Holocaust / Dan McMillan.
pages cm
Includes bibliographical references and index.
ISBN 978-0-465-08024-3 (hardcover : alkaline paper)—
ISBN 978-0-465-03664-6 (ebook) 1. Holocaust, Jewish (1939–1945)—
Causes. 2. Germany—Social conditions—1918–1933. 3. Germany—
Social conditions—1933–1945. 4. Germany—Politics and government—
1933–1945. I. Title.
D804.3.M398 2014
940.53'1811—dc23
2013051212

10 9 8 7 6 5 4 3 2 1

CONTENTS

INTRODUCTION

And we dare speak on behalf of our knowledge? We dare say: *"I know?"* . . . Answers: I say there are none.

—Elie Wiesel[1]

Why another book on the Holocaust? Because even the best histories of this catastrophe tell us how it happened, but not why. For each of the most important events of history—for example, the fall of the Roman Empire, the French Revolution, and World War I—there are many books that try to explain why the event occurred. Yet for the Holocaust we seek in vain for a book on its causes. To be sure, most narrative accounts of the Holocaust will touch on anti-Semitism, and some will also examine how Adolf Hitler managed to gain control of Germany. Yet, although Hitler and anti-Semitism were vitally important causes of the Holocaust, they form only part of the story, and not even the largest part. Even worse, the explanation of these causes usually gets lost in the mass of details that make up the narrative, and the frustrated reader finishes the book still having exactly the same question that moved him or her to start reading in the first place: Why did this happen?

It is not enough to narrate the blow-by-blow of events. A reader who wants to know why these events happened needs a book that clearly defines each cause of the Holocaust, explains its historical origins, and clarifies how it combined with the other causes to produce the most terrifying genocide in history. This book provides the first comprehensive analysis of the causes of the Holocaust. This is surprising, given the fact that professional historians understand the causes quite well. Ask any group of specialists, and they can easily produce a list of major factors: Germany's failure to become a democracy until 1918, decades after France, England, and the United States made that transition; the pointless slaughter of World War I, in which 10 million young men lost their lives; the rise to power of Adolf Hitler, without whom the Holocaust would not have happened; the increase in anti-Semitism during the four decades before Hitler took office, and its causes; the rise of "scientific" racism, the widespread belief that major genetic differences between races or nationalities was a scientifically proven fact; and psychological mechanisms that can make it easy for men to kill or allow bystanders to look the other way.

A book like this one should have been written a long time ago. If historians understand the several causes of the Holocaust, why is this book the first to pull all the causes together and explain them in straightforward language? Why have historians hesitated to undertake this vitally necessary task? Some fear that explaining the killers' motives and actions might seem to lessen their guilt. Auschwitz survivor Primo Levi warned against trying to understand the murderers, "because to understand is almost to justify." Yet every murderer acted with free will and had no reason to fear punishment if he refused to commit murder. No explanation can diminish the killers' terrible guilt. Others assume that it honors the victims and does justice to their suffering to say the Holocaust was so terrible that we cannot understand it. The Auschwitz survivor and Nobel laureate Elie Wiesel rebuked scholars who sought to explain the Holocaust: "You are fortunate, I ought to envy you, but I do not. I prefer to stand on the side of the child and the mother who died before they understood the formulas and phraseology which are the basis of your science." People also avoid explaining the Holocaust because it seems uniquely horrifying, and we worry what it may say about us, since people just like us carried out the murders.[2]

The Holocaust frightens people like no other event in history, evoking an instinctive horror and loathing that almost compel us to look away from it. The special horror of the Holocaust may derive from the way the Nazis completely denied the worth of human life. They declared a very large branch of humanity—many millions of Jews worldwide—to be a kind of vermin in human form that they intended to completely exterminate. "With anti-Semitism," said Heinrich Himmler, the chief organizer of the Holocaust, "it is exactly as with delousing. . . . It is a matter of cleanliness. . . . We will soon be completely free of lice." The Jews are the only large ethnic group to have been targeted for complete extinction, a fact that sets the Holocaust apart from all other genocides. Not only did the Nazis set out to murder every Jewish person they could find, but they also reduced them to material objects, processing their bodies for value as if they were animal carcasses: they cut off women's hair to make textiles, tore out teeth to harvest gold fillings, and used Jewish prisoners as laboratory animals.[3]

In the first years after World War II, observers dismissed the murderers as a relatively limited number of born criminals, social misfits, and the mentally unhinged. This comforting illusion soon evaporated, and historians found that the overwhelming majority of killers—who may have numbered as many as 200,000—were perfectly ordinary human beings who did not differ from us in their basic psychological makeup, or at least not until they began their careers as murderers. Even worse, many tens of thousands of murderers, far from being the dregs of German society, instead represented the educated elite: doctors, lawyers, university professors, government officials, military officers of all ranks, owners and managers of large corporations, titled aristocrats, and wealthy landowners.[4]

When normal men and women commit history's most radical assault on human dignity, we face terrible questions. Is every one of us capable of such boundless depravity? If the Nazis could completely deny their victims' humanity, does any human being have inherent worth and an unquestioned right to life? If civilization's fundamental moral standards could lose all of their authority, how can one find meaning and purpose to human existence? If one of the world's most advanced nations could sink this low, what kind of dark and violent future lies in store for humanity?

I first confronted these awful questions as a teenager in the 1970s, when I read a book about the Holocaust, Simon Wiesenthal's *The Murderers Among Us*. To be able to live with such questions, and to maintain the faith in human goodness that has always given meaning to my life, I needed to understand why the Holocaust happened, and what it did or did not say about humankind. This need has shaped the course of my life ever since: I became completely fluent in German, double-majored in history and German in college, spent my junior year at the Freie Universität in West Berlin, and earned a history PhD from Columbia University. I then taught history at universities in New York, New Jersey, and Illinois, read everything I could about the Holocaust, constantly refined my understanding of its causes, and searched relentlessly for ways to explain these causes as clearly and concisely as I could. Throughout, I never lost sight of the central question: What does it mean to be human in the aftermath of the Holocaust?[5]

As I soon realized, the better we understand why the Holocaust happened, the more we can look upon the human race and humanity's future with hope instead of despair. It took a perfect storm of broken people, destructive ideas, unbelievably bad luck, and the bleakest of circumstances to produce history's most frightening catastrophe. In almost every society, several sturdy barriers stand between a people and the perpetration of mass murder. Only a very long and violent chain of events managed to shatter these barriers in Germany. This book should show its readers why the Holocaust happened, and it should put this event in its proper historical perspective: yes, as perhaps the most terrible thing human beings have ever done, but no, not as proof that we are inherently "evil," or that we have made no moral progress during our short time on earth, and certainly not as evidence that humanity's future is anything less than bright and full of promise.

Although everything in this book is consistent with the best scholarship, this is not an academic treatise. This book is for everyone who has ever wondered why the Holocaust happened.

CHAPTER 1

POSING THE QUESTION

This is a glorious page in our history and one that has never been written and can never be written.

—Heinrich Himmler, head of the SS, speaking about the murder of the Jewish people[1]

What was the Holocaust? It was the determined attempt by the German government during World War II, aided by collaborators in most European countries, to murder every single person of Jewish ancestry on the European continent—some 11 million human beings by the Germans' own calculations. If Hitler had won the war, he almost certainly would have tried to destroy every remaining Jewish community on Earth. This goal of complete biological extinction, together with the degree of power the killers exercised over their victims and their complete denial of the victims' humanity, makes the Holocaust unique among all mass killings in history. Partly for this reason, I reserve the term "Holocaust" for the attempted extermination of the Jewish people, explicitly setting it apart from the Nazi regime's murder of millions of Gentiles, including, among others, more than 3 million Soviet prisoners of war; nearly 2 million Poles dead of varied causes under German occupation; as many as 220,000 Roma (Gypsies); many tens of thousands of handicapped patients in German hospitals and asylums; and thousands of homosexual men. Some of these Gentile victims have been named as part of the Holocaust, but doing so makes it hard to grasp the full horror of the Holocaust and spreads confusion about the true causes of all these crimes.[2]

Not only were the Jews the only group targeted for extinction, but in a very real sense they were, in Hitler's mind, the main reason for killing most of these other victims. For Hitler, World War II was a war against the Jewish people, who in his mind controlled the governments of Germany's enemies. In particular, he and his most dedicated followers believed that Jews, operating from Moscow, were responsible for the spread of communism everywhere. Had he not believed in this "Jewish-communist" conspiracy that supposedly threatened Germany, Hitler might have felt no need to start the war in the first place. Ultimately, all of the murders he ordered followed directly or indirectly from his decision to fight his "war against the Jews."[3]

By the late 1920s, Hitler had arrived at a comprehensive worldview, a lens through which he understood history and politics. This drastically simplistic belief system reflected his primitive cast of thought, his fascination with violence, and his burning desire to avenge Germany's defeat in World War I. Hitler embraced a philosophy best characterized as "racial Darwinism." He believed that history was the record of a merciless struggle for survival between the "races" of humanity. Superior races necessarily destroyed inferior races, a process that improved the human species in the same way that the struggle for survival had driven the evolution of primates into human beings.[4]

In this harsh struggle for survival, as Hitler saw it, the Germans, although supposedly the best part of a superior race

("Aryans"), suffered two terrible disadvantages. First, there were not enough of them and they did not have sufficient land and natural resources. Being too small a nation, with inadequate manpower and industrial capacity, the Germans could be crushed by a coalition of enemies, which is exactly how they lost both world wars. Second, the Germans suffered grievous internal divisions, caused mostly by the socialist and communist parties and their Marxist theory of class struggle. Behind these destructive internal divisions, according to Hitler, stood the Jews. Hitler believed that Jews fostered class conflict in order to divide and rule the societies in which they lived.

In Hitler's view, and that of his dedicated followers, the Jews' dangerous qualities were rooted in biology, in their genetic makeup. Their parasitic behavior was not a merely cultural phenomenon, which might be subject to change, but rather the inevitable outgrowth of a biological uniqueness that made them less than human. Therefore, Hitler and his accomplices commonly described Jews as bacteria or vermin to be eradicated by antiseptic methods.

Hitler believed he must take two steps to ensure Germany's survival amid the Darwinian combat of races. First, he had to eliminate the Jews from German society, and second, he had to acquire "living space" (*Lebensraum*) from the Soviet Union. He meant to annex huge swaths of western Russia, drive out or kill the Slavic inhabitants, and populate the territory with German farmers. Germany would gain fertile farmland for its food supply and raw materials for its military industries. Healthy peasant families, given unlimited land on which to prosper, would breed ample numbers of soldiers for the wars of the future. Conquering the Soviet Union would also kill two birds with one stone. Because the Soviet Union was a communist state, in Hitler's eyes that automatically meant it was controlled by Jews. By destroying the Soviet Union, he would eliminate the center of a worldwide "Jewish-communist" conspiracy.

3

Taking power in January 1933, Hitler set out to remove the Jews from German society, although he did not yet plan to murder them. The Nazi regime first aimed to eliminate "Jewish influence" on German society by segregating Jews from Gentiles, excluding them from the professions, government service, and cultural life; robbing them of their citizenship; and confiscating Jewish-owned businesses. This devastating assault on Germany's Jewish community found its most shocking expression in "Crystal Night" (*Kristallnacht*), a nationwide anti-Jewish riot of November 9–10, 1938. Using as a pretext the assassination of a German diplomat by a young Polish Jew, the regime sent instructions to rank-and-file Nazi Party activists all across Germany late on the evening of November 9. The entire country erupted in an orgy of violence. Nazi thugs, aided by thousands of other Germans who spontaneously volunteered, set synagogues afire and smashed the windows of Jewish-owned shops, the broken glass giving this episode its name. At least 91 Jews were murdered, and 25,000 to 30,000 Jewish men were arrested; roughly 20,000 of them were taken to concentration camps, where 400 died of hunger and abuse.[5]

The regime's comprehensive system of segregation and discrimination, inscribed in hundreds of laws and regulations, did much to make the Holocaust possible. By driving Jews from the schools and the workplace, by criminalizing sexual contact between Jews and Gentiles, and by pressuring Gentiles to abandon friendships with Jews, the Nazis completely isolated German Jews and destroyed the social and emotional ties that had bound them to their countrymen. Consequently, by the time the government began deporting German Jews to their deaths in October 1941, they had become strangers to their neighbors. German Jews' isolation helps us understand why tens of millions of Germans, who knew at least something about the killing, seem to have cared little about people who had once been valued coworkers, neighbors, and friends.[6]

The flood of anti-Jewish measures during the 1930s also paved the way to genocide by expanding the Nazi movement's power over German society and moving millions of Germans to compromise their moral and ethical principles. The erosion of principles took place gradually each time the German citizenry accepted a new set of anti-Semitic policies. In every sphere of life, anti-Jewish initiatives destroyed personal and institutional autonomy, with the state establishing its right to dictate even such personal choices as those concerning friendship and romance. The military, the civil service, and the business community abandoned their control over whom to hire, promote, or fire, dismissing their Jewish colleagues at the regime's request. Doctors, lawyers, and university professors, happy to be rid of their many Jewish competitors, agreed to their exclusion from these professions. German professionals thus abandoned the vital principle of meritocracy, a principle that justified the autonomy of these professions and their claim to exalted social status. The learned professions also compromised their intellectual integrity, with doctors affirming the rightness of racial theories and academics working to cleanse their disciplines of "Jewish thinking," an effort that produced such absurdities as the search for a "German physics" and a "German mathematics." Lawyers swiftly abandoned two core principles that had defined their profession: the rule of law and the legal equality of all citizens. The Christian churches, abdicating their proclaimed role as the moral conscience of society, largely shunned their parishioners who had "Jewish blood," even though most of these unfortunates had converted to Christianity long before.[7]

By the time Hitler started World War II in September 1939, his anti-Jewish policies had morally corrupted virtually the entire elite of German society, and tens of millions of other Germans as well, all of whom had accepted the Jews' persecution; many Germans, indeed, had profited from the policies, either by acquiring Jewish-owned businesses at fire-sale prices, or simply by being rid of competitors. Having badly compromised themselves morally, these Germans were psychologically ill-prepared to avoid participating in murder. One problem with making moral compromises is that doing the right thing becomes increasingly difficult: it requires admitting that one's earlier acts were wrong. In effect, to get clean, one must first get dirtier, a step that few proved willing to take.[8]

On the eve of World War II, the Nazi regime's policy was to abuse German Jews so badly that they would feel compelled to emigrate, and hundreds of thousands did manage to get out, although every other country, including the United States, accepted them only grudgingly and with many limitations. After Hitler invaded Poland on September 1, 1939, German policy toward the Jews evolved in 1940 into genocidal plans for expelling Europe's Jews to some kind of reservation, then to mass murder in the spring of 1941, and finally to the complete extermination of European Jewry, a decision taken in the fall of that year. Three factors, more than any others, drove this radicalization of policy.[9]

Probably the most important factor was Hitler himself. Hitler felt a deep and ferocious hatred for the Jews that was rooted in his belief that they had caused Germany's defeat in World War I. Paired with his predilection for extreme violence, this hatred meant that ever since the early 1920s, he had probably had it in him to order the Holocaust, and would happily have done so if circumstances had made it possible. Hitler saw the Jews as Germany's mortal enemies and as the ultimate embodiment of evil. In turn, he saw himself as entrusted with a divine mission to destroy them and thereby become the savior of Germany. Hitler's self-image as a kind of prophet predisposed him to welcome a truly final "solution" to the "Jewish question" as the fulfillment of his historic destiny.[10]

Hitler's subordinates constituted a second radicalizing factor. These men were mostly senior officers of the SS, the paramilitary formation that would later organize and carry out the murder of the Jewish people. They shared Hitler's belief that Jews were less than human, so they were always ready to escalate the regime's violence against the Jewish people. Equally important, these men saw that they could advance their careers by taking the initiative to radicalize policy even without orders from Hitler. This was because the Nazi state had disintegrated by the late 1930s into a kind of administrative anarchy in which multiple agencies competed for control over policy, and the only real source of power was Hitler. Pointing to Hitler's threatening statements about Jews, many of these men tried to further their careers by advocating even greater violence toward Jews than what already had been decreed, in the expectation that Hitler would eventually approve their actions.[11]

Germany's military victories during the first two years of World War II constituted the third radicalizing factor. Each new conquest increased the number of Jews under German control, making a nonviolent solution to the imaginary "Jewish problem" increasingly unattractive to Hitler and his henchmen. After overrunning Poland in the fall of 1939, the Nazis had more than 2 million Jews within their grasp. The earlier policy, of pressuring Jews to emigrate, could no longer solve their "problem": other countries would never agree to the immigration of these millions. This obstacle led Nazi planners to the idea of deporting all Jews to some kind of reservation, initially imagined for eastern Poland. Faced with the difficulty of feeding and resettling large numbers of people, they simply accepted that thousands would die of hunger and neglect. The unexpectedly swift German conquest of Western Europe in the spring of 1940 only compounded the Nazis' self-imposed Jewish problem. Victory brought many more Jews under German control while offering the exhilarating prospect of permanently "solving" their Jewish problem: shipping more than 6 million European Jews to the inhospitable island of Madagascar, where they would necessarily die in enormous numbers.[12]

In one of history's cruelest ironies, a few thousand valiant fighter pilots, by winning the Battle of Britain (fall 1940) and denying the Germans air superiority over the British Isles, may have helped make the Holocaust possible. Unable to invade Britain, the Germans discarded the Madagascar Plan, because British control of the sea lanes made it impossible to ship Europe's Jewish population to the island. Already skeptical about the prospect of invading Britain, Hitler turned now to fulfilling his ultimate goal: invading and destroying the Soviet Union, a goal made all the more urgent because the United States clearly intended to enter the war on Britain's side. Hitler now believed that, to prevent an unwinnable war against the British, the Soviets, and the Americans, the alliance that ultimately crushed Germany under the sheer weight of its manpower and arms production, he must destroy the Soviet Union immediately. Hitler's decision to invade the Soviet Union in 1941 all but sealed the fate of European Jewry.[13]

Attacking the Soviets with the largest invasion force yet seen in history meant a war without mercy against Hitler's imagined Jewish-communist conspiracy and its Moscow headquarters. German civilian and military authorities planned to starve tens of millions of Soviet citizens to death in order to make room for German settlement of their land. The German Army made little provision for the care of prisoners, with the result that 2 million Soviet soldiers starved or froze to death in German captivity by March 1942. Against the backdrop of this titanic bloodshed, Hitler would have seen no reason to spare the Jews, who, by his perverted logic, were responsible for the war he had started. Tens of thousands of men in mobile shooting squads followed closely behind the German troops that invaded on June 22. These men shot Jewish men and boys of military age, a policy enthusiastically welcomed by the German Army and justified by the claim that the Jews, allegedly all communists, would sabotage the German war effort if left alive. However, one may doubt that this "military necessity" excuse was the real motive for the murders: by mid-August, the death squads had expanded their killing to entire Jewish communities, murdering every man, woman, and child.[14]

Conquering the Soviet Union would now let Hitler strike at the entire Jewish population of Europe, making possible a policy radical enough to match his conception of his historic greatness. We will probably never know when Hitler made the decision to murder every Jew in Europe, or his state of mind when he did so. But the best evidence suggests that he crossed this Rubicon in the middle of October 1941, in a state of euphoria prompted by a month of spectacular military victories, triumphs which let him think that his ultimate victory—over the Soviets and the Jews—was at hand. On October 17 Hitler announced to two of his aides that "we are getting rid of the destructive Jews entirely," proudly declaring, "I proceed with these matters ice-cold. I feel myself to be only the executor of history." On October 25, speaking to Heinrich Himmler, chief of the SS, and Himmler's deputy, Reinhard Heydrich, Hitler boasted about the murder of the Jewish people: "We are writing history anew from the racial standpoint."[15]

By the end of 1941, German shooting squads had murdered some 600,000 Jews on the territory of the Soviet Union; roughly 1.5 million would die this way before the war was over. Deciding that murder by shooting was too slow, Hitler's aides began construction, in the fall of 1941, of death camps. Here they would murder their victims with poison gas. Ultimately they established six such extermination centers: Auschwitz and Treblinka are the best known and claimed the largest numbers of lives; the others were Belzec, Chelmno, Majdanek, and Sobibor. Auschwitz and Chelmno lay just inside the newly enlarged borders of Germany, on territory annexed from Poland. The other camps were established in occupied Poland.[16]

The German government had these extermination camps up and running by midsummer of 1942. Having already begun large-scale gassing at Chelmno in December 1941, they now proceeded to comb through all the territory they controlled, gathering up Jews from almost every European country, from Belgium and Holland in the West to the Aegean islands of Greece in the far Southeast. They packed their victims tightly into freight cars, usually without food, water, or toilets, frequently with standing room only, and shipped them along the rails to the killing centers. The dreadful journey could take as long as two weeks, and many perished along the way of thirst, exhaustion, or suffocation. Arriving at Auschwitz, Treblinka, or some other death camp, at any time of day or night, the captives were greeted by shouting SS guards and vicious trained dogs and driven to the entrances of gas chambers. They undressed, at gunpoint if necessary, and were forced into airless, windowless bunkers. Chelmno was the only exception: there the SS murdered their victims in the cargo spaces of large vans, into which the vans' engine exhaust was channeled.[17]

The gas chambers were disguised as showers, complete with fake water pipes and showerheads. The guards promised their victims that they would find paid work in German defense plants, telling them they needed to shower first and have their clothing disinfected. Surrounded by heavily armed men, grasping at any reason for hope, most victims seem to have accepted this explanation and entered the gas chambers without protest. Some Polish Jews, however, sensed that death awaited them: living near the camps gave them information that eluded victims from, say, France or Holland. Often, therefore, the Germans drove Polish Jews to their doom through sheer terror and a massive display of force.[18]

Even those victims who initially accepted the cover story about showers must have soon recognized their mistake: the rooms were packed almost to overflowing, and the SS turned off the lights. At

Auschwitz and Majdanek, the guards dropped crystals of hydrogen cyanide into the frightened throngs in the chambers. This was a commercially produced pesticide named Zyklon-B. The crystals rapidly vaporized, producing a deadly gas. At the other camps, the Germans poisoned their victims with carbon monoxide from truck or tank engines. Squads of Jewish prisoners then had to drag the victims from the gas chambers and feed them into giant crematoria, where the flames consumed their bodies.[19]

Before being sent to their deaths, hundreds of thousands of the Germans' victims survived for a year or longer in ghettos, where the Germans used them as slave labor. Fed a meager diet, packed into overflowing, unsanitary housing, they fought a desperate and losing battle for survival, many suspecting their ultimate fate. Hundreds of thousands more passed through the dozens of work camps erected as satellites of the Auschwitz killing center, or through countless slave labor camps elsewhere. There Jewish prisoners performed hard physical labor in every kind of weather and on a starvation diet, always under a sentence of death. Most survived only a few weeks or months before they died of exhaustion or the guards murdered them because they had become too weak to work. They lived under the watchful eyes of their killers, knowing they were marked for death, trying desperately not to show physical weakness—an impossible task for human beings who were overworked, underfed, and subject to frequent sadistic abuse.[20]

Some 1.1 million human beings are believed to have died at Auschwitz. Treblinka claimed another 925,000 lives, by the most recent estimate. This industrialized killing continued until November 1944, when Himmler called a halt to the gassing and prepared the evacuation and destruction of the camps in a vain effort to conceal his crimes. His plan was to use the surviving victims as hostages in negotiations with Germany's enemies. Tens of thousands of camp survivors died of hunger, exhaustion, or gunshot on

11

"death marches" during the last months of the war as the SS led them westward to concentration camps within Germany, such as Dachau and Bergen-Belsen. In these camps, thousands more, including fifteen-year-old Anne Frank, whose published diary later gained worldwide fame, died of hunger or disease only weeks or days before Allied troops liberated them. Between 5 million and 6 million Jews perished in the Holocaust. The exact tally of victims will never be known.[21]

To the limited extent that other books on the Holocaust explain why it happened, they confine themselves largely to the factors discussed in the foregoing pages: Hitler's racist and anti-Semitic beliefs, which were shared by thousands of the worst killers, and the institutional pressures and wartime context that radicalized Nazi Jewish policy between 1933 and 1942. Yet these elements of an explanation only beg further questions. This book attempts a comprehensive explanation of the Holocaust by answering them: by showing where Hitler's ideas came from and how they could have enjoyed support among so much of Germany's elite; how World War I could have produced a generation of men so hardened to human suffering that they would gladly kill millions in the service of these ideas; how a man like Hitler could come to power in Germany, but would not have had a chance in other Western democracies, such as France or the United States; how Hitler, once in power, could become so admired by his countrymen that many of them would have done whatever he commanded; what psychological factors could have allowed men who were not Nazis to murder defenseless civilians; and how other factors let tens of millions of other Germans who knew about the murders react with cold indifference.[22]

The Holocaust was far from the only mass killing in history. The Turkish government murdered as many as 1.5 million Armenians during World War I; some 1.7 million Cambodians—out of a total population of only 7.9 million—died under the Khmer Rouge regime between 1975 and 1979; and the Rwandan government murdered an estimated 500,000 of its own people in the spring of 1994, in only a hundred days' time. Yet people instinctively place the Holocaust in a class by itself, not only among mass killings, but among all historical events. It inspires in nearly everyone who encounters it a special kind of loathing and horror, even if we cannot say exactly why. Reading about the Holocaust, or seeing a film like *Schindler's List*, seems to paralyze the mind, making it difficult to imagine ever understanding this event. Referring to the creature from Greek mythology whose sight turned men to stone, historian Inga Clendinnen wrote of "the 'Gorgon effect'—the sickening of imagination and curiosity and the draining of the will which afflicts so many of us when we try to look squarely at the persons and processes implicated in the Holocaust."[23]

One can see this unique reaction to the Holocaust in the often heated debate, which has raged for decades among countless experts, over whether the Holocaust was "unique" among genocides. The existence of this debate does not prove that the Holocaust stands in a class by itself, but it does suggest that most of us see it that way. What is more, although the Holocaust was not the first genocide in history, it has become the yardstick for measuring all the others. As a distinguished historian of the Armenian genocide has observed, "every researcher of mass violence other than the Holocaust spent enormous amounts of energy trying to prove that the event they were studying shared similarities with the Holocaust, so as to strengthen the case for genocide."[24]

The most striking sign of the special status we grant the Holocaust is that many distinguished scholars claim or imply that we cannot explain why the Holocaust happened. One leading historian characterized Auschwitz as "incomprehensible"; another, after spending five years writing a major work about the Holocaust, confessed that he didn't understand it any better at the end of the project than he had when he had started his research. Doris Bergen, in the preface to her widely used short history of the Holocaust, listed three questions that her book would not attempt to answer: "Why did such horrible things happen? If there is a God, how could such atrocities have been possible? What are human beings that they can inflict such agony on other people?" Professor Bergen thus put the question "why"—the question this book tries to answer, and which historians have answered about every other major historical event—in the same category as an unanswerable question about the existence and intentions of God. No respected historian has made this claim about the Armenian, Cambodian, or Rwandan genocide, or about any other important historical occurrence.[25]

The most disturbing symptom of the unique effect the Holocaust has on people is the existence of an enormous Holocaust denial industry and the willingness of people in positions of responsibility to claim that this exhaustively documented catastrophe never happened. While the Turkish government continues to deny the reality of the Armenian genocide, and other genocides, including those in the Balkans during the 1990s, have inspired their own denialists, only in the case of the Holocaust can one find vocal deniers all across the world. I can claim little insight into this disgusting phenomenon, which in large part must be motivated by an especially vicious strand of anti-Semitism. But some Holocaust denial may stem from the unique horror the Holocaust inspires and from an unwillingness to accept that people just like us could have done this. I hope that this book, by explaining how something so unimaginable could have happened, might overcome the inability of many to believe that this catastrophe in fact occurred.[26]

What accounts for the special status of the Holocaust when compared to other historical events? If it frightens us in some way that is unique, what is the source of its special horror? How was the Holocaust different?

CHAPTER 2

A GENOCIDE LIKE NO OTHER

If you could lick my heart, it would poison you.

—Itzhak Zuckermann, second in command
of the Warsaw Ghetto uprising[1]

In 1971 the journalist Gitta Sereny conducted a remarkable series of interviews with Franz Stangl, who was then serving a life sentence in a West German prison. In 1942 and 1943, Stangl had served as the commanding officer of two death camps, first at Sobibor and then at Treblinka. There he supervised the murder of hundreds of thousands of Jews with carbon monoxide gas.

Stangl did not see his actions as murder. He referred to his deeds as his "work," insisting that he personally had no prejudice against Jews. Indeed, he claimed to have had "quite friendly relations" with Jewish prisoners in both camps. These prisoners—in the case of Treblinka, a floating population of several hundred—had been granted a temporary stay of execution so that they could serve the SS as slave laborers in the camp. Sereny asked Stangl if he had enjoyed any aspect of his "work." Stangl later circled back to this question, saying "that's what I enjoyed: human relations" (i.e., with prisoners). Stangl mentioned in particular a Treblinka prisoner from Vienna named Blau. "He was the one I talked to the most, he and his wife. . . . I'd made him the cook in the lower camp. He knew I'd help whenever I could."[2]

"There was one day when he knocked at the door of my office about mid-morning and stood to attention and asked permission to speak to me," said Stangl. "He looked very worried." Blau's eighty-year-old father had just arrived on a train from Vienna, and he would die in the gas chambers within the hour. "I said, 'Really, Blau, you must understand, it's impossible. A man of eighty . . .'" Blau's father was too old to work, so Stangl saw no excuse to spare his life.

Blau responded that he understood this. He just did not want his father to die in a gas chamber. He requested permission to take his father to the kitchen, serve him a meal, and then escort him to the so-called Infirmary. Stangl replied: "You go and do what you think best. Officially, I don't know anything, but you can tell the [guard] I said it was all right."[3]

After the elderly man's meal in the kitchen, Blau led his father to the Infirmary, a structure disguised as a medical facility by a large red cross painted on the wall. After parting with his son, the elder Blau would have been escorted down a long corridor by one or two Jewish prisoners who belonged to the camp's "red squad." As he walked, he may not have suspected that anything was amiss. At the end of the corridor, however, he rounded a corner and learned his fate. In front of his eyes lay a pit filled with decomposing corpses. A fire burned steadily in this pit, reducing the bodies to ashes so as to make room for the next round of victims. An SS guard, most likely the sadistic August Miete, directed him to stand on a wooden plank at the edge of the pit. The elder Blau then had to wait for Miete to murder him with a pistol shot to the back of the neck.[4]

Later that day, the younger Blau returned and thanked Stangl several times. Stangl replied: "Well, Blau, there's no need to thank me, but if you want to thank me, you may."[5]

The fate of this man and his father, and Stangl's notion that this event counted among the "human relations" he had enjoyed at Treblinka, say a lot about how the Holocaust differed from the other major genocides of the twentieth century. First, to a far greater degree than in other genocides, the perpetrators of the Holocaust denied their victims' humanity. Stangl regarded his nightmarish transaction with Blau as a normal interaction because he did not think that Blau was really human; thus he felt no guilt—or even discomfort—about killing Blau's father, or about "socializing" with Blau, even though he planned to later murder him along with all the other Jews in the camp. Second, the killers arguably exercised a more extreme degree of power over their victims than human beings have wielded over other human beings at any other time in history. Consequently, the victims of the Holocaust experienced what may have been the most terrible helplessness, degradation, and humiliation ever witnessed. Thus the younger Blau was reduced to thanking Stangl for the "favor" of having his own father murdered by gunshot instead of poison gas.

These differences hardly mean that the Holocaust was in some objective sense worse than the Armenian, Cambodian, or Rwandan genocides. Such a conclusion would hinge on value judgments that are hopelessly subjective: Who can say what kind of suffering is most terrible, which actions are morally most depraved? The Turkish government had tens of thousands of Armenians burned alive and many others drowned on barges sunk in the Black Sea. One could therefore argue that Armenians often suffered more terrible physical pain than did the victims of the Holocaust. Whereas most murders in the Holocaust were carried out in Poland or the Soviet Union, out of sight of most Germans, in Rwanda the killers shamelessly slaughtered their own neighbors—sometimes even their own relatives—in broad daylight with no attempt at secrecy. Perhaps this represented a uniquely terrible breakdown in a society's moral order. Under the Pol Pot regime, more than one-fifth of the Cambodians lost their lives, a higher proportion even than the fraction of Poland's population killed in the Holocaust, although a much lower one than the two-thirds of Europe's Jewish population who perished.[6]

If it makes little sense to claim that the Holocaust was worse than other genocides, the question remains: Why do we see the Holocaust as being somehow unique? I submit that the Holocaust evokes in us a special horror because it represents an implicit death threat against all of us, because it constituted history's most uncompromising assault upon the principle that every human being deserves to live. The Nazis embraced a racist ideology that defined their victims as less than human, as vermin in human form that they must completely eradicate, much as we exterminate rats and cockroaches. In language that finds only limited parallels in other genocides, they routinely described their victims as "bacilli," "microbes," "bacteria," and "vermin." And this way of seeing their victims constituted a central motive for the killings.

Human beings have slaughtered each other repeatedly down through the centuries, but always for some concrete purpose: for political power, out of perceived military necessity, to seize land and riches, or to enforce religious conversion. Only during the Holocaust have we come to murder a huge population solely for the sake of killing them. In other mass murders, targets of the violence could often save themselves by changing their behavior: converting to a new faith, surrendering their land and homes, obeying a new ruler, serving their persecutors as slaves, or taking flight. Even to their tormentors, the lives of these victims still had some value, however minimal.[7]

18

In Hitler's Europe, the lives of Jews had lost all value, and no change in their behavior could save them. Their very birth had condemned them all to death. Conversion to Christianity, a profession of loyalty to Hitler, the surrender of all possessions, or work as slaves—none of these actions could change their fate. Even flight was pointless: in October 1941, the regime banned all further Jewish emigration from German-controlled Europe, having decided to murder each and every one. The Nazis' denial of the value of human life was uncompromising and total.

The Nazis expressed this denial of human beings' worth by making the determined effort to murder every person of Jewish ancestry in Europe, while hoping one day to destroy every Jewish community on Earth. No Jewish population in Europe was small enough to escape the Nazis' notice, whether it was the 700 Jews of Norway, out of a prewar population of roughly 1,600, who were sent to Auschwitz, or the 96 captured in July 1944 on the tiny Greek island of Kos. In July 1942, Heinrich Himmler journeyed to Helsinki to meet with the prime minister of Finland in an attempt to catch about 200 foreign Jews who had found refuge in that country.

The Nazis' striving for complete biological extinction of the Jews has no parallel in history, despite claims to the contrary. Some have argued that the Turkish government aimed to exterminate the country's entire Armenian population, but the facts say otherwise: the killing largely ended in December 1916, leaving hundreds of thousands of Armenians alive, although the murderers remained in power for another two years. Had they wanted to exterminate the Armenians they easily could have done so, but they did not. A strong case can be made that the Rwandan government and the killers at the local level tried to completely wipe out the country's Tutsi minority. However, just as the Young Turk leaders had no plans to murder Armenians outside of Turkey's borders, so, too, did the Hutu government in Kigali harbor no homicidal designs against

Tutsi living in Burundi, Uganda, or other neighboring countries. An obvious rejoinder to this point might be that the Turkish and Rwandan governments lacked the military strength to commit genocide beyond their respective national borders; had they been powerful enough, would they not have done so? Yet the answer to this question is clearly no, further highlighting the uniqueness of the Holocaust.[8]

The Armenian and Rwandan genocides were both perpetrated by governments that faced an imminent loss of power and that resorted to genocide as a desperate, last-ditch measure. Turkey had lost almost all of its European territory in the Balkan War of 1912. In 1914, the major European powers forced Turkey to accept reforms that granted local self-government to Turkey's large Armenian minority, which was heavily concentrated in six provinces of the country's Anatolian heartland. All parties to the agreement understood that it was just the first step toward the creation of an independent Armenian state and the consequent dissolution of Turkey as an independent country. From the fall of 1914 through the spring of 1915, Turkey suffered disastrous military defeats. Fearing their country's imminent disintegration, Turkey's rulers set out to destroy nine-tenths of the Armenian population in an effort to forever thwart the creation of an independent Armenia at Turkey's expense. In Rwanda, the government in Kigali set the genocide in motion because it was losing a civil war against Paul Kagame's invading army of Tutsi exiles, an army that completed its conquest of Rwanda and ended the genocide a hundred days after the murders began. At the local level, the killers were motivated not by ideas of racial superiority, but rather by a fear that the Tutsi rebels posed an imminent threat to their own safety. If Turkey had won the Balkan War of 1912, its leaders would have seen no need for genocide. The Hutu leaders of Rwanda, had they been strong enough to threaten their neighbors, would not have resorted to murder, but instead

would have continued to control the Rwandan Tutsi through discrimination, as they had for decades. In other words, they were
acting from weakness rather than from strength. In contrast, the
organizers of the Holocaust acted from strength rather than from
weakness. The Nazis acted against victims who posed no plausible
threat, and not in a mood of fear and desperation, but rather in one
of exhilaration and joy.[9]

The perpetrators of the Holocaust expressed their ideological
conviction that Jews were subhuman in several other ways. First,
they reduced their victims to the status of material objects, processing them for value as if they were animal carcasses. The SS began
the process by systematically plundering Jews of their possessions:
cash, jewelry, and flatware; pocket watches and wrist watches;
fountain pens and cigarette cases; sheets, quilts, and blankets; cam-
eras and binoculars; mirrors, cosmetics, and baby carriages; eye-
glasses, toothbrushes, and false teeth; and anything else of value.
The Jews had to surrender even their clothes, forced to strip in front
of strangers of both sexes, before they died in the gas chambers or
shooting pits.[10]

But theft of their possessions was only the first step in this dehumanizing process. When Jews arrived at Auschwitz, SS doctors
quickly assessed each prisoner's physical condition. If the camp
needed a fresh supply of slave labor, the SS chose some young and
robust prisoners for this purpose, sending all others directly to their
murder by cyanide gas. Each newly chosen slave received a number
tattooed in blue ink on the left forearm, and this number replaced
the prisoner's name from this point forward. "You are only numbers," a guard told the freshly arrived Julius Ganszer. "A shot, and
the number is gone. Don't try to escape; the only way out of here is
by the chimney." The SS then put their slaves on a starvation diet
and systematically worked them to death, using them up as one
might any piece of equipment, and replacing them as needed from

the cattle cars full of Jews that arrived on an almost daily basis. While they still lived, Jewish prisoners might also find themselves used as laboratory animals in experiments conducted by the Auschwitz doctors.[11]

Whether they killed them at once or first used them as slaves, the SS always found uses for Jews' bodies. They sheared off women's hair to make industrial felt and other textiles; by February 1943, they had harvested more than 6,500 pounds of it. The SS pulled victims' teeth that had gold fillings and collected Jews' skulls and skeletons for anthropological research. For decades it was widely believed that the Germans rendered their victims' body fat in the crematoria, using it to manufacture soap. There is no truth to this legend, yet it shows that people intuitively grasp the radically dehumanizing nature of the Holocaust. This myth also makes sense: if the SS had found a profitable method for making soap from body fat, they would not have hesitated to do it.[12]

Looking forward to a world in which the Jewish "race" was extinct, the German government gathered artifacts and documentation of Jewish life for a Jewish Central Museum in Prague. Racial anthropologists panicked in late 1941, fearing that their "material" (i.e., Jews) might be killed before the researchers could photograph them. "If we wait too long," wrote Dr. Dora Maria Kahlich, "valuable material could escape us; mainly our material could be torn out of its family background and of its habitual environment." Kahlich and a colleague raced to German-occupied Tarnow to photograph Orthodox Jews and measure their bodies. Since some of these human "objects" resisted, Kahlich called on the German Security Police for their "kind" help in securing cooperation from this "material." Treblinka survivor Jacob Wiernik recalled the day Germans and Ukrainians put him and his family on a train to the death camp: "They photographed us as though we were animals from before the Flood."[13]

Committed to a racist ideology that defined Jews as vermin in human form, the German forces treated them as objects while they lived and after they died. Their faith in this racist belief system was so strong that they also lived, with no apparent discomfort, among men and women whom they had all condemned to death, sometimes for years. This may explain the attitude of Franz Stangl, the Treblinka commandant who fondly recalled his "human relations" with Blau and other prisoners.

In death camps and slave labor camps, hundreds of thousands of Jews lived side by side with the men and women who planned to kill them all, a kind of gigantic Death Row in which prisoners and guards mingled on a daily basis. The only counterpart to this remarkable phenomenon in other genocides might have been the Khmer Rouge's disastrous agricultural projects, where hundreds of thousands of Cambodians perished, mostly of starvation, but often by outright murder. Yet the differences outweigh the similarities: few of the Cambodian victims were condemned to death at the outset, whereas every Jewish prisoner, without exception, would inevitably be murdered, and both victims and killers understood this awful truth.[14]

The perpetrators of the Holocaust seemed to feel little, if any, discomfort in the company of their victims, and from their point of view, why should they? As they saw it, although Jews wore a human face, spoke a human language, and had a human intelligence and human feelings—all of which made it possible to interact with them in a superficially "normal" fashion—nonetheless they were not, according to the Nazi belief system, truly human, and could therefore be murdered without compunction, and often without anger. More than one witness testified that Franz Stangl never personally abused a prisoner. Sobibor survivor Stanislaw Smajzner stated that he "never saw Stangl hurt anyone. . . . What was special about him was his arrogance. And his obvious pleasure in his work and his situation." Other SS at Sobibor did not seem as contented in their work, although they behaved worse than Stangl did in other ways. Stangl "had this perpetual smile on his face. . . . No, I don't think it was a nervous smile; it was just that he was happy," said Smajzner.[15]

Most of the hundreds of thousands of Jewish camp prisoners performed unskilled physical labor and soon perished from exhaustion and hunger. Prisoners with special skills, however, could often work indoors at less strenuous tasks, draw more ample rations, or acquire valuables that they could trade for food. Such prisoners might survive for a year or more, and their work often brought them into frequent contact with the Germans in the camps. For some Germans, these Jews were professional peers with whom they shared advanced education or special skills. The infamous Auschwitz doctor Josef Mengele worked with several Jewish doctors as he performed his cruel experiments on prisoners. An SS colonel, Dr. Joachim Caesar, who ran the Auschwitz agricultural experiments, employed several academically trained Jewish women, who "were placed under 'historical monument' protection," in the words of the camp's commandant, Rudolf Höss. In Höss's view, Caesar treated these women "almost as colleagues." Höss complained that this practice impaired discipline, and observed that "when the necessary punishments were carried out, Caesar took it very personally."[16]

A larger number of Jews provided all manner of personal services to the SS and other Germans, mostly in the camps, but sometimes for the shooting units in the towns where they were based. Many, especially women and girls, were used as domestic servants. "Hermann G.," who helped shoot Jews into mass graves behind the lines on the Eastern Front, wrote home on July 7, 1941: "We don't need to do anything anymore. H.F. and I have a Jew and, each of us, a Jewess. . . . They do for us everything we want and are at our service. . . . The Jews are fair game. Everybody can snatch any of them on the street and keep them." He concluded that "one can only give well-meant advice to the Jews: Do not bring children into the world; they have no future anymore."[17]

In the camps the SS frequently used prisoners for entertainment. In Auschwitz, Belzec, Sobibor, and Treblinka, Jewish musicians played in ensembles or orchestras. Sometimes the music was used to soothe the victims as they entered the gas chambers; at other times, in concerts for the enjoyment of the SS. In Treblinka the orchestra played during the evening roll call, during which weak and ailing prisoners were culled from the ranks and taken to the Infirmary to be shot. Stangl's Treblinka deputy, Kurt Franz, also organized regular boxing matches between prisoners for the amusement of his comrades. All the other prisoners were forced to watch, and the prisoner orchestra and choir opened the "entertainment."[18]

Many SS adopted this or that prisoner as a kind of mascot, and the prisoner then often received special privileges. At Chelmno the Germans had thirteen-year-old Simon Srebnik stand in a boat on the Narew River and sing to them. Simon sang sentimental airs and Prussian marching songs while the SS supervised the unloading of gas vans and the burning of bodies. In the winter of 1942–1943, the celebrated conductor Artur Gold arrived on a train from Warsaw, and was plucked at the last moment from a crowd of naked men about to enter the gas chambers. Organizing the camp orchestra on orders from the SS, he became a favorite of the Germans, who fed him special rations and even threw a party for his fortieth birthday. The SS brought drinks and pastries from their kitchen, and the orchestra performed a special repertoire, the musicians dressed in their best clothes. Select prisoners and all the SS were invited. Only in the Holocaust have we witnessed such a grotesque spectacle: murderers and murder victims "celebrating" together in an atmosphere of apparent jollity.[19]

It seems clear that many Germans felt comfortable in their daily interactions with people whom they had condemned to death, just as Franz Stangl did. Some could even enjoy contact with their victims, not out of sadism, but rather out of indifference: they believed these Jews were less than human, hence nothing to get upset over. Murdering them was simply a job. Many SS men, however—perhaps the majority—treated their victims in a flagrantly sadistic manner. Paradoxically, this behavior may have reflected some residual belief in their victims' humanity. Seeing them as human could have aroused anger at Jews, because it would force the SS to see themselves as murderers. In most cases we will never know, since the killers have left so few diaries, letters, or other documents that might illuminate their state of mind. Still, the few surviving sources indicate that many were fully comfortable with their actions and even enjoyed their style of life in the death camps.[20]

By bringing their wives or mistresses to the scene of their crimes, the killers displayed an unforced acceptance of their own actions, an acceptance perhaps made easier by their denial of their victims' humanity. Every summer, hundreds of wives and girlfriends would visit their men of the SS in Auschwitz, often staying for weeks at a time. Auschwitz commandant Rudolf Höss lived in the camp with his wife and children; his fifth child was born there. Felix Landau, who helped lead a shooting squad in Ukraine in 1941, strove mightily to get his mistress transferred out to his base of operations. Captain Julius Wohlauf, who directed a shooting unit, brought his pregnant wife out to his base in Poland for their honeymoon. On August 25, 1942, she sat beside him as his men rounded up several thousand Jews in Miedzyrzec and crammed them into trains headed for Treblinka. His men deported roughly 10,000 Miedzyrzec Jews in the course of two days and acted with extraordinary brutality, shooting dead nearly 1,000 who were too frail to travel or who did not comply quickly enough with their orders.[21]

A medical doctor and SS officer, Johannes Paul Kremer, illus-trates the killers' emotional detachment from their victims. Kremer served as a medical officer in Auschwitz from the end of August 1942 until mid-November of that year. His detailed diary devotes a comparable amount of space to mass murder by cyanide and the pleasures of Auschwitz social life. On September 9 he hears that his divorce is final: "I can now see life in all its colors again. A black curtain has risen from my life! Was later present as the doctor at corporal punishment of eight prisoners and an execution with small-bore rifle." Kremer happily records the receipt of some soap, right along with his fourth gassing. The diary continues for weeks in this vein, moving between routine medical issues, Kremer's own medical research, mass murder, and the fine meals and cultural en-tertainments he enjoyed in the camp. On September 23 he records his sixth and seventh gassings and a festive dinner in honor of a visiting SS general: "There was baked pike, as much as you wanted, real ground coffee, excellent beer and open sandwiches."[22]

Kremer most fully revealed his emotional detachment from his victims when he testified after the war, at his trial in Poland, about his medical research in Auschwitz. He had wanted to study the effects of starvation on the human body by taking live tissue samples from badly malnourished prisoners. He found his subjects in the Auschwitz Infirmary, prisoners who would be sent to the gas chambers because they could not regain their ability to perform slave labor. After Kremer selected a prisoner, an orderly would put this "patient" onto a dissection table. "I would go up to the table," Kremer testified, "and ask the patient to give me some details essen-tial for my research." Superficially this interaction resembled a con-versation between patient and doctor. How much had the patient weighed before his "detention"? How much weight had he lost in Auschwitz? Was he taking any medication? Once Kremer had gath-ered this information, a medical orderly would kill the "patient" with a poisonous injection. Kremer then took tissue samples from the victim's liver, spleen, and pancreas. In his diary he mentioned doing this on five occasions during the two and a half months he stayed at Auschwitz.[23]

Kremer's "research" offers a harsh illustration of how thoroughly the perpetrators denied their victim's humanity: he viewed these prisoners as nothing more than sources of tissue samples, and he conversed with them—at least in his own telling—calmly and with little affect. He probably was comfortable in these conversations, judging from the diary entries that record his actions as routine.

Among Holocaust survivors, none have shed a more penetrating light on the killers than the Italian Primo Levi. A trained chemist, Levi was spared the gas chambers so that he could assist German engineers at a synthetic rubber plant that had been built with slave labor at Auschwitz. His life hung in the balance as he entered the office of a Dr. Pannwitz, who would test his knowledge of chemistry. If Levi passed the test, he could avoid the hard physical labor that killed most prisoners and go on to work in the shelter of the plant's laboratory. With bated breath he entered Pannwitz's office, took a seat in front of the German's desk, and waited. "When he finished writing, he raised his eyes and looked at me," said Levi.

Levi wrote that he hoped someday to see Pannwitz again, not to take revenge upon him, but "merely from a curiosity about the human soul." He was curious "because that look was not one between two men; and if I had known how completely to explain the nature of that look, which came as if across the glass window of an aquarium between two beings who live in different worlds, I would also have explained the great insanity of [Nazi] Germany."

"One felt in that moment, in an immediate manner, what we all thought and said of the Germans. The brain which governed those blue eyes and those manicured hands said: 'This something in front of me belongs to a species which it is obviously opportune to suppress. In this particular case, one has to first make sure that it does not contain some utilizable element.'"[24]

Many of the leading perpetrators of the Holocaust—men such as Franz Stangl, Rudolf Höss, or Adolf Eichmann—later insisted that they harbored no personal feelings of animosity toward their victims, that they did not hate Jews. While such claims strain credulity, it may be true that the emotion of hatred played only a small role in driving their murderous actions. After all, they would have said, what is the point in hating a virus? For that is exactly what they thought they saw when they looked at a human being of Jewish ancestry: a dangerous microbe or insect pest that only appeared to be human. Today people marvel at what they imagine to have been a boundless hatred that fueled the Holocaust. Yet the truth was often something far more frightening: not hot, passionate hatred, but rather indifference so cold that mass murder provoked no more emotion than the disgust one feels when stepping on a beetle.

The Holocaust differed from other genocides in another important respect as well: the degree of power the killers exercised over their victims. In other mass slaughters, power usually has been limited to the brief moment in which the killer took the victim's life. In the Holocaust, because the Germans stayed among their Jewish victims for extended periods of time, their power was not just briefly used, but rather *lived*, hour by hour, day by day, month by month, year by year. And this power assumed forms and dimensions that can only be characterized as grotesque.[25]

The killers' central power, and the basis of all other power, was their absolute control over life and death. In the camps, the SS exercised this power most obviously in "selection": that ritual in which they assigned some Jews to slave labor, and the remainder—usually the great majority—to the gas chambers. Prisoners faced their first and most important selection when they tumbled out of the densely packed cattle cars that had brought them to a death camp. Disoriented and exhausted from an arduous journey, very few understood what came next. At Belzec, Chelmno, Sobibor, and Treblinka—all pure extermination camps with no large slave-labor population attached—the SS took at most a handful of Jews from the mass of prisoners. The rest went directly to the gas chambers. From Auschwitz, in contrast, the SS provided the slave labor for a large network of satellite camps, a workforce consisting of more than 100,000 Jews. Overwork and malnutrition steadily consumed the lives of these prisoners, so the SS chose a large fraction of the captives from each trainload to replenish this workforce. According to Auschwitz commandant Rudolf Höss, the SS selected, on average, 25 to 30 percent of new arrivals for slave labor. The rest of the incoming prisoners met their deaths in the gas chambers within a few short hours.[26]

SS medical doctors, including the notorious Josef Mengele, stood at the railway siding and made the selection. Guards would form the prisoners into a line that would file past the doctor, who would simply motion each one to his right or his left, one side for murder by poison gas, the other side for slave labor. Robust men between the ages of eighteen and thirty-five had the best survival chances, as they would have the longest useful life as slaves. Healthy young women might also avoid the gas chambers for the moment, provided they had no children with them. The SS concluded that separating children from their mothers caused too much disruption during selection. Since all children younger than sixteen or thereabouts went to the gas chambers, the SS sent their mothers with them to avoid disorder at the rail siding. The aged, the infirm, the sick, the children and their mothers—all were condemned to die within hours. And this selection was only the first.[27]

Few prisoners understood the meaning of the first selection until they arrived in their barracks, where experienced prisoners would tell them why heavy smoke was always belching from the crematorium chimneys. At this point they learned that their loved ones, who had arrived with them on the train, had all been reduced to ash. Now they understood that their own lives were forfeit should they ever displease their Nazi masters, and the foundation for the Germans' power was firmly laid. Gerhard Erren, an administrator of occupied territory, made this point with brutal clarity in a January 1942 report. The SS had shot several thousand Jews in his district the preceding November, and he had put the remaining 7,000 Jews to work for the Germans. "They are working willingly," he wrote, "because of the constant fear of death. Early next year they will be rigorously checked and sorted for a further reduction." In the camps, such "further reduction" took place on an almost daily basis, repeatedly underscoring the Germans' total domination.[28]

When Auschwitz prisoners became weak from overwork and grew emaciated on their limited rations, guards would cull them and send them on to the gas chambers, which they had to enter fully knowing their fate. At Treblinka, Kurt Franz frequently staged selections at the evening roll call as the camp's prisoners stood at attention and were forced to watch. Prisoners who had broken camp rules, or whose physical vigor had become suspect, had to engage in "sport": running in circles, then dropping to the ground on command, then getting up to run again until at least some of them had collapsed from exhaustion. Those who failed to complete the sport were taken straightaway to the Infirmary and shot, to be replaced by healthy young men from the next trainload.[29]

Selection established the Germans' absolute power, and thereafter the guards lived among their victims with no fear of retaliation. Only on a few occasions did the victims rise in armed rebellion against the Germans: in the Warsaw and Bialystok ghettos and in prisoner uprisings at Auschwitz, Sobibor, and Treblinka. In the years since 1945, countless people have asked why Jews did not lash out more often at their tormentors, since they knew their own deaths were all but certain anyway. The answer is collective punishment: an individual act of rebellion would provoke the deaths of many other prisoners. At Treblinka, an Argentinian citizen who had been stranded in Warsaw, Meir Berliner, stabbed an SS man to death. In retaliation the guards shot ten men on the spot, then shot another 150 the following morning. Although any prisoner's chances of surviving a camp were extremely slim, open rebellion meant certain death, not only for the rebel but for hundreds of others as well.

Moving easily and comfortably among the condemned, the SS used them for numerous personal services: as maids, cooks, tailors, bootblacks, barbers, even doctors and dentists. Most remarkable of all, some had themselves shaved by Jewish barbers. Consider for a moment how shocking a scene this is. A murderer lets his victim, a man he has condemned to death and whom he inevitably will kill, hold a straight razor to his throat, relaxing in a barber's chair as the blade glides over his carotid artery. He is so fully in command of the situation, so confident in his absolute domination of this man whom he has compelled to serve him, that he prefers being shaved by his victim to shaving himself.[30]

Perhaps the ultimate expression of the killers' unlimited power was forcing Jewish prisoners to assist in the murder of their own people, including their families and friends. At Treblinka these prisoners were assigned to one of several established work details. Forty to fifty prisoners with blue armbands stood on the platform when the death trains arrived, removing the bodies of those who had died during the journey. Working in teams of two or three to a freight car, they cleaned the cars and removed any trace of the victims; the whole train had to be cleaned within fifteen minutes. About forty other workers, wearing red armbands, helped victims undress, then took the victims' clothing and luggage to a storage area. Those who were too weak to make the walk uphill to the gas chambers were carried into the Infirmary, where they were shot. Once undressed, the women went to the "Gold Jews," a squad of nearly twenty men, most of them former jewelers or bank clerks, to surrender their valuables. While the SS harried the naked men uphill to the gas chambers, the women entered the haircutting bar- racks, where a detail of sixteen or seventeen professional barbers awaited them. Working quickly with shears, the barbers removed the bulk of each woman's hair so that the Germans could use it to make textiles. This "haircut" typically lasted a minute or two.

Driven about a hundred yards to the gas chambers, the men died first, the women second. After murdering a batch of prison- ers, the SS turned their bodies over to several other prisoner teams. About a dozen men removed the bodies from the chambers and laid them on a concrete platform, from which the much larger "Body-Transport Detail"—about a hundred strong—carried the bodies away to burial ditches, and after a later date to a huge metal grill, atop which the bodies would be burned. Another team cleaned the gas chambers, while the twenty to thirty "dentists" yanked gold teeth from the corpses using pliers.[31]

Using Jewish labor to run the death factories allowed the SS to kill effortlessly, without having to witness violent death, and spared them unpleasant contact with the corpses. The victims removed their clothes on instructions that were often transmitted by Jewish prisoners who spoke the victims' language. The doomed Jews were told the soothing cover story that they needed to take a shower that would remove lice and disinfect them. Many victims had doubts at this point, but they had little choice but to obey, and who could imagine the reality of the gas chambers, unprecedented in history? So they walked into those windowless bunkers under their own power and died in the darkness, their death throes hidden from their killers. A single guard at Treblinka could extinguish more than 2,000 lives with no more effort than that needed to throw a switch, thereby starting a panel of engines that pumped carbon monoxide into a row of six chambers.[32]

As the death factories proceeded with their bloody work, some Jewish communities in German-occupied Eastern Europe clung to life, hoping to survive by making themselves useful to the German war economy. The German authorities confined them to badly overcrowded, unsanitary ghettos and appointed councils of Jewish elders to govern these ghettos for the Germans. While employment in war industries gave tens of thousands a temporary reprieve, the SS exerted constant pressure on the Jewish councils, demanding that those unable to work be surrendered for "resettlement," that is, shooting or murder in a death camp. Sometimes the ghetto elders knew the true fate of those who were "deported." Others had been warned but could not believe fantastical-sounding stories of mass murder by poison gas. Others lacked any concrete information, but even they had every ground for terrible doubts about the Germans' intentions.[33]

On a regular basis, the SS would demand that the ghetto authorities surrender some fixed number of residents for "resettlement"—1,000, or 2,000, sometimes 5,000 or more, as when the SS sent the bulk of the Warsaw ghetto to Treblinka from July 23 to September 21, 1942. Each time, the Jewish councils would have to draw up the lists of residents who would be deported, a task that caused them terrible anguish and which prompted Adam Czerniakow, leader of the Warsaw ghetto, to kill himself on the eve of the first deportation. At the beginning of September 1942, the German authorities informed Mordechai Chaim Rumkowski, the ghetto elder of Lodz, that he would have to surrender all adults over the age of sixty-five and all children under the age of ten. They were to be "resettled" to work camps, a cover story that made little sense: how could small children and the elderly work in war production? On

September 4, Rumkowski announced the Germans' decision, standing before the ghetto residents as a "broken Jew," in his words. "In my old age I must stretch out my hands and beg: Brothers and sisters, hand them to me, give me your children!"[34]

In death camps Jewish prisoners sometimes had to participate in killing. Shlomo Venezia, a Jewish Italian who had lived in Greece before the German occupation, worked in the "special squad" of Crematorium III, one of the Auschwitz gas chambers. Venezia and other members of this work detail had to convince the victims that the gas chamber was a shower bath, gather their clothing and possessions after they entered the death chamber, and feed their bodies into the crematorium once they had been murdered. At Crematorium III, the cyanide crystals were poured into the chamber through an opening high on the side of the building. A heavy cover closed this opening, so two prisoners had to lift this cover for an SS man, who poured the cyanide into the crowd of terrified victims.[35]

Some people arrived at Auschwitz too frail to walk to the gas chambers. When these victims were brought to Crematorium III, Venezia and his colleagues would have to help them undress, then walk them around a corner, propping them up, so that an SS man could step up behind them and shoot them in the back of the neck. "For us, this was by far the most difficult task to accomplish," said Venezia. "There couldn't be anything harder than taking people to their deaths and holding them while they were executed." Members of the so-called red squad (or "burial society") at Treblinka faced this horror on a daily basis, carrying or escorting prisoners down the corridors of the Infirmary to the burial pit where their executioner awaited them, although the sources do not say they held victims while they were shot.[36]

At the death camps many Jewish prisoners had contact with the trainloads of victims immediately before they were gassed.

Often they had to help the SS persuade these unfortunates that the death chambers were actually showers, and that they would not be harmed. At other times their participation was limited to avoiding the victims' questions, not telling them their fate. Two considerations above all compelled prisoners to act this way. First, if they warned the victims, their own lives were forfeit. Second, the victims were now trapped, locked inside a death camp and surrounded by heavily armed killers. There was no point in frightening them before they entered the gas chambers: they would be terrified soon enough, and the outcome was the same either way. Venezia told of how, as people undressed to enter the gas chambers, he tried to diminish the victims' suffering by "helping out so that everything would happen as calmly as possible." He added: "I don't know whether we can call it 'collaboration' when we were trying to reduce, to however small a degree, the suffering of people who were about to die." If people took too much time to undress, the SS would beat them. In helping the frail and the frightened remove their clothing, Venezia was striving to prevent this.[37]

The frequent encounters with the doomed victims put the Jewish camp personnel in a terrible position. Many avoided eye contact with the condemned and pretended not to have heard their searching questions. Sometimes, however, they could not escape a confrontation with those who soon would die. Abraham Bomba, a professional barber from Czestochowa, survived Treblinka because the SS needed him to cut off the women's hair at their last stop before the gas chambers. He had to cut their hair short, since the Germans wanted as much as they could get, but not so short that it would upset and frighten them: "We just cut their hair and made them believe they were getting a nice haircut," said Bomba. One day a group of women came in from his native Czestochowa. "I knew a lot of them," he said. "I knew them; I lived with them in my town. I lived with them in my street, and some of them were my

36

close friends. And when they saw me, they started asking me, Abe this and Abe that—'What's going to happen to us?' What could you tell them? What could you tell?"[38]

On another day, the wife and sister of one of his fellow barbers came in to be shorn. "They could not tell them this is the last time they stay alive, because behind them was the German Nazis, SS men, and they knew if they said a word, not only the wife and the woman, who were dead already, but also they would share the same thing with them," said Bomba. "But in a way, they tried to do the best for them, with a second longer, a minute longer, just to hug them and kiss them, because they knew they would never see them again."

So that was the full extent of the freedom of action that Abraham Bomba and his comrades had in the haircutting barracks: to linger over a loved one perhaps a minute longer than usual, but no more, and to spare them the terror of death for just a few more minutes.[39]

CHAPTER 3

WHY GERMANY?

They construct shelters and trenches, they repair the damage, they build, they fight, they command, they organize and they kill. What else could they do? They are Germans. This way of behavior is not meditated and deliberate, but follows from their nature and from the destiny they have chosen.

—Auschwitz survivor Primo Levi[1]

Why Germany? Why did Germans, and not some other nation, perpetrate what may have been the most terrible genocide in history? If their crime was unique, does it follow that the Germans were also in some way unique? Can one speak of some distinctive German pathology, some flaw in the "German character"? It is, of course, tempting to see the Holocaust as a distinctively or even uniquely German event: doing so creates an alibi for the rest of humanity and reassures us that such murderous potential does not reside within us. We must resist this temptation.

By and large, historians have rejected notions of a German

pathology. And given the enormous social, economic, and political diversity of German society during the first half of the twentieth century, it makes little sense to talk of national character, to refer to "the Germans," as if they were somehow all alike. Such generalizations make little sense when applied to any country, but they are especially ill-advised when talking about Germany during this period.[2]

One should also remember that although Germans instigated and directed the Holocaust, they found willing accomplices in virtually every European nation. As German troops rolled into Lithuania, local nationalists began murdering Jews with German encouragement. The Germans swiftly co-opted them and used them as auxiliaries in the extermination program. The same pattern repeated itself in Latvia and Ukraine. Over a one-year period beginning in June 1941, the Romanian government murdered between 280,000 and 380,000 Jews on territories under its control. Moreover, Turks murdered as many as 1.5 million Armenians, one Cambodian in five died under the Khmer Rouge reign of terror, and Rwanda's Hutu slaughtered 500,000 of their Tutsi neighbors. There is nothing uniquely German about genocide.[3]

The foregoing caveats notwithstanding, it also seems obvious that a French or British government, for example, could not have perpetrated the Holocaust. What was different about Germany? Germany stood apart in that a man like Adolf Hitler could not have gained mass support in any of the world's other major democracies, yet the Nazis won a full third of the vote in the last free German elections in November 1932. Something had gone badly wrong in the development of German politics. A large fraction of the German people had developed political attitudes and beliefs that were incompatible with democratic government. Combined with a large measure of bad luck, this specifically political dysfunction, and not some vague and global pathology in the German "national character," gave Hitler his opening and made the Holocaust possible. This chapter explains how German politics went so badly off the rails.[4]

Germany's political dysfunction can be traced back to one basic problem: the country did not become a democracy until the revolution of November 1918, in the final days of World War I. German voters' lack of experience with democracy helps to explain why so many of them voted for Hitler's Nazi Party. The failure to achieve democracy gave birth to a second problem: an aggressive, racist nationalism that not only helped to bring about World War I but also prepared millions of Germans to later vote for the Nazis. Indeed, Nazi ideas were mostly just a radicalized version of what German nationalism had been on the eve of World War I.

By the time the war began in 1914, Britain and France had both become stable parliamentary democracies, while Germany remained a semi-authoritarian empire. "Parliamentary democracy" means two things. First, it means that an elected legislature—the parliament—controls the executive branch of government. Members of parliament become the cabinet ministers, and the cabinet can govern only if it is supported by a majority of the members of parliament. Second, it means that the whole adult population, or at least, in historical terms, its male half, gets to vote for the members of parliament. (Women got the vote in most countries only after World War I ended in 1918, and in France not until after World War II.) Why did Germany not make the transition to democracy before the 1918 revolution?

Some argue that Germans, compared to other peoples, have been especially obedient to authority. This alleged inclination to obedience has been offered as an explanation for the behavior of some killers in the Holocaust, or for the delayed advent of democracy in Germany. No one has proved this theory by comparing the Germans to other nations in this regard, however, and a lot of evidence speaks against it. Revolutions in Germany in 1848 and

1918, and in East Germany in 1989, demonstrate that Germans are fully capable of rebelling against authority. Their extraordinarily high level of political engagement since the 1880s—whether measured by the percentage of the population that voted, the numbers who joined political parties, or activism in all manner of voluntary associations and pressure groups—shows a tremendous desire on the part of the German people to assert their will in politics. The stereotype of the obedient German also makes it difficult to understand how Germany could have become the thriving democracy that it is today. Conversely, over the past four decades, a relatively small number of wealthy individuals and a host of special interests have badly damaged democracy in the United States, purchasing influence with donations to politicians' election campaigns. One could argue that most Americans have been robbed of their vote by this flood of campaign cash. Yet no one would claim that the American people have lost their love of freedom or have become especially obedient toward authority.[5]

Rather than looking to an unproved theory and common stereotype of "obedient Germans," one can explain Germany's delayed democratization through more concrete factors. First, making the transition to parliamentary government has been a difficult and often dangerous undertaking for nearly every nation that has attempted it. Second, Germany's economic backwardness until the mid-nineteenth century delayed the country's political development. Third, through no fault of the German people, Germany was created as a unified nation-state in a way that created fearsome obstacles to democracy. Finally, the Germans were too divided against each other by religion, social class, and political partisanship to unite against their hereditary emperor and claim the power to govern themselves.

Most countries that became parliamentary democracies did so in two steps. First, the parliament, elected by only a propertied fraction of the people, wrested control of the executive branch from a hereditary monarch. Then, often in several smaller increments, parliament expanded the suffrage until it included all men, and later all women. Achieving the first step, parliamentary control of the executive branch, often required considerable violence.

England, for instance, made the breakthrough to parliamentary government in the seventeenth century, but only after some sixty years of instability and violence, including two revolutions, the beheading of a king, a bloody civil war, and a military dictatorship. In France, the revolution of 1789 led briefly to a kind of parliamentary democracy, followed by terrifying violence, the execution of a king and queen, a series of dictatorships, an intermittent European war spanning more than two decades, and the restoration of the monarchy, with the transition to parliamentary control occurring only in the nineteenth century. Further instability followed, with revolutions in 1830, 1848, and 1871. Parliamentary democracy found a stable footing in France only toward the end of the 1870s. In the United States, it took a revolution and several years of war against Great Britain to place governmental power in the hands of the people's elected representatives. It then took until 1840 for all white men to get the vote, until 1919 for women to gain the suffrage, and until the 1960s for most African Americans to establish their right to vote. This history should make it clear that Germany's slow progress toward parliamentary government does not mean that the Germans were politically passive or especially obedient to authority. This task has been difficult and dangerous for most nations that have attempted it.

Germany also got a later start toward parliamentary government than its neighbors did, mainly because it developed more slowly economically. Economic backwardness meant that it took German-speaking Europe longer to develop a middle class, including an upper middle class—that is, elites who were of common birth, rather than elites who were members of a hereditary aristocracy. In England, France, and the United States, such middle-class elites played an essential role in the drive toward parliamentary government and in the revolutions this movement helped to produce. It was not until the second decade of the nineteenth century that a critical mass of such elites had developed in Germany. Once this critical mass was in place, they moved forward, establishing a political movement called "Liberalism."[6]

Inspired in part by the ideas of the French Revolution, German liberals demanded a thoroughgoing reform of society and politics. Among their many goals, two took center stage. First, they sought active participation by the people in government. At the end of the Napoleonic Wars in 1815, Germany was fragmented into three dozen major and minor kingdoms, each governed by a hereditary ruler who did not answer to his citizens in any significant way. Liberals demanded the creation of elected parliaments that would share power with the ruling prince or king. They did not call for actual parliamentary control of the executive, that is, for the parliament to take all power away from the hereditary ruler; nevertheless, the power sharing they proposed represented a dramatic change.

The second main liberal goal was the creation of a single German nation-state. In this vision, Germans would no longer be citizens of Prussia, Bavaria, Saxony, or some lesser kingdom, but instead citizens of Germany, a single country for all speakers of German, just as the French had France. National unification was fundamentally a democratic demand, a call for national self-determination, a demand that Germans be governed by Germans. It was also a practical goal: divided into so many small states, the Germans were vulnerable to aggression from neighboring countries, as Napoleon had reminded them by conquering much of German-speaking Europe during the first decade of the nineteenth century.

National unification was a politically explosive demand, because it threatened the authority of every hereditary ruler of a German state. The kings of Bavaria or Saxony, for example, would lose some—maybe even all—of their power to a centralized national government, just as the governments of the separate American states had surrendered much of their authority to the government of the United States that was created in 1789. National unification also threatened the territorial integrity of one of the two most powerful German kingdoms. This was Austria, a multiethnic empire composed not only of several million Germans, but also of millions of Poles, Czechs, Hungarians, Serbs, Croats, and people of other nationalities. Uniting all Germans under one government would mean taking populous and wealthy German-speaking regions from the Austrian Empire so that they could join a unified Germany. Not surprisingly, Austria consistently worked to sabotage efforts toward German national unity. Although the liberal movement grew rapidly during the first half of the nineteenth century, and elected parliaments with limited powers were introduced in many German kingdoms, at the end of the 1850s the cherished goal of national unity seemed as distant as ever.

In the years between 1862 and 1871, German history arrived at a crucial fork in the road, and the unpredictable fortunes of war set the country on the path that led, eventually but not inevitably, to the Holocaust. In 1862 it came to a showdown between the king of Prussia and the liberal majority in the lower house of the Prussian parliament. Although the liberals did not call for parliamentary control over the executive branch, they did demand significantly expanded power for parliament. Crown and liberals had clashed over the parliament's right to help shape military policy. In 1860 the liberals refused to vote a regular budget; elections in December 1861 expanded the liberal majority. The deadlock continued, and in March 1862 the king dissolved parliament and called new elections. The elections, held in May, had the opposite effect to the one King Wilhelm I had intended, giving the liberals three-quarters of the seats in the lower house. Wilhelm seriously considered abdicating the throne.[7]

At this critical juncture, the greatest political genius in modern European history assumed control of the Prussian government. This man was the newly appointed prime minister, Otto von Bismarck. Bismarck took a hard line against the liberals. In flagrant violation of the constitution, he simply spent money without a budget from parliament, and did this for four years running. In the right circumstances, this protracted struggle might have led to a crisis and expanded power for the Prussian parliament. But instead Bismarck won the game by giving liberal voters a prize that their own leaders could not deliver: the unification of Germany.[8]

In a series of three short wars, all ending in complete victory for Prussia, Bismarck maneuvered the rulers of the smaller German states into a position from which they had to join a new German nation-state dominated by Prussia and excluding the German-speaking regions of the Austrian Empire. The turning point during the wars of unification, and in a real sense the hinge of modern German history, came on July 3, 1866, near the town of Sadowa in what today is the Czech Republic. Bismarck had cleverly provoked a war between Prussia and Austria, but Prussia found itself fighting against all of the other major German states as well. Informed observers predicted that Austria would win the war handily. In Paris the betting odds were four to one in Austria's favor. Public opinion in the German states was overwhelmingly hostile toward Prussia, and even more so toward Bismarck, whom they condemned for provoking needless bloodshed.

In the week before the Battle of Sadowa, the two Prussian armies were separated and in poor communication with each other, and both were quite confused about the location and intentions of the Austrian forces. On July 3, the commander of the Prussian First Army, without informing his commander in chief, launched a frontal assault on a large Austrian army whose existence he had discovered only the night before. Fortunately for the Prussians, the crown prince, leading the Second Army, arrived in time to stabilize the center of the Prussian line and outflank the Austrians on their right, driving the Austrians from the field. Although the Prussians had somewhat better weapons, the outcome of this decisive battle could easily have been different. As a member of the king's entourage said to Bismarck in the late afternoon of July 3, "You are now a great man. But if the crown prince had arrived too late, you would be the greatest scoundrel in the world."[9]

Prussia's swift defeat of France in 1870 let Bismarck finish the process of welding most of German-speaking Europe into a single country. Because he had delivered the long-sought goal of national unification, Bismarck was wildly popular among liberal voters, and indeed among many liberal parliamentary leaders. In a position of great political strength, he compromised with the liberals on many important points, but managed to create a constitution that kept the elected national parliament in a role clearly subordinate to that of the emperor. This outcome was far from inevitable. Had Prussia lost the 1866 war against Austria, Bismarck would have lost his job, the Prussian parliament would have gained power at the expense of the king, and the German Empire might not have been created at all, or could have been created, but without the authoritarian basis upon which Bismarck established it. As it was, the German people had lost the best chance they would have at parliamentary government for many years to come.[10]

Despite this setback for an evolution toward democracy, there was still a chance to reform Bismarck's political system. The national parliament was elected on a democratic suffrage, meaning that all adult males could vote. In turn, the parliament controlled the government's budget. Parliaments in other countries had used this "power of the purse" to gradually wear down the authority of hereditary monarchs until reaching the point where parliament could appoint the cabinet and control the executive branch of government. If the democratically elected parliament in Germany had used its budget authority to gain control of the executive branch, the country would have become a democracy. Why didn't this happen? This question has many answers, but probably the most important is that the parliament was fragmented into five or more major political parties, many of them deeply antagonistic to each other. At no time, from unification to the outbreak of World War I in 1914, was it possible for these warring parties to work together to expand the power of parliament.[11]

The degree of antagonism between Germany's parties was probably the most important difference between Germany's political development and that of France, Britain, and other Western nations. German society and politics fractured deeply along the jagged fault lines of region, religion, social class, and the urban-rural divide. Although no European great power had a culturally or socioeconomically homogeneous population, the Germans were exceptionally diverse and divided against one another. This was partly because the different German regions had developed over centuries as separate political units. Such divisions also reflected the extraordinarily rapid industrialization of the country after 1850. In consequence, the German Empire had not only the most reactionary and politically entrenched landed aristocracy in Europe, but also the largest and politically most militant socialist working class. Moreover, whereas most European countries were overwhelmingly either Catholic or Protestant, about 65 percent of Germany's population was Protestant and roughly 35 percent Catholic.[12]

Germany's socioeconomic and cultural divisions, in turn, gave rise to five (and then six) mutually antagonistic sociopolitical blocs, each represented by its own party: conservatives, Catholics, liberals, democrats (who were later replaced by left-wing liberals), socialists, and, finally, after 1918, communists. Their contempt for one another was matched only by the depth of the roots that each party struck in distinct segments of German society. Each party drew its support from a well-defined socioeconomic group: liberals, for example, depended on support from the Protestant middle class, while socialists relied on industrial workers. Frequently, each party's social base was geographically segregated from the electorate of the other parties.

Dense networks of social clubs and other organizations anchored voters' loyalty to a party and encouraged them to socialize only with those who shared their political outlook. This was a bit like the way American liberals today watch MSNBC, while conservatives prefer Fox News, only much more all-consuming. For example, an industrial worker who voted for the socialists would live in a working-class neighborhood, belong to a socialist labor union, take his refreshment at a socialist bar, seek recreation in a socialist swimming or gymnastics club, sing political songs in a socialist glee club, and get his news from socialist newspapers. The Catholic Center Party drew similar organizational strength from the numerous institutions connected with the Catholic Church. Making the divisions between political parties even worse, the German parties were very ideological: they offered their members and voters not only specific policies, but also quasi-religious worldviews that sometimes made the parties mutually incomprehensible to each other. For example, the liberals saw themselves as the enlightened agents of human progress; they were resolutely hostile to the Center Party because they saw Catholicism as a bulwark of superstition and backwardness.[13]

Of the antagonisms that separated the German parties, none ran deeper than the opposition between the socialists and everyone else. The socialists were perhaps the most ideological of Germans, deriving all their principles and policies from a single theory.

Sticking closely to arguments presented by Karl Marx, they predicted that competition from large industrial enterprises and department stores would wipe out the bulk of Germany's urban middle class, driving shopkeepers and craftsmen into the ranks of the "proletariat," workers who had nothing left to sell except their own labor. Mechanized agriculture, the socialists reasoned, condemned family-owned farms to the same fate. When this destructive competition had advanced far enough, so Marx had predicted, the proletariat would rise up, overthrow capitalism, and institute what Americans usually call "communism": government ownership of all businesses and centralized economic planning designed to make everyone equal economically. Needless to say, everyone outside the industrial working class lacked enthusiasm for this vision of their future.[14]

From 1878 to 1890, the Imperial Government, with the support of a majority in parliament, repressed the socialist party without entirely banning it. Thus, although socialist clubs were shuttered and their newspapers banned, men could still run for parliament on the socialist ticket. This repression backfired. It only made the party more extreme, convincing its leaders and members that complete opposition to the regime, and greater commitment to Karl Marx's radical vision, was the only way forward. In 1890 the government abandoned its failed policy of repression, and from there the party grew rapidly. Socialist clubs of every kind proliferated, a militant socialist press mushroomed in readership, and the socialist-dominated trade unions progressed rapidly. In elections to the national parliament, the socialists took 19.8 percent of vote in 1890, 27.2 percent in 1898, and 31.7 percent in 1903. In the 1912 elections, the last held before World War I, the socialists polled nearly 35 percent and took more seats in parliament than any other party. From 1890 onward, and ever more urgently after each election, the central problem of German politics was what to do about the socialists.[15]

The profound disunity of the German people had helped to delay the advent of democratic government for nearly fifty years—for how could the German people claim the power to govern themselves when they could agree on so little? And once democracy came, in the incomplete and fragile revolution of 1918, these divisions undermined the new Republic, discredited democracy, and helped open the door to Adolf Hitler in January 1933. The promise of overcoming these divisions constituted a central part of Nazism's appeal for the movement's committed members. It was also a leading theme in the Nazi Party's electoral propaganda.[16]

Although partisan antagonisms blocked the path to parliamentary democracy, the pressure for democracy and greater political participation was enormous, urgent, and growing fast. Germans' unusually high level of participation in politics, when compared to other nations in the last decades before World War I, proves their determination to have a say in how they were governed. The socialists, representing more than a third of the voters, demanded democracy insistently and loudly, while the more leftist of the two liberal parties, representing much of the Protestant middle class, also called for some democratic reforms.

For the elite of German society, most of whom shared the government's hostility to democracy and horror of socialism, this pressure for democracy presented a terrifying problem. They responded by using anti-Semitism and aggressive nationalism as political weapons against democracy and socialism. For reasons of their own, much of the German middle class responded to these dangerous ideas and sometimes expressed them in ways that made even the government uncomfortable. Among a substantial fraction of the German people, the demagogic use of nationalism and anti-Semitism produced anxiety bordering on paranoia, a conviction that they faced fearsome enemies both at home and abroad.

CHAPTER 4

A WORLD OF ENEMIES

What we need is to overcome the conflicts of interest between the different classes and occupations through the
national idea.

—Leading nationalist Heinrich Class, in his
manifesto *If I Were the Emperor* (1912)[1]

Beginning in the late 1880s, German politics became increasingly
nationalistic, and German foreign policy took on an aggressive,
bullying aspect that steadily worsened international tensions. One
source of this militant nationalism might be found in the dilemma
faced by much of the German middle class. On the one hand, these
people actively participated in politics, wanted a say in how they
were governed, and might have welcomed democracy if they could
have counted on people like themselves controlling the government.
But democracy was neither achievable nor even desirable anymore.
Actual democracy—real power for the national parliament—would
also mean power for the dreaded socialists. German elites and men
of the middle class therefore needed a substitute for democracy, an

outlet for their frustrated need for power. I propose that their substitute was an increasingly radical nationalism—an arrogant belief in national superiority and demands for an aggressive foreign policy. If they could not enjoy power and self-respect as voters who chose their own government, they could settle for being citizens of a powerful country and members of a nation that allegedly was racially superior.

This interpretation of German nationalism has the drawback that it is difficult to prove or disprove with documentary evidence. Obviously, no nationalist politician gave speeches saying, "Germany needs overseas colonies so that I will feel better about being powerless here at home." By its nature, this would have been a psychological process of displacing and refocusing painful emotions whose existence was easier to repress than to acknowledge. Such an internal emotional struggle necessarily leaves few traces in history's written records, although there is some indirect and circumstantial evidence. Although many historians may reject this argument, most do agree about another motive that drove the radicalization of German nationalism: the desperate need to undermine the socialist movement.[2]

Nationalist propaganda and an aggressive foreign policy were supposed to weaken the socialist movement in at least three ways. First, industrialists and merchants argued that colonies would expand foreign trade and thereby improve living standards in Germany. A better standard of living would, they hoped, convince workers to accept capitalism and lose interest in the socialist cause. Second, acquiring colonies and otherwise making Germany look like a great power would make the government more popular. Finally, and most importantly for understanding the later rise of Nazism, nationalists and their allies in government hoped to escape social conflict by persuading Germans to forget their differences by uniting against foreign enemies. They also hoped that socialist workers would forget the economic and social-status differences that separated them from the middle class and elites, and focus instead on what they had in common with the other classes, namely their "German blood," often defined by excluding German Jews and claiming that they were an alien nationality.[3]

Starting in the 1880s, more than half a dozen major nationalist pressure groups sprang up in Germany, each with membership in the tens of thousands, all promoting an intensified national pride and demanding that the government expand German power abroad or persecute ethnic minorities at home.[4]

The German Colonial Society was founded in 1887 with the aim of calling on Germany to acquire overseas colonies. The organization, which reached a membership of 39,000, argued that gaining colonies would secure raw materials for German industry and captive markets for German products. The colonialists also claimed that Germany's explosive population growth drove too many Germans into emigration, where their skills and energies were lost to Germany. Instead, or so they imagined, these surplus Germans could settle in colonies and remain part of Germany. These nationalists also wanted colonies for prestige: colonies were status symbols among nations, a sign that a country had become a major power.

The Eastern Borderland Association, founded in 1894, devoted itself to persecuting Germany's Polish minority, which lived mostly in eastern Prussia. By 1900 this pressure group had 54,000 members in roughly 400 local clubs. Prussia had acquired most of its Polish population in the eighteenth century when it had joined Russia and Austria in carving up Poland between them. At the end of the nineteenth century, more than 3 million Poles lived in eastern Prussia. Nationalists feared Poles as a threat to Germany's territorial integrity in the region bordering on Russia: as Poles increasingly embraced their national identity, Germans feared a revival of the Polish nation-state that had been extinguished in the eighteenth century. A restored Poland, which was in fact established after World War I, could only come into being by taking territory from Germany, Russia, and Austria-Hungary. The men of the Eastern Borderland Association wanted nothing less than to completely "Germanize" the Polish minority, to eradicate the Polish language and culture and destroy the Poles' identity as a nationality distinct from the Germans. They hoped to ban the Polish language, even from churches and private clubs, and to reduce most Poles to landless agricultural laborers who could not practice urban occupations. Thus Poles should be forbidden to move into cities, and the government should confiscate Polish-owned farms so that they could be sold to German settlers.

The association energetically spread ideas of Slavic racial inferiority, and the government gave these men a lot of what they demanded. A 1904 law empowered the government to block Polish attempts to purchase land. A 1908 law allowed the state to confiscate Polish farms after compensating the owners. Other laws banned the Polish language in schools, government offices, courtrooms, and some private clubs. These discriminatory policies, and the virulent anti-Slav racism that was used to justify them, paved the way for some of Nazi Germany's greatest crimes during World War II: the lethal mistreatment of Poles in areas under German occupation, and the German Army's murder of more than 3 million Soviet POWs.[5]

The most radical, viciously racist, and intellectually influential pressure group was the Pan-German League, founded in 1891. The Pan-Germans believed in the racial homogeneity of all Germans and in Germans' clear superiority to other "races." They demanded overseas colonies in part to settle a supposed surplus population; in addition, they promoted German settlement in central and southeastern Europe, saying it would anchor Germany's economic domination of that region. The Pan-Germans appointed themselves

advocates for the allegedly abused rights of German minorities else-
where in the world—for example, in Latin America—envisioning a
German protectorate over these minorities, eventually as part of a
German "world empire."[6]

German elites' strategy of using nationalism to fight socialism
was a miserable failure. Undeterred by facts, however, Germany's
ruling class continued to cling to this failed policy. A tragic consequence of this chest-thumping nationalism was World War I. The
war had many causes, but none weighed more heavily than Germany's aggressive foreign policy after Bismarck left office in 1890.
A prime example is Germany's construction of heavy battleships
after 1898, which challenged British naval supremacy and set off
an arms race between the two countries, driving Great Britain into
an informal alliance with France. Germany's interest in acquiring
overseas colonies was also dangerously provocative. Other European powers had acquired most of their colonies long before a unified Germany came into being in 1871. By 1900, almost the entire
world had fallen under the direct or indirect influence of the United
States or of Germany's neighbors, so Germany could usually acquire colonies only at the expense of another country. One consequence was risky diplomatic confrontations, such as the Moroccan
Crisis of 1911, in which the German government foolishly challenged France's established influence in that North African country.

The Moroccan Crisis ended in an embarrassing defeat for the
German government and drew the French, British, and Russians
closer together in their alliance against Germany. In January 1912,
Germany's ruling elites suffered an even more devastating blow: the
socialist party took more than one-third of the vote in the national
elections, becoming Germany's largest party. The Moroccan crisis
and the election of 1912 demonstrated the complete failure of nationalist politics. Germany was surrounded by powerful military
enemies whom she had alienated by her bullying foreign policy.

At home, Germany's ruling elites faced greater pressure for democratic reform than ever before, and a socialist revolution seemed eminently possible. Their backs against the wall, most of these elites dug in their heels against any reform, and many adopted a more radical set of ideas, ideas that foreshadowed the core beliefs of Nazism. Drawing together strands of thought that had been developing on the German Right for over a decade, Heinrich Class articulated these ideas in 1912 in a manifesto entitled *If I Were the Emperor.* Class was chairman of the Pan-German League. His book went through five editions before war broke out in 1914.[7]

Class anticipated all the major elements of Nazi ideology along with much of Hitler's domestic political strategy once he took power in 1933: the hope for a harmonious national community, devoid of class conflict and cemented by strong feelings of national identity; identification of the German nation as a race that was genetically superior to other races; condemnation of the Jews, a supposedly destructive race, for all conflicts between Germans, and promotion of a national community defined by excluding them; rejection of democracy as being destructive of the national community; and belief that a charismatic leader could unite the nation and suppress social conflict by acting as a dictator.

Shortly before the outbreak of war in 1914, Class saw Germany's situation as desperate. He invoked the fall of the Roman Empire, and asked whether Germany, too, would not sink into chaos. "It is not yet too late to save a noble people," Class declared histrionically, "but we cannot delay much longer." Germany's foreign policy position had worsened, and domestic political divisions had intensified. Class worried that the country's leadership lacked the will to make the "brutal decisions" that would be needed to solve these problems.[8]

Of the "brutal decisions" Class demanded, the most important was to take the vote away from the German working class.

Whereas all adult males could vote in national elections, Class wanted to limit the suffrage to men who paid taxes. As he saw it, universal male suffrage silenced or "disenfranchised" Germany's elites, drowning the voices of society's natural leaders in the chorus of the propertyless and uneducated. Even worse, lower-class voters acted on primitive "mass instincts" and were easily misled by unscrupulous demagogues. Class argued that Jews were entirely responsible for the rise of the socialist party and the labor movement. Using their alleged control of the press, Jews had cleverly manipulated millions of German voters by exploiting their ignorance and appealing to their baser instincts. Thus the constitution would have to be changed to deprive these misled masses of the vote. This change would have to come "at any price," including a coup backed by military force. "Our people is deathly ill," he warned, and compared a coup to a father forcing a sick child to undergo a painful operation.[9]

Further steps would eliminate the harmful influence of Jews and gradually wean the German worker from socialism and bring him back into the harmonious national community. Class wanted to stop all Jewish immigration; deport all Jews who were not citizens; take away Jews' right to vote; bar them from the civil service, the military, the legal profession, school-teaching, and theater; and forbid them to own banks and rural land. Most importantly, any newspaper with Jewish staff had to be clearly identified as a "Jewish newspaper"; the rest of the press would be marked as "German" and would not be allowed to employ Jews. The government should also replace the "poisonous" Jewish press with cheap newspapers, published at state expense, to help "win the masses back to the Fatherland." Continuing to believe the right-wing fantasy that national pride could be a substitute for democracy and social justice, Class advocated frequent patriotic gatherings in which elites would strive for reconciliation between the warring social classes.

"Patriotic festivals for the people" would help accomplish the same end. It would take some years to restore "peace and harmony" between Germany's social classes, "once the virus causing discord has been eliminated."[10]

By "virus," Class meant Jews, and they were absolutely central to his thinking. Just as Germany's elites had tried to unite the country against foreign enemies, now the Jews would serve as a treacherous enemy against whom the nation could rally. By invoking the Jews' alleged "nature," Class marked the transition on the German Right to the specifically racist, biological anti-Semitism that would later inspire Hitler to seek the complete extinction of the Jewish people. Jews, it was now believed, could never be persuaded or forced to act in a manner less harmful to Germany. Their genetic makeup determined their destructive behavior, and they were unable to change it. Therefore, Germany had to eliminate them, whether by harsh discrimination, as Class proposed, or by outright murder, as Hitler ultimately decided. Class argued that thousands of Jews automatically acted in the same destructive way, according to their nature. The Jews were a race, he insisted, and "the race is the source of the dangers." Throughout, Class described the Jewish people in the language of medicine and hygiene, as "the ferment of decomposition" sickening the body politic, so that if action were not taken soon, "no doctor can help anymore." He complained that the authorities allowed "these strangers to corrupt and poison our people," and had no doubt that "wherever sickness shows itself in the body of our nation, we find Jews who foster and nurture it."[11]

Class believed that many elites did see the danger and were ready to take "decisive action." To inspire their efforts, they needed only a charismatic leader to rise up and guide them: "If today the Leader arises, he will wonder at how many loyal followers he has—and what valuable and selfless men rally to him." Class described this indispensable man using the same word that became

Adolf Hitler's title: the Leader (*Führer*). "If salvation does not come soon," Class warned, "then we will fall into chaos." Only a great "Leader of the Germans" could save the day, a man who would impose Class's "reforms" at the point of a gun if need be, including taking the vote away from millions of working-class Germans.[12]

Class looked to Otto von Bismarck, founder of the German Empire, as the model for the charismatic leader. Bismarck's extraordinary popularity and outstanding role in German politics helps explain why so many German opponents of democracy hoped that a charismatic leader would solve their problems. However, Bismarck's precedent was probably not the most important reason why Class and countless other right-wingers longed for a mighty Leader. "Charisma" comes only partly, if at all, from the attractive personal qualities of a political leader. After all, many of Bismarck's and Hitler's personal qualities were unattractive in the extreme. Charisma comes above all from situations of severe crisis, when the political system has broken down, and the only remaining hope for the desperate seems to be a man of superhuman strength and skill.

For Heinrich Class, and probably for most of Germany's elite in 1914, the political system seemed irreparably broken, leaving them vulnerable to socialism at home and military defeat abroad. Yet their desperation went even further than naïve hopes for a superhuman Leader: some actually hoped for war between the great powers of Europe, thinking that war would resolve Germany's political crisis and allow them to break through the ring of enemies that surrounded them. Surely, they thought, war would unite all Germans behind their leadership. Facing war on two fronts against three enemies, even socialist workers would give up their claims to economic justice and democracy, and begin to see themselves as Germans and not as workers. Moreover, a war would keep them from rising in rebellion when people like Heinrich Class arrested their leaders and took away their right to vote. The narrowness of vision among the German elites, their selfishness and arrogance, and their capacity for self-delusion might even be funny had their behavior not had such tragic consequences.

In the 1912 edition of *If I Were the Emperor*, Class praised war as "the awakener of all good, healthy, strong energies in the nation," a political tonic that would bring to life "everything that is great and prepared to sacrifice, and thus is selfless," cleansing the German soul of selfish "pettiness." To Class and his allies, of course, the German worker's demands for fair wages and democratic government sprang from the selfishness and materialism with which Jews had supposedly poisoned the lower class. Class wanted this war even though he recognized that Germany's enemies could deploy superior resources, and that it would take the nation's "entire strength" to win. However, victory promised rich rewards: an election would send a nationalist majority to parliament, and this parliament would enact Class's antidemocratic reforms. He expected "the most vehement resistance" to his reforms from "those whose imaginary rights would have to be diminished by the reform of the Empire." He thought that resistance to his "reforms" could be overcome—and the reforms pushed through using the normal constitutional process—by the "spiritual uplift of an overwhelming experience," that is, a general European war. "Thus," he reasoned, "a war that a statesman undertook in service of this domestic political goal would be justified." Class wanted to inflict the calamity of war on Europe's millions in the hope of blocking democracy indefinitely.[13]

Class's views were extreme, but he was hardly alone in holding them. Many tens of thousands of men from German society's elite, quite possibly a majority of the country's most influential citizens, joined and led the many nationalist pressure groups that so badly poisoned German political life on the eve of World War I. These were owners and managers of corporations, titled aristocrats, military officers, wealthy landowners, and especially men who worked in occupations that required a university degree: higher civil servants, doctors and lawyers, and teachers at college preparatory high schools. Fully one-half of the Pan-German League's leaders came from this educated sector of society. More than 15,000 such educated men belonged to the German Colonial Society at one point, more than 22,000 to the Eastern Borderland Association, and probably tens of thousands to other nationalist leagues. Since there were only about 135,000 university-trained elites in Germany in 1914, it seems clear that a huge fraction of Germany's best-educated men belonged to such groups. Especially given that educated elites tended to dominate the nationalist groups they joined, it seems probable that most of Germany's elites of education, or at least those who were politically most active, had committed themselves to radical nationalism by the eve of World War I. These pressure groups thus prepared a whole generation of Germany's leading citizens to support the most radical nationalist of all, Adolf Hitler.[14]

During the twenty-five years before World War I, the future perpetrators of the Holocaust were born. They spent their formative years influenced by Imperial Germany's poisonous political climate and by the world war that it produced. Adolf Hitler first saw the light of day in German Austria on April 20, 1889. Many of his future henchmen were also born before 1900, grew to manhood before the end of World War I, and witnessed the war's massive slaughter as combat soldiers. Rudolf Höss, although born late enough (1900) to have escaped the fighting, lied about his age to get into the army, saw combat, and went on to become the commanding officer of the Auschwitz death camp. A slightly younger generation, consisting of men born between 1900 and 1910, supplied most of the leading organizers of the Holocaust, including Heinrich Himmler, future head of the SS, and his deputy, Reinhard Heydrich. Although too young to fight in the war, they absorbed a German nationalism made all the more ferocious by the hatreds born of bloody warfare. Not experiencing firsthand the terror of combat, they eagerly glorified the war and the hardened men who had fought it, modeling themselves on a new and brutal ideal of what the German soldier should be.

Germany's political conditions before 1914, as badly dysfunctional as the system had become, were not yet extreme enough to transform normal men into the slaughterers of millions. Although Heinrich Class dreamed of a military coup to make the German Empire less democratic, not even he was calling for murder, nor was anyone else among Germany's frightened ruling class. World War I would change that decisively.

CHAPTER 5

HARDENED BY WAR

So began for me, as probably also for every German, the greatest and most unforgettable time of my earthly life. Compared to the events of this most tremendous struggle, everything before it receded into a stale nothingness.

—Adolf Hitler, on his years as a soldier in World War I[1]

Thanks to Germany's irresponsible and provocative foreign policy, a major war had become reasonably likely by 1914. Yet it was far from inevitable, and had it not broken out, history would have taken a very different course in the twentieth century from that which it followed. World War I helped cause the Holocaust in two important ways. First, it inflicted terrible damage on Germany's already dysfunctional political system, intensifying the social and political conflicts that divided Germans from each other. The radicalization of German politics goes a long way toward explaining why a third of German voters later gave their ballots to Hitler in the country's last free elections. Second, the war produced a large group of violent men who would later murder millions without hesitation. Ten million men died in combat, including 2 million Germans, and they died in fighting that seemed utterly meaningless, fighting in which the deaths of these young men became almost an end in itself. This pointless slaughter drastically cheapened human life, producing a cohort of genocidal killers who accepted that mass death was simply a normal part of human existence. Without World War I, the Holocaust could never have happened.

On June 28, 1914, a Serbian nationalist named Gavrilo Princip shot dead the heir to the throne of the Austro-Hungarian Empire, which was Germany's only real ally. This desperate act set off a chain reaction that drew all the great powers of Europe into war by August 4. Germany and Austria-Hungary fought against the alliance of Britain, France, and Russia. The Germans promptly executed their war plan: a vast, counterclockwise flanking invasion, sweeping down through Belgium into the north of France, aiming to fall upon the French armies in their rear. The Germans believed that Russia needed more time to mobilize its troops than did France. Germany therefore sent the great bulk of its forces into France, hoping to knock France out of the war within the first weeks of fighting. With their western front secure, the Germans could then turn all of their energies to defeating the Russian foe in the East.

Germany's invasion of France failed at the Marne in early September 1914, and the war in the West rapidly settled into the pattern it maintained for almost four years: trench warfare. The horrifically pointless and destructive nature of the fighting helps explain why World War I had such devastating consequences. "Trench warfare" meant that the opposing armies each maintained their troops in trenches 8 to 10 feet deep, dug out of the muddy soil. Between the enemies' front lines lay an open space—sometimes as wide as half a mile, other times only a few hundred yards. Strewn across this space lay barriers of barbed wire that each army had created to keep enemy troops from advancing toward its own trenches. Aptly named "no-man's-land," this space between the trenches was a place where no man could long survive.

Technology, namely the machine gun, had made the horrors of trench warfare possible. Machine guns had been invented in the last decades of the nineteenth century. The American Gatling Gun was an early, primitive version. By 1914 they had developed into fearsome weapons. Whereas an infantry soldier could fire no more than fifteen bullets in a minute, a machine gun fired six hundred shots per minute or more. Positioned strategically atop the trenches, machine guns swept no-man's-land with withering fire, cutting down enemy soldiers in waves as they tried to advance, like a scythe mowing down sugar cane, reaping a grim harvest of human lives whenever either side was foolish enough to launch an attack.

The first day of the Battle of the Somme, July 1, 1916, illustrates the terrible consequences of trench warfare for the foot soldier. The British prepared their attack by firing artillery shells at the German trenches around the clock for seven days. The British had two goals: to destroy the Germans' barbed wire in no-man's-land and to kill the German machine gunners. The Germans, for their part, sheltered their gunners in sturdy bunkers constructed twenty feet or more below the surface of the earth. The British artillery did not kill them, just as it did not fully cut the wire in no-man's-land. Just before daybreak on July 1, the British silenced their artillery. Their men climbed out of the trenches and charged the German lines. A race had begun between the German machine gunners, who were climbing out of their bunkers to set up their weapons, and the charging British soldiers. The finish line was the front edge of the German trenches. Whoever lost the race would die.[2]

The German machine gunners, having to move only forty or fifty feet, won this fatal race. The British assault failed. Twenty thousand British soldiers paid for their generals' stupidity with their lives; another 40,000 were wounded. This horrible scene was re-peated numerous times over the course of the war. Unable to break through their enemies' lines, the European armies then settled into a war of attrition. Each side fed more and more men and ammuni-tion into the bottomless pit of trench warfare; the war could end only when one side ran out of the men or weapons to fight it. Erich von Falkenhayn, head of Germany's armies, embraced this terrible reality when he started the other great battle of 1916: Verdun.[3]

Verdun was a historic complex of French fortifications sur-rounded on three sides by German trenches. Falkenhayn reasoned that the French, in part out of considerations of prestige, would make every sacrifice to hold Verdun. Surrounding the French posi-tion with artillery, he would turn Verdun into a killing ground. The German offensive would, as Falkenhayn put it, "compel the French to throw in every man they have. If they do so the forces of France will bleed to death." Informally, German officers referred to the Verdun battle plan as the "blood pump."[4]

"Operation Judgment," as Falkenhayn named his offensive, commenced on February 21, 1916, and continued until July 11, with two bursts of later fighting in October and December. Falken-hayn's plan failed miserably, as it cost the Germans as much as it did the French. Already by the end of June, more than 200,000 men had been killed or wounded on each side, and some 20 million ar-tillery shells had been fired. The surrounding territory had become a wasteland, with entire forests and villages erased and the surface of the earth reduced to a moonscape of overlapping shell holes.[5]

As contemporaries recognized, the battles of the Somme and Verdun, both in 1916, inaugurated a new and unprecedented kind of fighting, the "battle of materiel" as the Germans called it. In this war of attrition, in which each side sought to exhaust the other's supply of young men, armies fired titanic volumes of artillery shells in barrages that could last for days, while machine guns swept battlefields bare of any men who rose up from the trenches that had sheltered them. The men who endured this horrific and pointless fighting were forever altered by it.[6]

In their diaries and reminiscences, soldiers spoke of the overwhelming fire as a force of nature, an insuperable obstacle, or a colossal machine crushing every man in its path. In a reference to this awful power, the German veteran Ernst Jünger gave his celebrated war memoir the title *In Storms of Steel*. Reflecting on one battle, Jünger recalled how he "stared long into the glowing witches' cauldron, whose visible border was formed by the piercing muzzle flashes of the English machine guns," and how "the thousand-headed bee swarm of these bullets, which flooded over us," doomed the attacking German troops. Others called the machine-gun fire "hail" or "steely rain." Friedrich Bethge recalled how his men assaulted the British trenches, moving closely behind a creeping barrage that crushed the enemy's position under a "fiery steamroller"; after crossing the first line of British trenches, they ran into a "wall of steel" in the form of the British artillery's blocking fire.[7]

In one battle, Jünger wrote, "from nine to ten [P.M.] the fire reached a crazy intensity. The earth shook, the sky looked like a seething giants' cauldron. Hundreds of heavy batteries thundered in and around Combles, countless shells crisscrossed howling and hissing over us. Everything was shrouded in thick smoke, ominously lit by colored rocket flares." Pounding pain rent the soldiers' heads and ears; they could communicate only in brief, shouted commands. "The capacity for logical thought and the sensation of gravity seemed suspended. One had the feeling of the inescapable and of absolute necessity, as when faced by an eruption of the elements. A non-commissioned officer of the third platoon went raving mad."[8]

The massive fire transformed the battlefield into a nightmarish wasteland of shell craters. Soldiers described the killing fields as

"Hell," an "Inferno," and a "desert" devoid of all life. The stench of rotting corpses filled every man's nostrils until it became a familiar part of the background. Bodies lay unburied in the open, while the dirt thrown up by exploding shells buried others, many alive. In late August 1916, Ernst Jünger led his company to a forward German position in the Battle of the Somme, into which the British had continued to pour men and munitions since the failed attack of July 1. The German line, more a shallow groove than a trench, "looked like nothing more than a row of giant craters, filled with shreds of uniforms, weapons, and dead men," wrote Jünger. "The surrounding terrain was, as far as the eye could see, completely unearthed by heavy shells. Not a single forlorn blade of grass showed itself to the searching gaze. The uprooted battlefield was ghastly. Between the living defenders lay the dead. Digging foxholes, we noticed that the dead were layered in strata. One company after another, hunkered down together during the artillery barrages, had been mown down, their corpses buried by the masses of earth hurled upward by the shells, and the relief troops had taken the place of the dead. Now it was our turn."[9]

Under prolonged artillery fire, men experienced a feeling of utter helplessness and vulnerability. Veteran Otto Germar described lying "for hours, days, for an eternity in a shell crater, occupied with no other thought than: this shell went to the left, that one behind me, this one in front—now, now must it land on me. . . . These thoughts, focused for days on this wretched and pitiable self, were what undermined the nerves, indeed, the strength of mind, bit by bit." Together with this helplessness came a feeling of the near-certainty of death and the recognition that it could and did strike at any time. Hans Henning Grote recorded in his diary how his unit moved into a fiercely contested sector of the Somme battlefield on August 28, 1916, going "out of the frying pan into the fire." "Our mission," he continued, was "to let ourselves be ingloriously shot to pieces." After summing up a day's losses, naming many individual deaths, Grote summarized the brutal calculus that determined how long his men would stay in the front line: "But we know, yes, that a monstrous percentage [of men killed] still has to be reached before they release the shattered remnant of my command from this Hell. Don't think, do your duty!" Grote's valued comrades had been reduced to an arbitrary percentage, eloquent testimony to the degree to which the war had cheapened human life.[10]

Soldiers reacted to such horrors in different ways. Some were simply broken psychologically. Many others, probably the majority, reacted the way we think that any sane person would have to react: with revulsion, with hatred of war, with condemnation of this pointless slaughter of millions. The thirty-seven-year-old painter Ernst Noppe, writing in his diary after the Battle of Longwy in August 1914, summed it up this way: "Ghastly impressions, one cannot describe these disgraceful horrors. The human being is an animal of the lowest kind, merciless." A Lieutenant Henckel, writing a letter from the Verdun battlefield on March 24, 1916, put the matter with brutal clarity: "This is no longer war, but rather butchery of human beings."[11]

Although many more German veterans became pacifists than warmongers after 1918, nonetheless there was a distinct minority of combat soldiers who came to love the fighting and who gloried in the ways it had transformed them. Among German veterans, Ernst Jünger wrote most eloquently of the thrill of combat and the emotional intensity that came with confronting death. He spoke of gaining a sense of mastery over one's own emotions and of experiencing a new, crystal-like clarity of wholly dispassionate thought. Describing a new kind of man that emerged from the war, he used such adjectives as "hard," "coldblooded," "sober," "dispassionate," and "objective." And these terms were not mere description, but rather an ideal toward which many young men, notably men who were active on the radical nationalist Right of German politics, continually strove. They celebrated their emotional distance from the victims of the right-wing violence of the early 1920s, saw renewed warfare as an objective necessity, and later expressed pride in their ability to take the "tough" decisions that would spell doom for millions of Hitler's victims. In short, the brutalizing combat of World War I gave birth to a genocidal cohort made up of hundreds or even thousands of men who had enjoyed combat, as well as many from the generation that followed who were too young to have experienced the war's horrors, but old enough to worship the hardened men who had.[12]

Many future perpetrators of the Holocaust surely read Jünger's popular memoir of combat. During the 1920s, Jünger was the most prominent and respected intellectual among right-wing nationalists in Germany. In his graceful prose, he acknowledged the horror, the death, and the devastation that surrounded him, but also prized the exhilaration and heightened sensory perception he experienced when death was near. Noting the "thick stench of corpses" that hung over dangerous sectors of the battlefield, he recalled how he and his comrades "ran as a matter of life and death, and as I sensed these fumes while running, I was hardly surprised—it came with the territory." Jünger found that this odor was "not solely disagreeable; it provoked, closely mixed with the piercing smoke of the explosives, an almost clairvoyant excitement, which only the greatest proximity to death can produce." Amid this nightmarish run across a corpse-strewn battlefield, he "sensed in these moments no fear, but rather a great and almost demonic lightness." And combat gave him something else that other veterans welcomed, a calm indifference toward his own death and that of others, an equanimity in the face of mortality that might be regarded as a kind of inner peace.[13]

During a day of ferocious fighting in July 1917, in which his company suffered heavy losses, Jünger was hurled back into a shell hole by two bullets, shot through lung and shoulder. He lay unattended for thirteen hours, finally had his wounds bound by a medic, and was carried back to the hospital by stretcher bearers who dropped him several times to take cover from incoming shells. Doctors treated him, and finally he could rest. "In the deathly exhaustion in which I found myself," he wrote, "an awareness of happiness came over me, a happiness which intensified more and more, and which stayed with me for weeks. I contemplated death, without being troubled by the thought. All of my affairs seemed astonishingly simplified, and with the feeling 'You're all right' I glided into sleep."[14]

Other combat veterans gained their acceptance of death by varied paths and in differing degree. For Hans Henning Grote, desperation seems to have wrought this crucial metamorphosis as he stood in a foxhole full of muddy water, exposed to relentless artillery fire and strafing by British fighter planes: "At one blow a great and deeply shaking indifference won dominion over me," he wrote. "I could care so little, it would be best if they got me!" Others contemplated the sheer randomness of death and found solace in the equality of chances between men, or in a submission to Fate. Otto Germar's men were supposed to be relieved from the front line by fresh troops at 4 o'clock in the morning. The relief troops came two hours late, and in the interim, a shell's explosion buried three men alive. Their comrades dug frantically for them, found them all blue from lack of air, and managed to revive only one. Germar vividly recalled one of the dead, a man who had recently returned from furlough after proposing marriage to his sweetheart, of whom he proudly carried a photograph. But Germar quickly discarded the idea of complaining to the late-arriving relief unit. "Had they come on time, they would have the dead now, and another mother, another bride would have to weep." He painted an image of death leaping about the battlefield, landing at random, "and thus one stands here in another's place, one dies here for the other."[15]

The titanic firepower of the new "battle of materiel," grinding the individual into insignificance, seemed to transform some men, purging each soldier of his inner frailties, making men "hard," "coldblooded," "sober," "dispassionate," and "objective." According to the new concept of warfare, the soldier must become as precise, objective, and hardened as the great "machine" of battle, constructed by scientific military planning. He must be reduced to an extension of the artillery, the machine guns, the trench systems, and the logistics which alone could bring victory. "The man no longer employs the machine," wrote one essayist in 1925, "but rather the machine makes use of the man." The thunderous and unceasing artillery barrage, as Otto Germar put it, gave "this war its objective, dispassionate character, murderous of heart and nerves."[16]

Veterans wrote of the entire German army being winnowed of weaker elements and becoming hardened. Ferdinand Beingolf, in his aptly named essay "The Horror," tells how he had to dig graves in a French cemetery at midnight and then bury the cruelly mangled bodies of his comrades, working alone in darkness. "From this kind of burial duty you don't come back as a momma's boy, but rather as a broken man—or as a soldier." Adolf Hitler recalled in *Mein Kampf* his own metamorphosis from "a young volunteer to an old soldier." Joining up in the first days of August 1914, he was carried away by the "romanticism of battle," but this illusion was soon replaced by "the horror." Enthusiasm "gradually cooled off," and "the gushing jubilation was suffocated by the fear of death." He and his comrades now had to fight a battle between "the instinct of self-preservation" and the commandments of duty. "I also was not spared this struggle," Hitler wrote. "Always, whenever death was on the prowl, an unnamed something within me tried to rebel, presented itself to the weak body as the voice of reason, yet it was only cowardice."[17]

In the winter of 1915–1916, after more than a year in combat, "this struggle within me was decided," wrote Hitler. "My will had finally become the unchallenged master. If I greeted the first days of battle with laughter and jubilation, now I was calm and resolute. This was what endured. Only now could Fate put me to the ultimate test without my nerves breaking or my wits failing." "This transformation," Hitler concluded, "had consummated itself in the whole army. It had come out of the unending battles old and hard, and whoever could not endure the tempest was broken by it."[18]

Ernst Jünger described his first encounter with this new type of hard and coldblooded soldier, who had appeared at night amid a deafening artillery barrage at Combles to lead Jünger and his men to the front line, saying, "He struck me at once as the inhabitant of a foreign and harder world." Asking their guide about the fighting, Jünger received "a monotone account of crouching for days in shell craters with no connection [to others], of constant attacks, of fields of corpses and maddening thirst, of the pining wounded and of more." He wrote: "The motionless face framed by the helmet's steel rim, the monotone voice accompanied by the clamor of the front, made an eerie impression upon us. A mere few days had put upon this messenger, who would lead us into the kingdom of the flames, a stamp that seemed to separate him from us in a way that defied expression." This ghostly messenger, telling them their fate, said: "If you're killed, there you lie. No one can help you there. No one knows whether he'll come back alive. They attack every day, but they're not getting through. Everyone knows that this is a matter of life and death." Jünger was moved and inspired by this man's example. "Nothing was left in his voice but a complete equanimity; it had been burned out of him. With men like these, one can fight."[19]

Only the searing experience of such combat, and the newly forged ideal of the coldblooded soldier who calmly accepted the war's massive slaughter, can explain how men of Jünger's generation could later murder innocent millions without remorse or even anxiety. The celebrated "front soldier ideal," best known to a generation of radical nationalist Germans through Jünger's writings, inspired Heinrich Himmler's definition of the ideal SS officer. Born in 1900, Himmler joined the army in the last year of World War I but never made it to the front. He saw himself very much as a failure for having neither seen combat nor achieved officer rank. This "failure" was made all the more bitter by the triumphant return of his brother Gebhard, who emerged from the fighting unscathed and was promoted to lieutenant and decorated for valor with the Iron Cross. Himmler became a classic member of the "war youth generation"—men born too young to fight, but swept up in the nationalist enthusiasm of the war and the radical nationalist politics of the first postwar years. These men were especially ready to glorify warfare because they had not seen its horrors firsthand. Himmler thought of himself as a soldier for his entire adult life, waging permanent and merciless war against the internal and external enemies of Germany, real and imagined, and he imparted the "martial virtues" of veterans like Jünger to the men of his SS.[20]

Speaking to high-ranking SS officers in October 1943, Himmler addressed what he and his men called "The Final Solution to the Jewish Question." Although he and his comrades could discuss it frankly among themselves, he said, "we will never speak of it publicly." Even members of the Nazi Party would not have the stomach to support this necessary policy, Himmler believed. "It is one of those things which are easy to talk about. 'The Jewish people will be exterminated,'" every party member would say. "'It's clear. It's in our program. Elimination of the Jews, extermination and we'll do it.' And then they come along, the worthy eighty million Germans, and each one of them produces his decent Jew. It's clear the others are swine, but this one is a fine Jew."

Himmler found this kind of compassion contemptible. About Germans who would make an exception for some Jews, he said: "Not one of those who talk like that has watched it happening, not one of them has been through it." Using imagery eerily reminiscent of trench warfare, Himmler observed: "Most of you will know what it means when a hundred corpses are lying side by side, or five hundred or a thousand are lying there. To have stuck it out, and—apart from a few exceptions due to human weakness—to have remained decent, that is what has made us hard. This is a glorious page in our history and one that has never been written and can never be written." Murdering by the millions did not mean that the men of the SS were brutal or immoral, much less criminal, in Himmler's view. It did not make them the worst of German society, he thought, but rather the very best, for only they were strong enough and hard enough to carry out this psychologically burdensome task. "All in all," he concluded, "we can say that we have fulfilled this most difficult duty for the love of our people. And our spirit, our soul, our character has not suffered injury from it."[21]

The ghastly battlefields and massive slaughter of World War I produced a generation of violent and hardened men, men who could accept the deaths of millions as a normal fact of political life. Yet men of many nations fought in the war without becoming murderers. It took the special role of nationalism and anti-Semitism in German politics, and the intensification of both in wartime Germany, to give these men the political convictions that made them so dangerous. It took the polarizing impact of the war on Germany's already dysfunctional political system, the crushing blow of Germany's defeat, and the political and economic chaos that followed to make Hitler's rise to power possible. Only then could the horror of the trenches find its fatal echo a generation later in the death camps and killing fields of the Holocaust.[22]

CHAPTER 6

DIVISION AND DISASTER

It cannot be disputed that in some circumstances it is the moral and political duty of a government to use war as a political tool.

—General Friedrich von Bernhardi,
Germany and the Next War (1912)[1]

When war broke out in August 1914, radical nationalists like Heinrich Class thought their hour had finally struck. The long-desired war would unite all Germans against a common enemy, weaken the socialist movement, and open up rich opportunities for territorial and economic expansion. The mood of the German public seemed to confirm their fondest hopes for national unity and the suppression of class conflict. When the war began, in every combatant society voices called for all citizens to rally round the flag and set aside the political conflicts that had divided them during the years before the war. In France this domestic political truce was called the "sacred union." Germans called it the "peace of the fortress," evoking a beleaguered community sheltered in a castle and surrounded by enemies. This "spirit of 1914" had great emotional resonance for Germans because their country had been so badly divided in the last years before the war, with the socialists declaring their intention to destroy the Imperial political system, and the nationalist Right constantly denouncing the socialists as traitors. As it happened, the sequence of events leading to war smoothed the way for the socialist party and labor unions to come in from the cold and join the national community.

Because Russia called up its troops before Germany did, the German government could persuade the socialists that Germany was fighting in self-defense. What is more, since the Russian Empire was even less democratic than Germany, and was viewed by most Germans as culturally backward, socialists gladly rallied to the flag. No one wanted to lose a war to "barbaric," autocratic Russia. In the almost fifty years of the party's existence, the socialists had proclaimed their rejection of the Imperial system by voting against every single budget. Now, on August 4, with Germany at war on two fronts against three enemies, the government asked them to vote for war loans. Joining a unanimous parliament, the socialists voted to support the war effort and were welcomed—at least for a while—into the national community. To thunderous applause from a crowd of 300,000 in front of the Imperial Palace, Emperor Wilhelm II declared: "I know no more parties. I know only Germans."[2]

Hatred for Germany's enemies helped cement the new bonds of national unity and social peace. Ernst Lissauer, a German-Jewish poet, expressed these ideas in his celebrated "Hate Song Against England," written shortly after the war began. Like many German nationalists, Lissauer harbored a special grudge against England. These men did not understand that Germany's bullying behavior and construction of battleships had driven the British into an alliance with France, so they accused Britain of entering the war for the sole purpose of destroying an economic competitor. The final verse of Lissauer's poem celebrates the unity of all classes of Germans, bound by love for each other and hatred for the English:

> *You we will hate with a lasting hate,*
> *We will never forgo our hate,*
> *Hate by water and hate by land,*
> *Hate of the head and hate of the hand,*
> *Hate of the hammers and hate of the crown,*
> *Hate of seventy millions choking down.*
> *They love as one, they hate as one,*
> *They have one foe and one alone—*
> *ENGLAND*

The Germans might be choking on their hatred, but finally, or so hoped Lissauer and other nationalists, the socialist working class ("the hammers" and "the hand") were united in common purpose with educated elites ("the head") and the Imperial government ("the crown").[3]

Yet if nationalists hoped that the war would bring political harmony and a tamed socialist party, German workers soon had other ideas. They made terrible sacrifices for their country during World War I: they died in the trenches by the hundreds of thousands, suffered massive additional deaths from malnutrition amid food shortages, worked extra shifts in armaments factories, and saw their wages eaten up by inflation when the government printed money to finance the war effort. Naturally, they expected a reward for their patriotic service: full citizenship through reforms that would finally give them a say in how they were governed. Many wars have brought about democratic reform, and for exactly this reason. Women finally got the vote, just after the end of World War I, in Germany, Britain, and the United States. This was partly because their contributions to the war effort—for example, by working in munitions factories—strengthened their claim to full citizenship. In the United States, the voting age was lowered from twenty-one to eighteen in 1971 because eighteen-year-old Americans were dying in the Vietnam War, and could no longer be denied the right to vote.

In Germany, World War I sharpened the conflict between the people's democratic aspirations and their rulers' determination to block all reform. Tensions worsened so markedly that by the time Germany lost the war, massive civil violence was almost inevitable. Right-wing politics during the war also paved the way for making German Jews the scapegoats for Germany's defeat, because conservative nationalists had long blamed Jews for the rise of the socialist party, and most critics of the war came from the socialist ranks.

Early in the war, Germany's rulers recognized that workers' sacrifices would increase pressure for democracy, which they wanted to thwart at all costs. So, they set out to fight reform with the same strategy they had followed for the two decades before 1914: using nationalism and anti-Semitism as weapons against democracy. The ruling elites offered national triumph—in this case victory at war—as a substitute for real political participation, attacking as unpatriotic anyone who criticized the government. During the war, they refused to even consider negotiating a compromise peace with Germany's opponents. Instead, they insisted on a crushing German victory that would let Germany take land and resources from its neighbors and force the nation's defeated enemies to pay the cost of the German war effort. Such a "victory peace," they imagined, would make the government wildly popular, and perhaps even allow them to crush the socialist party once and for all. This wishful and irresponsible thinking was neatly stated by Alfred Hugenberg, a wealthy businessman and prominent member of the Pan-German League. Hugenberg warned that workers who had fought at the front would come back to work resisting "factory discipline" and the power of business owners. Hugenberg's answer to this problem? "It would therefore be well advised . . . to distract the attention of the people and to give fantasies concerning the extension of German territory room to play."[4]

Already in September 1914, with the war barely a month old, Germany's prime minister, Theobald von Bethmann-Hollweg, drafted a confidential outline of Germany's war aims that was breathtaking in its arrogance and greed. Leaders of industry, of the nationalist pressure groups, and of the military produced their own war aims plans. And although the details varied, the basic thrust of the plans did not: France and Russia would be permanently reduced to the status of second-rate powers, and Germany would become the unchallenged master of the European continent. Germany's defeated enemies would have to surrender some of their overseas colonies. Germany would annex or otherwise control all of Belgium, mainly for its coal and steel industries and the strategic value of its coastline for naval warfare. Germany would likewise gobble up large industrial regions of northern France and a gigantic swath of the western Russian Empire, including the Baltic region (Lithuania, Latvia, and Estonia), Ukraine, Russian Poland, and more. Whether it was directly annexed or indirectly controlled, Ukraine would become Germany's breadbasket, while Russian coal and iron mines would give Germany a permanent and crushing superiority in arms production. Germany's military leaders saw a further benefit to these massive thefts of land in the East: Germany's surplus population could settle on farms taken from Slavic peasants. Prospering on large farms, these Germans would raise large and healthy families, breeding the soldiers who would be needed for future wars against the Slavic peoples of Eastern Europe and Russia.[5]

Germany's rulers, especially the military leadership, had thus embraced a set of ideas that would profoundly influence Adolf Hitler, and which led in a straight line to Germany's genocidal war against the Soviet Union in 1941. They assumed, first, that future wars were inevitable, and second, that Germany had to secure sufficient land and resources—and breed enough soldiers—to defeat numerically superior enemies. They embraced racist ideas about the inferiority of the Slavic peoples, ideas that justified the most ruthless treatment of these peoples if it helped ensure Germany's survival. No one knows for sure exactly how Hitler came to adopt this thinking as his own, and to follow it to its most extreme conclusions, but by serving as a propaganda officer in the German Army directly after World War I, he would have been exposed to these ideas in one form or another. The communist revolution in Russia in November 1917 further radicalized these anti-Slavic imperialist ideas in the military and throughout the right wing of German politics, as fear that communism might spread to Germany only intensified hatred toward the Russians. This shift ensured that when German forces invaded the Soviet Union in June 1941, they would show no mercy. Within the context of this murderous war against the Soviets, it became possible to imagine the most extreme racist project of all, the complete extermination of the Jewish people.

By insisting on expansionist war aims, Germany's ruling class thus continued its well-worn strategy of using aggressive nationalism to block democracy, but now in a far more extreme and violent fashion. None of the major powers fighting World War I was seriously interested in a negotiated peace, but German policy made any compromise inconceivable. Germany's leaders would fight to the bitter end, hoping vainly for a total victory, no matter how heavy the toll in lost and ruined lives.[6]

Predictably, Germany's leaders and right-wing nationalists branded all critics of the war as traitors, and any call for a negotiated peace as a betrayal of the patriotic dead. Especially after the "turnip winter" of 1916–1917, when a failed potato crop caused hundreds of thousands of Germans to die of malnutrition, socialist workers increasingly called for a compromise peace and democratic reform. A large strike in the Berlin munitions factories in January 1918 crystallized a mass movement against expansionist war aims, and in favor of reforms that would make Germany a democracy. "Peace, bread, and freedom" became the slogan of the day. It came as no surprise to anyone that Germany's rulers accused the striking workers of lacking patriotism. More radical voices on the Right talked of executing labor leaders. Yet they could take this kind of argument only so far, because German workers did their duty in the factories and at the front, while the socialist party continued to vote for further war loans. It would be a hollow kind of national unity to rally the country against the entire industrial working class, which made up over a third of the population. At least in part for this reason, Germany's leaders sought to restore the fleeting sense of harmony of the first two war years by uniting the country against a small and unloved minority: German Jews, whom they had long accused of dividing the country by instigating socialism.

In late 1917, already bitterly divided by the war, the Germans entered a nightmarish seven-year period in which one traumatic event followed another. This cascade of hammer blows drained much of Germany's wealth, amputated large swaths of its territory, reduced the country to the status of a second-rate power, and drastically intensified the economic and political conflicts that divided Germans. Together with the war, these traumatic and disorienting events made the German people even more extremist and divided, and even more desperate for a charismatic leader who could draw the country together. The first and in some ways most important of these events occurred outside of Germany in November 1917, when the communists, or Bolsheviks, seized control of Russia in a violent uprising.[7]

The communist revolution in Russia made a vivid reality of the nightmare that had long terrified generations of Europeans, especially in the middle and upper classes. European socialist parties had long challenged the capitalist economic system and threatened private property, but they had largely confined themselves to non-violent methods. The Russian Bolsheviks, in contrast, proceeded to destroy capitalism and confiscate property at the point of a gun, provoking a bloody civil war that lasted four years and took the lives of as many as 10 million people. Militant communist parties, many of them loyal to Moscow, sprang up all across Europe, and Germany's communist party became one of the largest, taking 12.6 percent of the vote in the elections of May 1924 and an alarming 16.9 percent in the last elections held before Hitler took power, in November 1932. German elites, and probably most of the middle class as well, now saw in Russia a terrifying vision of the future that awaited them if they did not take decisive measures to crush communism. Fear of a communist revolution inspired a great deal of right-wing violence in the early 1920s, and it later moved millions of Germans to vote for the Nazi Party in 1932 and applaud Hitler when he locked up socialist and communist leaders in 1933.[8]

Almost exactly one year after the Bolshevik revolution in Russia, Germans had their own revolution and lost World War I. After German sailors mutinied at the end of October 1918, German cities and the German Army erupted in largely peaceful rebellion, with workers and soldiers ceasing to obey the elites who had commanded them for so long. Because Germany seemed to be dissolving into chaos, and because he hoped to prevent a violent revolution by communists, the socialist Philipp Scheidemann stepped to a balcony of the parliament building on November 9, announcing to an expectant crowd that Germany had undergone a revolution and would henceforth be a democracy. Scheidemann's improvised revolution lent a focus to the popular rebellion and kept it in peaceful channels. A provisional government was swiftly established, and nationwide elections were called for January 1919 to elect a convention that would draft a democratic constitution for Germany. Because the constitutional convention met in the historic city of Weimar, Germany's first democracy became known as the Weimar Republic.[9]

Like any new system of government, the Weimar Republic faced a crucial problem: how to establish its legitimacy. A government has "legitimacy" when its citizens automatically accept that the government and its officials have the right to make and enforce laws. Governments can establish their legitimacy in several ways; one of the most important is by following rules that everyone accepts when choosing the leaders of the government. In the United States, this means picking the president, the members of Congress, and other officials in democratic elections. Since almost all Americans agree that democracy is a fair and just system, they normally obey laws that are made and enforced by democratically elected officials, even when they disagree with this or that particular law. An equally important source of legitimacy is time. Governments establish their legitimacy with the passage of years and by force of habit, as their citizens get used to obeying the government and its laws. If a government functions reasonably well for enough years, eventually most of its citizens will accept its authority. Unfortunately, the Weimar Republic never got this crucially important breathing space; it didn't get the time it needed to establish its legitimacy. No sooner had the Republic been founded than it had to face a string of severe political and economic crises, shattering blows that would have shaken even the most long-established of governments. Even worse, the German people had had no prior experience with the rules that make up democracy; from the outset, at least a quarter of the voters, including most of the country's elite, were downright hostile to the democratic form of government.

Until the revolution of 1918, all German men had been able to vote for a parliament, but their votes had not given them any real influence on the decisions made by the government: the parliament, and the parties represented in it, had held very little power. In this sense, although Germans had practice in voting, they had no real experience of democracy. Before 1918, only the much-maligned socialist party had demanded that the country become a democracy. This fact had automatically discredited the idea of democracy for much of the rest of the country. Although the socialists had become very moderate in their policies by 1914, they had still talked about destroying the capitalist system—and they had become the largest political party. Germans who might otherwise have welcomed democracy and demanded a say in government for themselves had no use for democracy if it meant giving the socialists real power. Germany's ruling class was especially hostile to democracy. After all, under the authoritarian constitution of the empire (1871–1918), they enjoyed far more power than the rest of German society, and they would lose much of this power if Germany became a democracy. As wealthy property owners, they had also had the most to lose if the socialists gained any say in government.

Because of this antidemocratic legacy from the politics of the empire, the Weimar Republic suffered a serious lack of legitimacy from its very beginning, not only in the country at large, but precisely among the most articulate and influential members of German society, including the civil service, the legal system, and the military—namely, the people it needed to enforce its laws and guarantee its security. This deficit of legitimacy was all the greater not only because democracy had been associated in everyone's mind with socialism during the years of the empire, but also because the socialist party had led the revolution and dominated the provisional revolutionary government during its first months. For millions of Germans, socialism and democracy were therefore one and the same.

Despite these serious handicaps, the Republic got off to a promising start in the January 1919 election for the constitutional convention. Of the parties fielding candidates for this convention, three took a clear stance in support of democracy: the Socialists, the Catholic Center Party, and the Democrats. This "Weimar Coalition" of pro-democracy parties scored a resounding triumph, taking over three-quarters of the vote: 37.9 percent for the Socialists, 19.7 percent for the Center, and 18.5 percent for the Democrats. If this election is any indication, the German people (though not the country's elite) were willing to at least give democracy a chance. Two serious misfortunes seem to have ruined that chance and changed many voters' minds about the Republic. The first blow was losing the war in November 1918; the second was the peace treaty that the winners of the war imposed on Germany in June 1919. Conservative elites, in their typically unscrupulous fashion, managed to blame both disasters on the Republic, often going so far as to accuse the Socialists, Center, and Democrats of outright treason. These accusations simply continued the strategy of Germany's ruling class, begun in the 1890s and used with greater intensity during the war, of attacking democracy and socialism as unpatriotic. Erroneous beliefs about Germany's defeat and the peace treaty gained widespread acceptance in part because of the unfortunate timing of Germany's surrender and the revolution in 1918.[10]

By late September 1918, the German military High Command, chaired by Erich Ludendorff and Paul von Hindenburg, had recognized that Germany had lost the war and that the German Army was on the brink of collapse. Germany had faced a coalition of powerful enemies—Britain, France, and the United States—and its soldiers were hopelessly outnumbered and outgunned. When the shooting stopped, about 3.5 million German and Austro-Hungarian troops faced nearly 6.5 million Allied soldiers. On September 29, Ludendorff told the emperor that the war was lost and advised him to seek peace terms. Germany's request for a cease-fire was published on October 3, which gave the German people the first inkling that their long-promised victory was not in prospect. However, the High Command had carefully censored information from the front, and few citizens suspected that Germany had no cards left to play and would have to surrender unconditionally. The armistice negotiations proceeded in secret, while the German people harbored naïve hopes concerning their outcome. Meanwhile, the country erupted in rebellion and the emperor abdicated, and it was in this context that on November 9 the socialist Philipp Scheidemann proclaimed the revolution. Only two days later, on November 11, the new government announced Germany's humiliating surrender, which had been signed not by the emperor or by the generals who had directed the war, but by representatives of the new civilian government.[11]

This close coincidence in time between the revolution and the surrender gave a surface plausibility to the accusation that the democratic revolutionaries had betrayed the country, surrendering out of cowardice or even worse motives. General Paul von Hindenburg gave this grotesque myth its most pithy formulation in his testimony before a parliamentary committee in November 1919. The Germany Army, declared Hindenburg, had not been defeated by the Allies. Rather, it had been "stabbed in the back" by the home front. Criticism of the war, and political agitation among the troops by socialist conspirators, had allegedly destroyed the German Army's morale. Jews, long accused of instigating socialism, came under especially vicious attack. Adolf Hitler's ferocious hatred toward Jews drew much of its fury from his belief that they had engineered Germany's defeat.[12]

This enormously destructive "stab in the back legend" gained further credibility when the right-wing parties stuck the Republic's supporters with the responsibility for signing the hated Treaty of Versailles. The peace imposed on Germany at Versailles was in truth not nearly as unjust as most Germans thought, but nonetheless it was perceived as humiliating and deeply unfair. The terms of the treaty were not remotely as harsh toward Germany as the peace terms that the German government had imposed on Russia in

March 1918, and that it had planned to force on Germany's other enemies if Germany had won. Although Germany had to pay billions of marks in reparations to the victors, this financial burden did not cripple Germany's economy during the 1920s, although some observers argued that it did.[13]

Seen objectively, the Treaty of Versailles was grossly unfair in only two respects, although these were important. First, the Germans had to sign the so-called war-guilt clause, in which they and their Austro-Hungarian allies accepted all blame for causing the war. This paragraph of the treaty was not only historically inaccurate, but for Germans it was deeply humiliating. The second unfair aspect was that the treaty deprived Germany of the means to defend itself against foreign aggression. Germany could have no air force, no submarine fleet, only a very limited navy, and an army of only 100,000 men. The Germans could also maintain no fortifications and station no troops on their territories located on the banks of the Rhine River. Their border with France was thus unprotected. As long as they abided by the terms of this treaty, the Germans were defenseless.

By not even inviting Germans to the peace talks in Paris, the victorious Allies further demeaned Germany. They made not even the faintest pretense of negotiating. Instead, they announced the peace terms on May 7, 1919, and gave the German government only twenty-one days to respond in writing. On June 16, the victorious powers gave the Germans the treaty's final text and only seven days' time in which to sign. Should the Germans refuse, Allied troops stood ready to invade Germany and impose even harsher terms. At this crucial juncture, when Germany was forced at gunpoint to sign a treaty that all Germans angrily condemned, the only responsible course of action would have been a unanimous vote in the constitutional convention to approve signing the treaty. In this way the German people would know that their political leaders had no choice but to sign the treaty, even though every German politician hated having to do so. Instead, while 237 delegates voted to sign the treaty, 138 voted against and 5 abstained. Most of the votes against signing came from three parties. The great majority of the Democrats voted against it, and their party left the government, which henceforth was led by only two parties, the Catholic Center Party and the Socialists. All delegates from the two right-wing parties, the People's Party and the Nationalists, voted against signing. Before long, both of these parties began attacking the others who had voted to sign, questioning their patriotism. The more extreme right-wing party, the Nationalists, soon accused the Center Party and the Socialists of outright treason. Branding the signers of the treaty as traitors became a favorite tactic of the Nazi Party.[14]

Once the democratic constitution had been written, elections were held for the new parliament. The results of the June 1920 elections showed that the Republic's fragile legitimacy had already been severely compromised by the "stab in the back legend," the signing of the Treaty of Versailles, and a year and a half of political violence, including four leftist uprisings that were brutally suppressed by right-wing paramilitaries. The Weimar Coalition—the parties that embraced democracy—fell from the 76 percent of the vote it had polled in January 1919 to under half of the electorate, taking only 43 percent of the seats in parliament. The two right-wing parties, the People's Party and the Nationalists, together took 28 percent, and both were openly hostile to the Republic, as were the Communists (7 percent) and many of the members of the Independent Socialists (13 percent), a short-lived party whose members and voters later gravitated to the Communists or Socialists.[15]

When a government is widely perceived as illegitimate, violence often follows, because if there are no generally accepted rules that determine who shall have power, power is up for grabs. Consequently, all means to getting power seem acceptable, and no one feels obligated to obey the law. This is why many revolutions that begin with little violence—the French Revolution of 1789, or the democratic revolution of March 1917 in Russia, for example—end in massive bloodshed. Revolutionary governments, being completely new, have to struggle to establish their legitimacy, often facing armed challenges from opponents who do not accept that the revolutionaries have the right to govern.

The potential for political violence was especially great in Germany after the November 1918 revolution, because four years of war had produced a surplus of violent young men with military training. After Germany's surrender on November 11, the army largely disbanded, and the young Republic had no military force to guarantee its security. Consequently, its leaders permitted the creation of the Free Corps, private armies recruited by veteran officers. Because militant nationalists were probably the only soldiers who wanted to continue fighting after such a horrible war, the Free Corps became magnets for right-wing activists, many of them traumatized combat veterans who were addicted to violence and unable to adjust to civilian life. In most cases, the Free Corps were ferociously hostile to socialism and communism. They became increasingly alienated from the Republic, especially after the Treaty of Versailles was signed in June 1919. The treaty made their wartime sacrifice seem pointless.[16]

In 1919, Free Corps units suppressed two poorly organized leftist uprisings in Berlin, one in January and the second in March. Neither rebellion seriously threatened the government, but the Free Corps, only nominally under the government's control, acted with shocking brutality. In January one unit murdered two widely admired communist leaders, Rosa Luxemburg and Karl Liebknecht. In March the Free Corps killed roughly 1,200 people in Berlin's working-class neighborhoods. In Munich shortly thereafter, communists established their own government in opposition to the national regime in Berlin. Free Corps and regular army units invaded the city at the beginning of May, slaughtering real or suspected communists as they marched in, and frequently executing men who had already surrendered. At least 600 people lost their lives, more than half of them civilians. In March 1920, Free Corps units mounted a coup against the democratic government in Berlin, which in turn called a nationwide general strike in a bid to paralyze the economy and thwart the coup. The coup fell apart within days, but the strike gave birth to a communist "army" in the industrial Ruhr Valley in western Germany. Seeing no alternative, the government sent Free Corps units into the Ruhr to crush this latest rebellion from the Left. No one knows how many people they killed, but all estimates run into the thousands.[17]

This series of leftist uprisings, suppressed with needless brutality by right-wing paramilitaries, profoundly embittered the German working class. Millions of workers turned against the moderate Socialist party, which dominated the government that had ordered in the Free Corps. These angry workers found their new political home in the Communist party, which had been only a tiny radical clique before the shocking murders of Luxemburg and Liebknecht, now transformed into celebrated martyrs. The communists were relentlessly hostile to democracy and took their marching orders from the Soviet regime in Moscow. At the same time, although the leftist uprisings were easily crushed, they ratcheted up the general fear of communism to a state of hysteria among all levels of German society outside the working class, and even among moderate socialists. Fear of communism, fury at the loss of the war and the Treaty of Versailles, and the bloody precedent set by the Free Corps—all these factors stoked a campaign of political murder that ravaged the Republic during the first years of its existence.

During the period 1919–1922, right-wing activists committed at least 354 political murders in Germany. Nothing inhibited the killers, who did not hesitate to assassinate the Republic's top leaders. Many focused their hatred on Matthias Erzberger, leader of the

Center Party, who had signed the German surrender in 1918 and had rallied his party to sign the Treaty of Versailles. The leading Nationalist politician Karl Helfferich published a pamphlet, entitled "Away with Erzberger!" unfairly accusing him of corruption, and claiming that Erzberger would lead Germany into "complete annihilation" if he was "not finally stopped!" Erzberger sued Helfferich for defamation in early 1920. A war veteran shot Erzberger in the shoulder during the trial, perhaps encouraged by a description of the plump Center politician in the right-wing press as "round like a bullet, but not bulletproof." In June 1921, two former Free Corps officers caught Erzberger taking a stroll in the scenic Black Forest and gunned him down. In their fury, they fired twelve shots at him as he lay helpless on the ground, taking flight only after they had emptied the clips of their pistols.[18]

On June 4, 1922, an assassin armed with cyanide tried to murder Philipp Scheidemann, the socialist who had proclaimed the democratic revolution in November 1918. Then, on June 24, two former naval officers shot down Walther Rathenau, Germany's brilliant foreign minister, a man of unimpeachable patriotism who had helped organize the German economy during World War I. Rathenau's murder followed inflammatory statements by right-wing politicians and repeated calls for his murder in radical nationalist circles. The nationalists hated him not only for his prominent role in the Republic, but also because he was Jewish. A popular chant expressed hatred for Rathenau and Prime Minister Joseph Wirth:

> *Bash Wirth always soundly,*
> *Bash his skull, so that it clatters.*
> *Rathenau, also, Walther,*
> *Will not get much older.*
> *Gun down Walther Rathenau,*
> *The goddamned Jewish swine!*

Two other crises contributed to the general sense of lawlessness and underscored the Republic's vulnerability and lack of legitimacy. The first was the inflation that had wiped out Germans' life savings and deeply devalued their wages by early 1922, and then escalated into complete economic chaos the following year. The second was the French and Belgian invasion of western Germany in January 1923.[19]

Unwilling to raise taxes, and unable to borrow on international financial markets, the Imperial government had financed much of the war effort by simply printing money. Germany's rulers planned to undo the damage by winning the war and forcing Germany's enemies to foot the bill. When Germany lost, the inevitable consequence was that inflation, which had already robbed the country's currency of two-thirds of its value by the summer of 1918, accelerated dramatically after the war's end. This wartime policy, followed by the inflationary policies of the Republic's first governments, reduced the German mark to only 5 percent of its prewar value by January 1922. Assets denominated in German currency—such as war bonds, mortgages, and pensions, which constituted the life savings of millions of middle-class Germans—had thus lost 95 percent of their worth. The cost of living consistently outran the growth of wages, so that the real value of salaries for higher civil servants had fallen by January 1922 to only 36 percent of their prewar value.[20]

As if the young Republic did not have troubles enough, in January 1923 French and Belgian troops crossed the German border and occupied the Ruhr Valley, the center of Germany's coal and steel industries. The French gave as their excuse the German failure to deliver reparations payments on time: they would extract reparations directly from the production of German coal mines and steel mills, managing these enterprises themselves. Their ultimate goal, however, was to establish the entire Rhine-Ruhr region as a separate political entity, as a way of whittling Germany's military potential down to size. The conflict in the Ruhr rallied radical nationalists once again, giving angry young men opportunities to take violent action in a campaign of sabotage directed against the French occupation. It also ignited the final, catastrophic phase of the German inflation.

Prime Minister Wilhelm Cuno called for a campaign of "passive resistance" against the French, whereby every German in the Ruhr would stop working and the German government would pay the strikers' salaries. The resistance campaign earned Cuno a short-lived popularity, but the government could not afford it, and ended up just printing money to pay the striking workers. At this point, the German mark began losing value so rapidly, from one day to the next, that it could no longer be used as a means of exchange. The economy began to break down altogether, and unemployment rose sharply. In Berlin, a kilogram (2.2 pounds) of potatoes, which had cost 20 marks in January 1923, sold for 90 *billion* marks in November. In December of that year, a kilogram of bread cost 467 billion marks. Eggs and cigarettes replaced the mark as a kind of currency, and one could get more heat by burning banknotes than from using the coal that they could buy. A government official who—unlike most people of his social class—supported the Republic, asked despairingly: "How is one supposed to convince a people of the worth of democracy, in such a witch's Sabbath?"[21]

The war and its terrible aftermath had two important consequences. First, this traumatic series of events undermined the legitimacy of the Republic and gave democracy a very bad name. Even during the years of relative political stability (1924–1930), at least a third of the voters supported parties that clearly rejected the democratic form of government. In the election of December 1924, the Nationalists polled 20.5 percent, the Communists 9 percent, and the Nazis, together with other right-wing fringe parties, 3 percent.

In the 1928 election, the Nationalists took 14.2 percent, the Nazis 2.6 percent, and the Communists 10.6 percent, and 13.7 percent of the vote went to an array of single-issue parties whose support for the Republic was doubtful at best. The only parties that unambiguously embraced democracy—the Weimar Coalition of the Socialists, the Democrats, and the Catholic Center Party—never took a majority of the vote after the election of January 1919.[22]

The war also shaped the man who would lead Germany into yet another war and bring about the Holocaust. Before World War I broke out in 1914, Adolf Hitler had known nothing but failure. He imagined himself to be an artistic genius, but failed the entrance examination of the Viennese Academy of Fine Arts in September 1907. So deep was his humiliation that he told neither his mother nor his only friend, August Kubizek, of his failure. Hitler's mother died of cancer in December of that year, and he moved to Vienna in February 1908, living off his inheritance and planning to reapply to the academy that fall. Chronically lazy and self-deluding, Hitler did nothing to prepare for the impending examination; instead, he frittered away his time attending the opera, going to museums, and pursuing a series of fantasy projects, each dropped soon after it was barely begun: writing plays, turning a Germanic saga into an opera, and trying to create a new drink to replace alcohol, to name only a few. In October, the Academy of Fine Arts decided not to even let him take the entrance examination a second time. Perhaps unable to face his friend after this failure, Hitler moved out of their shared lodgings without leaving Kubizek a forwarding address.[23]

When his money ran out in the autumn of 1909, Hitler lived on the street for several months, finding his way in December to a homeless shelter. In the words of his leading biographer, "the twenty-year-old would-be artistic genius had joined the tramps, winos, and down-and-outs in society's basement." In early 1910 Hitler managed to stabilize his living situation with a cash gift from an aunt, moving to a more respectable men's dormitory. There he lived for more than three years, earning his money by painting postcard-sized images of Vienna landmarks that a partner sold to tourists and frame shops. As before, he lacked all direction and purpose. In May 1913, Hitler fled to Munich to escape punishment for having avoided service in the Austro-Hungarian Army. There he resumed the aimless life he had lived in Vienna. In the summer of 1914, Hitler was living at the margins of society, a man without friends and without prospects. When war broke out in August, he promptly volunteered for the German Army.[24]

World War I was the best thing that ever happened to Adolf Hitler. It rescued him from a pointless existence and gave him a regular job, a sense of belonging, and a purpose for his life—the German victory for which he fought. The war also gave him his first meaningful successes: two medals for bravery under fire, the Iron Cross Second Class and First Class. During the war that he had unleashed on Europe in 1939, Hitler fondly recalled his years of trench warfare as "the one time when I had no worries." He served on the western front as a dispatch runner until he was temporarily blinded by mustard gas in October 1918, displaying a fanatical commitment to the war effort and an unswerving faith in Germany's inevitable victory. The revolution that toppled the emperor, and the armistice that confirmed Germany's loss of the war, coming two days apart in November 1918, fell upon Hitler as a crushing double blow. His entire world and his identity as a soldier had collapsed.[25]

Like so many on the right wing of German politics, Hitler came to blame the loss of the war on the revolution, and on the socialists and Jews who had supposedly brought the revolution about. Although he probably did not reach these conclusions until some point in 1919, in *Mein Kampf* Hitler backdated his political awakening to the day of Germany's surrender, as he lay in hospital recovering from poisoning by mustard gas. "There followed terrible days and even more terrible nights—I knew that all was lost," he wrote. "In these nights hatred grew within me, hatred against the perpetrators of this deed." Hitler had acquired the thirst for revenge that would drive his every action for the remainder of his bleak and violent life.[26]

Hitler published the second volume of his manifesto, *Mein Kampf*, in 1926. Although he did not know that he would one day try to murder every person of Jewish ancestry in Europe, he had articulated the fundamental beliefs that would lead to the Holocaust. By this point, all of the leading perpetrators of this crime had reached adulthood and acquired the political views and character traits that would make them into killers. The war, and the political violence that followed, especially service in the Free Corps, had hardened their hearts to the suffering of others and made them into fanatical adherents of an unspeakably violent ideology. Yet they lacked the opportunity to make their terrible ideas a reality. They were wholly excluded from power.

CHAPTER 7

WHY HITLER?

From that day on I could never violate my allegiance to
Hitler. I saw his illimitable faith in his people and the desire to set them free. His conviction upheld us, whenever
we weakened amid our trials; we leaned upon him in our
weariness.

His never-to-be forgotten speech affected me as the words
of a prophet.

—Two active members of the Nazi Party,
recalling speeches by Adolf Hitler[1]

Without Hitler there would have been no Holocaust. Yes, German
democracy had faltered badly by the end of the 1920s, and an authoritarian government might well have established itself. Without
Hitler, however, it is hard to imagine such a government perpetrating genocide. Hitler's bizarre and obsessive hatred for Jews was at
first particular to him, and was only later adopted by some of his
followers under his influence. Germany's cautious military leaders

eventually followed Hitler into world war with enthusiasm, but only after his early victories persuaded them of his "genius." On their own, they would never have undertaken the conquest of Europe. Yet Hitler's central role in the Holocaust only raises a larger question. How could a man like Adolf Hitler gain control of one of the world's most advanced societies? Hitler's coming to power is all the more remarkable when one considers not only his shocking moral depravity, but also his limited abilities and unattractive personal qualities.[2]

In personal terms, Hitler was not only unimpressive, but indeed downright repulsive. He seemed devoid of empathy, cared little for other human beings, and had no concern for the boundless suffering he inflicted upon them. In his entire life Hitler did not have a single friendship that most people would consider healthy. His two "romantic" relationships with women—Geli Raubal and Eva Braun—both ended with the women committing suicide, Braun taking poison by his side as he shot himself amid the ruins of Berlin.[3]

Far from developing nuanced insight into political affairs, Hitler let his thinking congeal into a handful of primitive obsessions that could be summarized on the back of a postcard. Unfortunately, these simplistic ideas were at least partly in step with the more sophisticated thinking of many of his contemporaries. The combination of his hate-fueled passion and endlessly repeated slogans and his uncanny feel for the mood of his audiences produced Hitler's only real talent, public speaking. This one skill carried him into politics and made his career.[4]

After World War I ended, Hitler faced the terrifying prospect of returning to civilian society and the unbroken record of failure that he had suffered before the war. Seeking desperately to remain in the military as long as he could, Hitler found employment with the army as a propaganda officer. Trained to spread nationalist and anticommunist ideas among the troops, Hitler discovered his gift for public speaking. During the crisis-laden five years that followed Germany's defeat in November 1918, Hitler steadily gained prominence in radical right-wing politics in Munich, the capital of Bavaria and a center of hostility to the young Republic. Discharged from the army in March 1920, Hitler threw in his lot with an obscure radical faction, the National Socialist German Workers Party, later to be known as the "Nazis," an abbreviation derived from the German pronunciation of the word "national." Being far and away the best public speaker in Munich, Hitler became the head of the Nazi Party in 1921, since only he could draw crowds to the party's rallies. By late 1923, the party counted 55,000 members, up from a few hundred when Hitler had joined in 1920. Hitler had become the most visible public figure calling for Bavarians to lead a coup against the democratic government in Berlin. Yet Hitler's understanding of politics began and ended with his ability to rouse the hateful passions of nationalist true believers.[5]

Hitler's record during his early career is one of political incompetence, displaying a complete cluelessness about the ways and means of acquiring power. Nowhere was Hitler's ineptitude more obvious than in the farcical episode known as the "Beer Hall Putsch." During the crisis year 1923, galloping inflation and the French-led invasion of the Ruhr made the dissolution of the Republic seem a real possibility. On November 8, Hitler and a group of his followers stormed a political meeting being held in a Munich beer hall. Hitler waved a pistol and forced the leaders of the Bavarian government and the local army commander into a private room. Facing death threats from Hitler, they promised to support his half-baked plan: Hitler would march on Berlin at the head of the Bavarian contingent of the German Army, topple the Republic, and declare himself leader of Germany.[6]

After one of Hitler's accomplices made the mistake of releasing the Bavarian leaders, they reneged on their promises to Hitler, and his coup, or *Putsch*, swiftly collapsed. The next morning Hitler made a final delusional attempt to inspire the Bavarian troops to mutiny against their officers and follow him to Berlin. As he marched his supporters into central Munich, shooting broke out between the police and Hitler's followers, leaving eighteen men dead, including four police officers. By all rights, Hitler's career in German politics should have ended then and there: conviction on charges of high treason, a long prison term, and then deportation to his native Austria, as he had never gained German citizenship.

Not for the last time, an astonishing stroke of good luck saved Hitler from failure and well-deserved obscurity. A flagrantly biased trial judge and enemy of the Republic, Georg Neithardt, ignored procedural rules and let Hitler turn the trial into a circus, giving political speeches from the witness stand over the prosecutor's objections. The trial catapulted Hitler to national prominence, and his absurdly lenient sentence—five years—shocked even conservative opponents of the Republic. Unfairly credited by a supportive prison warden with good behavior, Hitler was released in December 1924 after only thirteen months in custody, and efforts to have him deported led nowhere. Official favoritism toward Hitler was only one example of how conservative elites deliberately undermined the Republic, but it was one of the most consequential.[7]

His trial for treason was a triumph for Hitler. It persuaded both Hitler and his dedicated followers that he was the charismatic Leader destined to be the savior of Germany, the one long dreamt of by the nationalist Right. Over the next four years, the Nazi Party was transformed into a new kind of political organization, a "Leader party" in which Hitler's authority was unquestioned, and in which loyalty to him papered over all disagreements between followers. During this period, the party spread beyond its Bavarian stronghold to build a national organization, refined its methods of agitation, and increased its membership, which passed the 100,000 mark in October 1928. Throughout these years Hitler played a hands-off role, leaving vital organizational matters to subordinates, of whom Gregor Strasser was the most important. Hitler's detachment partly reflected his own chronic laziness, indecision, and lack of executive ability. It also sprang from his need to protect his charismatic image, his main contribution to the growth of the party, by placing himself above intraparty conflicts. Now unshakable in his messianic self-image, Hitler resolutely insisted on his dictatorial control over the Nazi Party. His supreme confidence, together with his brilliant public speaking, convinced enough followers of his genius that his control of the party became complete.[8]

Despite the Nazi Party's development of a tight organization and an effective propaganda apparatus, until 1930 Hitler and his party remained an insignificant splinter group, more a nuisance than a danger. The Nazis polled only 2.6 percent of the vote in the election of 1928. All this changed when the American stock market crashed on October 29, 1929, setting off the Great Depression.[9]

Throughout the world, the Depression shuttered businesses, closed banks, wiped out life savings, and put millions out of work. But it struck Germany with exceptional fury. By January 1933, the German unemployment rate stood at a shocking 30 percent. Including hidden unemployment and workers on shortened hours, almost half the labor force was wholly or partially unemployed. However, Germany's economic collapse, and the resulting failure of democratic government, were not inevitable, but instead resulted in large part from foolish decisions made by Germany's rulers.[10]

Germany's president, Paul von Hindenburg, had long hoped to force the Socialists out of government and destroy parliamentary democracy. Germany's top general in World War I, Hindenburg had promoted the lie that the democratic revolutionaries of 1918 had lost the war by stabbing the army in the back. When a conflict broke out in March 1930 between the Socialists and the People's

Party over unemployment benefits, Hindenburg used it as an excuse to carry out his long-standing plan. He installed a new prime minister, Heinrich Brüning, who bypassed parliament by issuing emergency decrees that Hindenburg signed into law. The constitution allowed an emergency decree to become law as long as a majority of the parliament did not vote to overturn the decree. On July 16, the parliament did just that, rejecting one of Brüning's measures. Rather than accepting the majority's decision, Brüning and Hindenburg took a fatal step, one that would prove a turning point in German history: they dissolved the parliament and called an election for September 14, naïvely thinking that the election would produce a more cooperative parliament.[11]

In the September 1930 election, the Nazis made their breakthrough: they polled over 18 percent of the vote, up from only 2.6 percent in 1928, and 107 deputies in brown-shirted Nazi uniforms marched into parliament. From this point forward, it would have been extremely difficult to create a parliamentary majority that could choose a cabinet and prime minister. Brüning continued to govern using emergency decrees signed by Hindenburg, and the moderate parties decided not to vote against his decrees, fearing that new elections might bring even more Nazis into parliament. Germany had ceased to be a democracy.[12]

Brüning's policies only worsened the situation, severely damaging the German economy and deepening the suffering of the German people. In part because he believed that balancing the budget would help the economy recover, Brüning raised taxes and slashed government spending. However, even after everyone could see that his policies had done terrible damage, Brüning stayed the course. His second, overriding aim was to show that even after taking such drastic measures, the German government could not come up with the reparations payments required by the Versailles Treaty. In other words, he accepted the suffering of the German people in the hope that it would help him persuade the victors of World War I to release Germany from its reparations obligations. Pensions, salaries, and unemployment benefits were all cut to the bone. This deflationary policy led to a further contraction of the German economy, and helps explain why unemployment rose higher in Germany than in any other major industrial economy. Not surprisingly, Brüning became almost universally hated: his government had little support in the elected parliament, and the economic situation had gone from crisis to catastrophe.[13]

By May 1932, Hindenburg and his advisers could see that Brüning had become a dangerous liability. At this point, Hindenburg could have chosen to govern with support from parties that supported democracy by granting emergency decrees to a coalition of moderate parties that had polled almost 43 percent in the 1930 elections. However, such a coalition would have included the Socialists, and Hindenburg had no intention of granting them any role in government. Besides, he was determined to destroy parliamentary democracy. So he looked instead for ways to create an authoritarian government that, unlike Brüning's cabinet, would have meaningful support from the German people. In this course of action, Hindenburg could count on the approval of much of Germany's elite—big business, large landowners, the titled aristocracy, and the military and higher civil service. Although these groups differed among themselves as to strategy, they agreed that some kind of authoritarian system should replace the hated Republic.[14]

Hindenburg replaced Brüning with Franz von Papen in mid-1932 and called an election for July, having secured a promise from Hitler—soon to be broken—that the Nazis would not join a vote to topple the Papen government. Hindenburg and Papen believed that they could "tame" the Nazi movement and harness it to their government. The July 1932 election was a disaster. The Nazis reached their all-time peak of 37.3 percent of the electorate. Making matters worse, the Communists polled 14.3 percent. The two extreme parties now made up a majority of parliament; if they voted together (as they sometimes did), they could block Papen from governing by emergency decree. The way back to democratic government by parliamentary majority was now definitively blocked, and even government by emergency decree could no longer be continued in conformity with the constitution. At this point Hitler saw his opening.[15]

Hitler began to woo Hindenburg, asking that the president make him prime minister and let him form a government. Hindenburg mistrusted Hitler and refused for the time being. But the government's problem remained: it did not seem safe to continue governing without any popular support, especially as the Nazis and Communists both had large paramilitary organizations that might rise in rebellion. The Papen government, known as the "cabinet of barons" because of its elite membership, had almost no support in parliament or in the country at large.[16]

A second election, in November 1932, brought the government only a small bit of good news: the Nazi vote had fallen 4 points, to 33.1 percent. Hindenburg wanted Papen to continue in office, if need be by declaring a state of emergency in outright defiance of the constitution. At this crucial juncture, the army weighed in during a December 2 cabinet meeting, presenting the results of a recent war games exercise. Lieutenant Colonel Eugen Ott explained that the army would not be able to maintain order if confronted by widespread strikes and an uprising by Nazi and communist paramilitaries, especially if they were combined with a Polish attack on Germany's eastern borders, which was at least possible. The army's judgment was probably overly pessimistic, but it had its effect on Hindenburg, who replaced Papen with General Kurt von Schleicher. However, the temptation to bring Hitler into the government was now even greater: the threat of a Nazi uprising would be banished, the government could now use the Nazis' popular support to buttress its own legitimacy, and Hindenburg could claim to be acting in a manner permitted by the constitution. Even so, Hindenburg resisted this step, not wanting to give so much power to a man he mistrusted and a party that used so much violence to achieve its aims.[17]

At the end, Franz von Papen played the fatal role. He was a favorite of Hindenburg, who seemed to regard him with fatherly affection. Papen persuaded Hindenburg to let Hitler form a minority government of Nazis and Nationalists. The Nazis would have only three officials in the cabinet: Hitler as prime minister, Wilhelm Frick as national minister of the interior, and Hermann Göring as Prussian minister of the interior. Papen, serving as deputy prime minister, would be tasked with keeping an eye on Hitler. Hitler was a political amateur, Papen assured Hindenburg, and Papen would exploit Hitler's popular support while retaining real control over the government. It was the worst mistake in history. Hindenburg said yes, and Adolf Hitler became prime minister of Germany on January 30, 1933.

The German people did not choose Nazi rule by a majority vote. The Nazi fraction of the electorate peaked at 37.3 percent in July 1932, and fell to 33.1 percent in the last free elections in November. Nonetheless, the Nazis had become the country's largest party, and so it is important to ask what Germans were voting for when they marked their ballots for Hitler. It is also essential to understand what motivated the nearly 850,000 activists who belonged to the Nazi Party on the eve of Hitler's taking power.

A very unusual set of documents reveals a lot about what motivated dues-paying members of the Nazi Party. An American sociology professor, Theodore Abel, gathering data for a book on the Nazis, went to Germany in 1934, a year and a half after Hitler had taken power. Abel sponsored a contest inviting party members to write essays in which they explained why they had become Nazis. Over six hundred Nazi Party activists submitted essays, and Abel awarded modest cash prizes to the best entrants. Their beliefs, and their reasons for joining the party, continued the basic themes of German nationalist politics. Their ideas were not new; they had already been established before World War I, and had become more popular among the middle class thanks to the terrible strains and intensified conflicts of the war and its aftermath.[18]

The Nazi belief system, as expressed by Abel's essayists, boils down to three mutually reinforcing elements: the ideal of a national community, the leadership principle, and anti-Semitism. The central concept of community was, as Abel aptly explained, "an untranslatable term which combines the meaning of 'unity,' 'devotion to the community,' mutual aid, brotherly love, and kindred social values." Although the family represented the primary form of community, the Nazis wanted it to encompass the entire German nation. This ideal expressed the Nazis' most important stated ambition: to overcome the divisions of religion and social class and to replace the distinct identities of each social group with the sole identifier "German." The ideal of the national community was partly rooted in militant hostility to the socialist and communist parties, which supposedly divided German workers from the rest of society. "While I was in the army," wrote one activist, "I found that the best soldiers came from the working class; now I had to witness these workers being alienated from the Fatherland. Why then should Germany rend itself? . . . At the same time . . . [Nazism], with its promise of a community of blood, barring all class struggle, attracted me profoundly."[19]

Even as they rejected the Marxist idea of class struggle, ardent Nazis resented the elaborate status hierarchy that prevailed in German society and expressed a faith that the new national community would banish social injustice and elite snobbery. For many, this hope for unity and belonging went back to their experience fighting in World War I, which they idealized as a time of harmony and mutual respect among comrades who came from every walk of life. As one veteran put it, "the war had taught us one lesson, the great community of the front. All class differences, staunchly entrenched before the war, disappeared under its spell. Out there it was what a person *was*, not what he seemed to be, that counted. There was only a people, no individuals."[20]

Militant German nationalism, and visions of national greatness, formed the necessary complement to this utopian vision of social harmony. Overcoming Germany's humiliation by the Treaty of Versailles demanded unity among Germans, while intense national pride would replace an individual's identity as member of a particular social class. "Seldom was our people united and great," wrote one of Abel's essayists. "But whenever it was strongly unified, it was unconquerable. This then is the secret of our idea, and in it lies the power of [Nazism]: unity is the goal of our Leader, who wants to make the people strong, so it may become powerful again."[21]

The "leadership principle" further anchored the idealized national community. Within the Nazi Party, officials at every level of the hierarchy were called "leaders," each receiving obedience from those below. At the top stood "the Leader" (*der Führer*), Hitler, who would command the whole nation. No interest, no social class, no autonomous group, could pursue its narrow desires in a manner harmful to the national community, because Hitler imposed order upon the entire nation. Germans had expressed a longing for such a leader long before Hitler entered politics, and many of Abel's essayists voiced this hope. "Around 1923," wrote a high-school teacher, "I reached the conclusion that no party, but a single man could save Germany." Hitler's spellbinding oratory won numberless converts to his movement, convincing them that he was the long-sought Leader who could unite the nation. "I heard Hitler in Bonn, in 1926," wrote one Nazi. "What he said, in clear, concise phrases, had long agitated the feelings of every good German. The German soul spoke to German manhood in his words. From that day on I could never violate my allegiance to Hitler. I saw his illimitable faith in his people, and the desire to set them free."[22]

Anti-Semitism, the third element, bound each part of the national community together by offering a common enemy, one that could be blamed for the country's divisions and all of Germany's recent setbacks. Nazi racial doctrine assumed both the genetic unity of the German people and irreducible differences between Germans and the "destructive" Jews. Being loyal only to other Jews, including Jews in foreign countries, Germany's Jews had supposedly instigated World War I, profited from the war economy at Germany's expense, and divided Germans by manipulating the political parties, especially the socialist and communist parties. One of Abel's essayists declared that "these Jews made use of the different parties to divide the German people against each other, while their leaders all subscribed to the same hidden purpose: namely, the exploitation of German workers." "I began a searching inquiry into the Jewish question," wrote another Nazi. "I read a great deal, and it became increasingly clear to me that international Marxism and the Jewish problem are closely bound together. In this fact I recognized the cause of the political, moral, and cultural decay of my Fatherland."[23]

Members of the Nazi Party varied somewhat in which element of the movement's belief system was most important to them. Of Abel's activists, roughly a third were principally motivated by hopes for a socially cohesive national community. Another third had responded mainly to ultranationalist themes in the party's propaganda, such as attacks on the Treaty of Versailles, although militant nationalism can be seen as the necessary complement of the idealized national community. Although anti-Semitism has been justifiably described as the "ideological cement" holding the Nazi movement together, for most members it was not the highest priority. A full two-thirds of these members expressed hostility toward Jews, but only about one member in eight said that anti-Semitism was his principal motive. Almost one-fifth of the sample said that their worship of Hitler was their chief reason for joining the movement. Looking at Abel's sample another way, namely, by asking who they hated most, two-thirds were "predominantly anti-Marxists." Over half hoped that Germany would be "reborn" and become "free of the system," meaning the system of divisive party government under the Weimar Republic.[24]

Explaining why 33.1 percent of the electorate voted Nazi in November 1932 is more difficult than explaining why people joined the party, since there were no public opinion polls. No one asked the voters why they had cast their ballots for the Nazis. One can make only an educated guess based on the timing of the Nazi electoral successes, the leading themes of the party's campaign advertising, and the socioeconomic backgrounds of the Nazi voters. In the first place, one must remember that the party polled only 2.6 percent of the vote in 1928. Although the Nazis made significant gains in some local and regional elections in 1929, it seems that the Great Depression, more than anything else, permitted their breakthrough at the national level. Hindenburg's imposition of a de facto dictatorship only served to further alienate the voters from their government. The government's economic failures gave the Nazis a tremendous advantage, because they had never borne any responsibility in the government of the Republic, and thus could not be blamed for any of the other parties' policies. Having never voted for a specific policy, the Nazis were free to make unrealistic, often mutually contradictory promises to different economic interests. The Nazi Party was therefore the ideal vehicle for protest, that is, for the expression of the voters' discontent.[25]

As a party of protest, the Nazis placed great emphasis on negative themes in their campaign advertising. Attacks on the socialists and communists were by far the most important and consistent theme in Nazi electoral propaganda. This assault on the Marxist parties reinforced a second central theme of Nazi Propaganda: that the multiparty democracy of the Weimar Republic—which the socialists had done so much to create—divided Germans against each other to the point of national paralysis. In the campaign leading to the Nazis' breakthrough in 1930, Hitler emphasized, again and again, that Germany had become fatally divided by antagonisms between the parties; only the Nazi Party could transcend these divisions and unify the nation. In the elections of July 1932, the Nazis again took up this theme, which had brought them success in 1930: only they could unite the country. Luise Solmitz, a Hamburg schoolteacher, wrote in her diary after seeing Hitler speak: "How many look to him in touching faith as the helper, savior, the redeemer. . . . To him, who rescues the Prussian prince, the scholar, the clergyman, the peasant, the worker, the unemployed out of the party into the people." To his claim for national unity through Nazism, Hitler added, with greater emphasis, the idea that the other parties had presided over the ruin of Germany, and that only the Nazi Party could save the country. To make this argument in 1932, Hitler had only to point to the flailing Brüning and Papen governments, whose policies worsened their people's suffering.[26]

Although the Nazi Party eventually drew members and voters from every walk of life and both major Christian denominations, the Protestant middle classes were heavily overrepresented in the Nazi electorate and the membership of the party. Protestants predominated largely because the Center Party was able to maintain its long-standing ties to the Catholic population and its organizational base in associations linked to the Catholic Church. Middle-class Germans were overrepresented partly as a result of the decade of economic misfortune that had begun for much of the middle class in 1914: the planned war economy that benefited big business and organized labor, but hurt family farms and urban small businesses, and then the hyperinflation that peaked in 1923, reducing the life savings of millions and the value of pensions by 85 percent. When the government ended the inflation in 1923 and 1924, reestablishing the value of all debts and pensions at only 15 percent of their prewar value, the established parties of the Protestant middle classes began to lose voters to dozens of new "splinter parties." Most of these parties represented very specific economic interests. A host of "revalorization" parties demanded that debts and pensions be revalued at some level higher than 15 percent of the prewar level, perhaps even at 100 percent. Other parties represented tenants or landlords, peasants or craftsmen, and so on. Such parties took 7.8 percent of the vote in the elections of December 1924, 13.7 percent in 1928, and 14.4 percent in 1930.[27]

While each splinter party demanded different policies, most of them had certain beliefs and attitudes in common and emphasized themes that also predominated in Nazi campaign advertising. They were especially critical of "the system" of parliamentary democracy. In particular, they complained that social-welfare spending, for example on health insurance, was too generous, and that their taxes were too high. These parties generally displayed not only a ferocious hostility to socialism and communism, but also a resentment of "big capitalism," for example, in the form of department stores that competed with small businesses. None of these tiny parties could accomplish anything in parliament on its own, but they represented a collective vote of protest. They reflected a profound alienation from the established middle-class parties and from the democratic form of government by voters who now lacked a political home. In the last free elections of the Republic, during the darkest depth of the Great Depression in 1932, these voters seem to have found their new political home in the Nazi Party. In the July 1932 balloting, the Nazis rocketed to 37.3 percent of the vote, while the splinter parties fell to 3.2 percent, far below their 1930 total of 14.4 percent. The three larger parties that had previously represented the Protestant middle classes had shrunk to only 8.1 percent of the vote, down from 36.9 percent in the election of December 1924. Most likely, the bulk of their lost voters had gone over to the Nazis.[28]

The history of the splinter parties, which reflected profoundly antidemocratic attitudes among much of the electorate, shows that the Great Depression by itself did not cause Hitler's rise to power and the collapse of German democracy. After all, although the Great Depression affected the entire world, established democracies such as the United States, France, and Great Britain never faced a serious challenge from an extremist movement comparable to the Nazi Party. An equally important factor was that much of the German electorate, and probably most of the country's elite, did not believe in democracy. German elites, in part because they feared socialism, had energetically fought against democratic reform from the 1890s on. As for the voters, they had had no experience of democracy before the 1918 revolution, and thereafter most of what they saw was simply bad. In the July 1932 election, nearly three-quarters of the voters chose parties that had explicitly rejected parliamentary democracy: not only the Nazis (37.3 percent), the Communists (14.3), and the Nationalists (5.9), but also the Catholic Center Party (15.7 percent), which had once been a mainstay of the Republic, but had now moved sharply to the right. In sum, three factors were needed to put Hitler in office: the Great Depression; Hindenburg's blunders and determination to destroy the parliamentary system; and the hostility of millions of Germans toward democracy. Had any one of these factors been absent, Hitler would have remained an unimportant agitator on the margins of German politics.[29]

When Hitler became prime minister in January 1933, he soon finished the task that President Hindenburg and Heinrich Brüning had begun in 1930: destroying Germany's first democracy. With that step a crucial barrier against genocide had fallen. Functioning democracies do not perpetrate genocide: although majorities have voted to discriminate against minorities (as in the American South), voters would never support mass murder. With Hitler in office, World War II and the Holocaust were now at least conceivable. Yet for Hitler to radicalize his Jewish policy to full-blown genocide, and to launch his murderous war against the Soviet Union, he needed to become far more than a dictator. To unleash this unprecedented violence, Hitler in fact needed more than his countrymen's passivity and failure to rebel against him. He needed their enthusiastic support, and he needed the country's elite—including professionals, businessmen, higher civil servants, and military officers—to actively participate in the murder of the Jewish people. When Hitler took power, most of these men were not Nazis; most of them were nationalist conservatives who disdained Nazism as a lower-class movement, and who looked down on Hitler because of his vulgarity and limited education.[30]

By the time Hitler invaded the Soviet Union in June 1941 and began the mass murder of Jews behind the German lines, he had become much more than a tyrant, although he was that also. Millions of Germans had come to worship him, believing that his judgments were infallible and that his commands were a historical necessity. This near-deification of Hitler was a cause of the Holocaust in its own right. How did it come about?

CHAPTER 8

FROM DICTATOR TO DEMIGOD

As my "creator," his portrait hangs both in my workplace
and in the living room at home. A look at him has often
produced in me what "pious people" allegedly feel when
deep in prayer.

—A 1939 letter about Hitler to a German newspaper

I will go down as the greatest German in history.

—Adolf Hitler, March 15, 1939[1]

By the time the Holocaust began in 1941, Hitler had become, in
the eyes of millions of his people, a mythic figure, known by the
quasi-religious title "the Leader" (*der Führer*), whose every command deserved obedience. This "Hitler myth" was composed of
a set of beliefs that others held concerning him: that he was im-
pervious to ordinary human appetites and needs, whether for love,
companionship, sex, or luxury; that he was the first servant of his
people, devoted to them and nothing else; that he embodied the

German nation and its special destiny; and that he was a political and military genius of superhuman abilities, even an instrument of divine Providence.[2]

The belief in Hitler's magical qualities drew strength from many sources: the long-standing hope among countless Germans that a charismatic leader could heal the nation's divisions and solve all problems; the German people's desperation amid the terrible crisis of the Great Depression; Hitler's gifts as a public speaker; the new medium of radio, which brought his voice into German homes; the skillful use of propaganda to burnish Hitler's image; and, above all, from Hitler's astonishing run of dramatic successes, beginning with the suppression of socialism and communism in early 1933, and ending only with the failure of German armies to capture Moscow in December 1941.[3]

Belief in the magical qualities of a charismatic leader usually takes root in conditions of crisis, when it seems that only someone of superhuman abilities can master the challenges of the day. In the world's two largest democracies, the economic suffering caused by the Great Depression was especially severe, and both countries saw the rise to power of leaders who were seen by their people as stunningly charismatic, although they could not have been more different in other respects: Adolf Hitler in Germany and Franklin Delano Roosevelt in the United States. In Germany the crisis was far more frightening than it was in the United States, because on top of 30 percent unemployment (25 percent in the United States), Germans suffered a complete loss of faith in their county's political system. In contrast, Americans never doubted the continued existence of their democratic form of government, which had endured for nearly a century and a half, and which had not faced any threats to its existence since the Civil War some seventy years earlier. Perhaps because the Germans faced a much more terrible crisis after 1929, they rewarded Adolf Hitler's later successes with a childlike adulation that may have exceeded even Roosevelt's extraordinary popularity.[4]

Besides the severity of the economic and political crisis, a second factor prepared the German people to accept the myth of Hitler's magical abilities: they were looking for him long before he arrived. Otto von Bismarck did much to create the expectation that a brilliant leader could solve all problems. He had led Prussia through the three victorious wars that had resulted in the creation of the first German nation-state, the German Empire, in 1871. As prime minister, Bismarck then wholly dominated the politics of the empire for another nineteen years. There is no counterpart to Bismarck in American history. At most one could say that he combined George Washington's accomplishment as the father of his country with the tactical cleverness and political longevity of Franklin Roosevelt. Even that comparison, however, is faulty, as Roosevelt governed for only twelve years, in contrast to Bismarck's twenty-eight. After Bismarck died in 1898, he became an object of worship for Germans who believed that another great leader could magically resolve the conflicts dividing their country. Between 1900 and 1910, enthusiasts for this Bismarck cult erected some five hundred "Bismarck towers" in every corner of Germany.[5]

As seen in the example of Heinrich Class, right-wing nationalists were calling—already before World War I—for a ruthless "Leader" who could suppress conflict and prevent the advent of democracy. The war only worsened the divisions within German society, and the 1918 revolution established the long-feared democratic political system and gave the hated socialists a share in power. With a feeling of severe crisis now widespread among the middle class, hopes for an all-powerful Leader spread far beyond the ranks of extreme nationalists. The massive "Steel Helmet" veteran's organization called for a "strong hand" to banish the "plague" of democratic government, insisting that Germany needed "a dictator . . .

who would sweep out the entire muck with an iron broom." The idea of a charismatic Leader had become so common during the 1920s that an analyst of the German automobile industry concluded that it could be saved only by "a superior leader personality, a man of strong action."[6]

Hitler's impressive talent for public speaking also did much to create the myth of his superhuman qualities. His impact on audiences can only be described as electrifying. One Nazi Party member affirmed that "his never-to-be-forgotten speech affected me as the words of a prophet." Another declared that "no one who has ever looked Hitler in the eye and heard him speak can ever break away from him." Amplified by the new and exciting medium of radio, Hitler's oratorical gifts reached into millions of homes, winning him enthusiastic admirers and fanatical converts among all social classes. A parallel to President Roosevelt's popular Fireside Chats on American radio seems obvious. The Germans are not the only nation that has come to idolize a charismatic leader during a time of crisis.[7]

In promoting the myth of his special qualities, Hitler had an immensely skilled helper, his Propaganda Minister Joseph Goebbels. Using film, radio, posters, the press, and carefully staged rallies and marches by the party members, Goebbels nurtured the myth of Hitler's infallibility. He promoted as well the illusion that Hitler knew the hopes and struggles of every German, cared deeply for each of his people, and might intercede for them personally, much in the manner of the loving Christian God. However, given how few Germans wrote letters to Hitler—perhaps not many more than 100,000, as compared to as many as 30 million Americans who wrote to Franklin Roosevelt during the same time period—one may question how many Germans were actually fooled by photos of gentle "Uncle Adolf" surrounded by adoring children, and other images supposedly demonstrating the Leader's kind benevolence.

Far more important than Hitler's oratorical gifts or Goebbels's propaganda in shaping the Leader's image was Hitler's unprecedented run of political and military successes.[8]

Hitler's record of success began when a mentally unbalanced Dutch communist burned down the German parliament building on the night of February 27–28, 1933. Arguing that the fire was the signal for a general communist uprising, Hitler secured from President Hindenburg a set of emergency powers that allowed Hitler to unleash the Prussian police and his own storm troopers upon the leadership and active cadres of the socialist and communist parties. Within weeks, these men were in captivity, hiding, or exile. At one stroke, Hitler had banished the specter of communist revolution that had terrified the great majority of the population. Moving rapidly, Hitler suppressed all political parties other than the Nazi Party and crushed the labor unions. Harmony among Germany's warring social classes was thereby imposed from above, to the enthusiastic approval of everyone outside the working class. The mass media were rapidly brought under Nazi control. After Hitler gained control of the army in August 1934, he ruled Germany as an unchallenged dictator.[9]

From these beginnings, Hitler moved from strength to strength. When he had become prime minister on January 30, 1933, unemployment in Germany had exceeded 30 percent of the labor force. Hitler promptly embarked on a program of deficit spending that massively funded the armaments industry, producing countless jobs throughout the economy. Combined with a cyclical upswing in the economy that began shortly after Hitler took office, this military spending produced full employment in Germany within only four years. This policy did not reflect any economic sophistication on Hitler's part, for he understood nothing of the study of economics. Rather, Hitler pumped money into armaments because he planned to start another major war. Few Germans could understand his intentions, given Nazi control of the media. The German worker knew only that he had his job back. Among the major industrial economies of the West, whether in Europe or North America, only Germany escaped the Great Depression during the 1930s. For millions of Germans, including many of the socialist and communist workers who had opposed the Nazis during the Weimar Republic, Hitler appeared to be a miracle worker, a man who brought bread, jobs, and prosperity.[10]

Beyond Germany's economic recovery, a series of seemingly brilliant foreign policy breakthroughs cemented Hitler's image as political genius. In a series of bold initiatives during the 1930s, Hitler reversed several terms of the hated Treaty of Versailles. Here again, these victories reflected no genius on Hitler's part, but instead resulted from the combination of his violent instincts and circumstances that rewarded aggression. As Hitler's leading biographer explained, Hitler had only one strategy throughout his political career. Incapable of compromise, he took aggressive action or threatened force if his demands were not met, which worked only as long as his opponents backed down. This was not the strategic wisdom of a statesman, but rather the impulsive brutality of a thug.[11]

Circumstances favored Hitler in that the most hated terms of the Versailles Treaty rested on questionable moral foundations. The treaty limited Germany's army to the tiny size of 100,000 men, reduced the German navy to a sort of glorified coast guard, and forbade Germany from building an air force or submarine fleet. Germany could not defend its border with France, because it was also forbidden to station troops or build fortifications on either side of the Rhine River. Why should Germany, alone among the countries of Europe, be denied the right to defend itself from military aggression? The peace treaties following World War I contained a further element of hypocrisy. A central principle behind all the

treaties was "national self-determination," the idea that each nation—Czechs, Poles, Hungarians, and so on—should govern itself
in its own country. Yet the Germans who made up the population
of Austria, in violation of their wishes and those of the Germans,
were not allowed to become part of Germany, because this would
have made Germany larger and more powerful than the war's victors wanted it to be. Germany and Austria therefore remained separate countries until Germany annexed Austria in 1938. Especially
in Great Britain, elite opinion had come to recognize that parts
of the treaty could not be maintained. The leaders of Britain and
France chose a policy of appeasement, believing that by agreeing to
"reasonable" German demands, they could ensure peace. They had
no way of knowing that Hitler's aggressive moves during the 1930s
were only the first steps of his plan to dominate Europe.[12]

Hitler had another major advantage as he proceeded to tear
up the Treaty of Versailles: far from fearing war, he welcomed it.
Indeed, Hitler may have been the only man of any influence in Europe during the 1930s who looked forward to another major war.
After the horrors of World War I, the peoples of Europe had had
enough. Public opinion in France, Britain, and Germany clearly
opposed another war, but with a crucial difference. France and
England were democracies, whose governments acted on their citizens' fervent desire to avoid another armed conflict. As a dictator,
Hitler could safely ignore his people's wishes, counting on them
to obey his commands once war had broken out, when he could
call on them to "defend the Fatherland." Time and again he gladly
risked war, and his French and British opponents backed down.[13]

Hitler reinstated a military draft in March 1935 and announced that Germany would build an army of over half a million men. He guessed, correctly, that France and Britain would take
no military action to punish this violation of the treaty, yet this
was no mature and careful judgment on his part. Before making

this potentially risky move, Hitler did not even discuss it with his military or foreign policy advisers. The German people held their collective breath. Did this mean war? When the French and British did nothing, anxiety gave way to euphoria. An intelligence agent of the socialist underground grudgingly reported that "the whole of Munich was on its feet. People can be compelled to sing, but not forced to sing with such enthusiasm. . . . The trust in the political talent and the honest will of Hitler becomes greater all the time. He is loved by many."[14]

Almost a year later, in March 1936, Hitler marched German troops into the Rhineland, which had been demilitarized under the Versailles Treaty. Anticipating this step, the French and British governments had already decided against responding with force. Among the German people, dread of war soon gave way to enthusiasm when war did not come. Luise Solmitz, a Hamburg housewife whose husband and daughter had been stripped of their German citizenship because of their part-Jewish ancestry, spoke for many when she confided her thoughts to her diary. Not long before, "when demoralization ruled amongst us," she declared, "we would not have dared contemplate such deeds. Again and again, the Leader faces the world with a *fait accompli*. Along with the world, the individual holds his breath. Where is Hitler heading, what will be the end, the climax of this speech, what boldness, what surprise will there be? And then it comes, blow on blow, action as stated without fear of his own courage. That is so strengthening. . . . That is the deep, unfathomable secret of the Leader's nature. . . . And he is always lucky." The Leader, Germans were told, was a man of peace, an incomparable genius who had restored their nation's pride and rightful place in the world without bloodshed. His successes seemed to bear out the myth.[15]

When Hitler annexed Austria in March 1938, he sent troops into that small country in an act of naked aggression. Or was it?

After all, very many Austrians greeted the German forces, and later Hitler himself, with raucous enthusiasm. When he drove into Austria not far behind his invading troops, Hitler found his motorcade repeatedly delayed by the enthusiastic crowds that lined the roads. Reaching Vienna, the capital, on March 14, Hitler encountered an enthusiasm that "defied all description," in the words of a Swiss journalist. An English observer remarked: "To say that the crowds which greeted [Hitler] were delirious with joy is an understatement." Hitler had to appear, again and again, on the balcony of his hotel to satisfy the crowd, which shouted, "We want to see our Leader." In annexing Austria, Hitler was pushing on an open door. France and Britain did nothing to oppose him, in part because Hitler's actions could be reconciled with the spirit of the peace treaties, and were welcomed by a very large fraction of the Austrian people. In German regions that bordered Austria, where fear of war had been especially acute, officials noted "heartfelt jubilation" everywhere, "above all because our Leader has pulled it off without bloodshed."[16]

Even the October 1938 annexation of the Sudetenland, a German-speaking region of western Czechoslovakia, could be rationalized as another expression of the principle of national self-determination. Hitler took bold, decisive action, and his reckless gambler's temperament was rewarded by French and British inaction. Yet again, the German people briefly feared war—especially since this time he had threatened war—but when war did not come, and the annexation was accomplished, they rejoiced in the triumph of their Leader, a "man of peace" who had restored Germany to her rightful status as a great power, without firing a shot.[17]

Nothing cemented the myth of Adolf Hitler's magical abilities like the swift and crushing victory over France in June 1940. In World War I, the Germans had fought the French for four years of bloody stalemate, lost 2 million of their young men, and lost the war. Now, Hitler had crushed the hated enemy and avenged the defeat of 1918 in six weeks of exhilarating triumphs at the cost of only 30,000 German soldiers killed. Yet happenstance, arguably more than any other factor, had played the decisive role.[18]

Hitler had started World War II by invading Poland on September 1, 1939. As they had warned, the French and British governments promptly declared war on Germany. Yet Hitler had attacked Poland without making any plans for war against France and Britain; he had no military strategy and no blueprint to gear up the German economy for long-term armaments production. Hitler then compounded this flagrant recklessness by demanding that the German Army march into battle in the West only a month after the conquest of Poland was finished, while his army was short on ammunition and half its armored vehicles were out of action. Their objections overridden by Hitler, the generals prepared to invade southward through Holland and Belgium into France, but the operation was repeatedly delayed through the fall and winter by bad weather, which would have kept the German air force from giving tactical support to Hitler's tank armies.[19]

These postponements of the invasion infuriated Hitler, but they proved to be his salvation. The French and British expected the Germans to invade by exactly the route that Hitler's generals were planning throughout the fall of 1939. Their expectation was further confirmed when a German officer's plane made a forced landing in Belgium and he could not fully destroy the documents he was carrying. These documents were based on the original plan, which was soon replaced by an entirely different strategy. Two enterprising generals, Heinz Guderian and Erich von Manstein, challenged an assumption long held by the senior leadership of both the French and German armies, namely, that the dense Ardennes forest in Luxembourg and Belgium could not be crossed by tanks. In fact, a network of logging roads would allow German tank armies to roll through in stealth, partly hidden from sight by the thick spring foliage. Bucking opposition from the Army High Command, Manstein secured a fateful meeting with Hitler on February 17, 1940, and presented his plan: a smaller German force would invade through Holland as originally planned, and serve as bait to draw the French and British off balance. The main blow would be delivered through the Ardennes, in tank columns that would slice through northern France, driving to the English Channel and cutting the Allied forces in two.[20]

Hitler deserves some credit for accepting Manstein's brilliant plan. He correctly feared that the Allies would expect the main thrust to come from the north. Yet all through the fall of 1939 he had insistently pressed for war, before the German Army had even recovered from the Polish campaign, and using the High Command's unimaginative strategy. Only bad weather had given Manstein time to develop his plan; only repeated postponements gave Hitler the chance to hear Manstein out. Hitler's fateful decision came not from military expertise, which he utterly lacked, but in large part from his natural preference for bold gambles and shocking surprises, combined with a large measure of good luck.[21]

The German armies attacked on May 10, 1940. As the northern prong of their invasion force drove into Holland, the Allies took the bait. The British sent almost their entire force, and the French sent their best and most mobile units northward to meet the German forces. Meanwhile, German tank armies rolled through the Ardennes unseen, exploding into the rear of the Allied forces. Covering 150 miles in only ten days, German armor reached the English Channel during the night of May 20–21. Cut off from their lines of supply, under attack from two directions, the Allied armies were lost. Cutting their losses, the British hastily assembled an armada of navy ships and private vessels, which rescued 340,000 French and British troops at Dunkirk during the last week in May, ferrying them across the Channel to safety. Paris fell on June 14 and France surrendered on the 22nd.[22]

Terrified that the war begun in September 1939 might turn into a repeat of World War I's horrific slaughter, Germans were overjoyed at the swift and stunning victory over France and Britain. They marveled at what they imagined to be Hitler's inexplicable genius. After the French surrender, the governor of the Swabia region reported that all "well-meaning" citizens saw "wholly, joyfully, and thankfully the superhuman greatness of the Leader."[23]

Thanks to his undeniable successes, popular adulation of Hitler soon took on the quality of a religious faith. Hitler's position as a kind of secular god would later convince many members of the SS, and others as well, to carry out the extermination of the Jews without feeling that they had to consider ordinary laws and morals. A minor Nazi Party official in Upper Bavaria reported, in autumn of 1935, the words of a woman who had formerly belonged to the communist party: "Look here, there's the picture of the Leader hanging in our one-time communist hovel, and beneath the picture I've taught my girl the Lord's Prayer. I, who left the Church in 1932. Every day my girl has to say the Lord's Prayer for the Leader, because he has given us back our daily bread." In the autumn of 1936, a Nazi Party member wrote a letter to Hitler containing this declaration of faith and love: "My Leader! . . . I feel compelled by unceasing love to thank our creator daily for, through his grace, giving us and the entire German people such a wonderful Leader. . . . It is a pleasure for me, not a compliment, not a hypocrisy, to pray for you, my Leader, that the Lord God who has created you as a tool for Germanity should keep you healthy."[24]

Not only was Hitler worshipped in a quasi-religious fashion, but over time he became the sole source of legal authority in Germany. Legal scholars and jurists would outbid each other in efforts to proclaim the Leader's unique place in legal theory and practice.

"The Leader is the supreme judge of the nation," declared Hans Frank, head of the German Academy of Law, in a 1938 speech to jurists. "Whether the Leader governs according to a formal written Constitution is not a legal question of the first importance. The legal question is only whether through his activity the Leader guarantees the existence of his people."[25]

Unconditional loyalty to the Leader was a supreme value within the ranks of the SS, who oversaw the extermination of the Jews and committed most of the murders. "My honor is loyalty," read the watchword of the SS. As Himmler explained to his men in a 1935 speech, loyalty was the SS man's supreme virtue. This included not only loyalty to friends and family, but also "loyalty to the Leader, and thereby to the German, the Germanic people." An SS man owed a duty of unconditional and unhesitating obedience to every order from the Leader. Himmler never tired of proclaiming his loyalty to Hitler in things both grave and trivial: "The Führer is always right, whether the subject is evening dress, bunkers, or the Reich motorways."[26]

Considering Hitler's growing status as the source of all legal authority, and the heavy emphasis within the SS on obedience to his commands, it seems plausible that Hitler's countless accomplices, who participated in murder in varied ways, both direct and indirect, found a special kind of comfort in the myth of Hitler's infallibility and godlike attributes. If Hitler stood above all law, whether human or divine, then so did they as instruments of his will. Acting on his orders, they operated within a space in which conventional moral principles did not apply.[27]

Karl Kretschmer, who served in a shooting squad in German-occupied Russia, confessed in a letter to his wife that his bloody work left him shaken. Nonetheless, he affirmed his belief that the Jews posed a mortal danger to Germany, and declared that "our faith in the Leader fulfills us and gives us strength to carry out our

difficult and thankless task." Erich Naumann commanded a shooting squad of several hundred men operating in territory that today
is Belarus. At his postwar trial, he claimed to have had "misgiv-
ings" about his actions, stating that "it was contrary to my nature
to kill defenseless people." However, when asked by the judge if he
had thought his actions were wrong, Naumann responded: "Not
wrong, Your Honor, because I was given the authority to do so,
because there was a Leader Order."[28]

A "Leader Order" had a sacred quality, enjoyed automatic legitimacy, and justified any action. Although commands to kill were
usually delivered verbally rather than in writing, every participant
in the Holocaust understood that a Leader Order demanded the
murders. The Auschwitz commander Rudolf Höss, who evidently
accepted his impending execution and made little effort to deny his
guilt, recalled that "I could not allow myself to form an opinion
about whether this mass extermination was necessary or not. At
the time it was beyond my frame of mind." Since "the Leader himself had ordered 'The Final Solution of the Jewish Question,' there
was no second-guessing for an old [Nazi], much less for an SS officer." Höss received his orders verbally from Himmler, and for the
SS, "Himmler's person was sacred. His orders in the name of the
Leader were holy."[29]

On August 15, 1941, as the shooting squads raged behind the
German Army's front lines, wiping out Jewish communities day
by day, Himmler visited the Byelorussian city of Minsk. Himmler
asked Artur Nebe, commander of a death squad, to shoot a hundred Jews as a demonstration, so that Himmler could see how
the process worked. Once the killing was done, SS General Erich
von dem Bach-Zelewski commented that this grisly task was emotionally and psychologically difficult for the shooters. In response,
Himmler addressed these men. Himmler assured them that their
consciences should be clear because they were soldiers who had to

obey every order without question. He alone had responsibility before God and Hitler for everything they had done.[30]

The men in the SS and other Nazi organizations who planned and carried out the murders did not just follow orders, although they did do that without fail. Frequently, they also acted on their own initiative, even pressing their superiors for permission to act with greater brutality. This phenomenon, like the tendency to unconditionally follow orders, was rooted in the central role that Hitler played in German law and politics. Because the Leader was the ultimate source of all authority, and increasingly the only source of authority for many men in the German government and Nazi Party, the legal system and traditional legal norms lost relevance over time, and government degenerated into a state of lawlessness. Hitler accelerated this process by creating administrative chaos, establishing multiple, competing governmental agencies for many areas of policy. He also undermined the legal system by giving Himmler, the SS, and secret police (which was part of the SS) free rein in combating Germany's "enemies," whether these were political dissidents, Jews, or "socially harmful elements," such as homosexuals or people deemed to be "work shy." Thus a defendant might win acquittal in court, only to have the secret police bundle him off to a concentration camp for an indefinite term of incarceration and hard labor.[31]

Recognizing this general lawlessness and administrative chaos, activists at all levels in the Nazi hierarchy acted on their own initiative. They found justification for their actions in the notion that their deeds were consistent with Hitler's general statements of purpose. Such men took the position that "the Leader would approve if he knew what I was doing." Werner Willikens, an official in the Prussian Agriculture Ministry, explained this dynamic in a routine speech. "Very often," Willikens complained, "it has been the case that individuals . . . have waited for commands and orders."

Instead, he admonished, "it is the duty of every single person to attempt, in the spirit of the Leader, to work towards him." An official "who works correctly towards the leader, along his lines," would eventually enjoy the "finest reward" of "suddenly attaining the legal confirmation of his work."[32]

When it came to the treatment of Jews, eager subordinates who wanted to "work towards" the Leader could point to Hitler's many violent and threatening public statements about the Jewish people—for example, his "prophecy" of January 1939, broadcast on national radio, that a second world war would result in "the annihilation of the Jewish race in Europe." Activists at all levels of government could cite such declarations by the Leader to advocate ever more violent measures, whether out of a desire to build their careers or out of genuine ideological commitment.

The German treatment of Poles and Jews in territories newly annexed from Poland, after Germany's conquest of that country in October 1939, illustrates the process of working towards the Leader. Albert Forster, administrator of Danzig and West Prussia, and Arthur Greiser, who oversaw the Wartheland district, were both high-ranking Nazi Party officials. Greiser and Forster raced against each other to see who could first manage to "Germanize" his district, that is, to rid it of Polish and Jewish "influence," and eventually to remove the Poles and Jews altogether. Whereas Forster worked toward his goal in part by reclassifying many Poles as ethnic Germans, Greiser forced the Wartheland's Jews into cramped and unhealthy ghettos. At the same time, he subjected the Poles to a nightmarish regime of discrimination and abuse, wiping out Polish cultural institutions, arresting and murdering Catholic priests, and forcibly resettling Poles to make room for German colonists, all at the threat of summary execution. "The Pole is for us an enemy," Greiser declared, "and I expect from every officer . . . that he acts accordingly. The Poles must feel that they do not have the right to put themselves on the same level as a people of culture." He exhorted his subordinates to be "brutal, harsh, and again harsh" in the "ethnic struggle."[33]

In late autumn of 1941, Greiser again took the initiative. When German Jews were slated to be deported to the overcrowded Lodz ghetto, located in Greiser's territory, Greiser asked—and received— Himmler's permission to "liquidate" some 100,000 Jews. The murder of Jews by poison gas began at Chelmno on December 8. Some months later, Greiser sought permission to murder 30,000 Poles who suffered from incurable tuberculosis. Told that Hitler would have to be consulted on this decision, Greiser exemplified the process of working towards the Leader when he replied: "I myself do not believe that the Leader needs to be asked again in this matter, especially since in our last discussion with regard to the Jews he told me that I could proceed with these according to my own judgment."[34]

Such initiatives by Hitler's subordinates did not "cause" the Holocaust, because Hitler made all of the important decisions. However, the widespread tendency to work towards the Leader helped radicalize all levels of the government and Nazi Party, ensuring that Hitler could easily find men who would carry out his criminal orders. And, to a degree that no one can measure, his subordinates' initiatives could have radicalized Hitler's own thinking as well, by showing him that even in his most extreme policies, he could count on active support.[35]

Unconditional loyalty to the Leader, as drilled into the SS, helps explain the behavior of many killers. So, too, does the widespread myth of the Leader's infallibility and Hitler's position as the sole source of law and political legitimacy in Nazi Germany. This "Hitler myth," and Hitler's role as the source of law, dissolved legal and moral norms and radicalized Hitler's subordinates by encouraging them to take actions they thought he would approve.

However, these beliefs and practices can hardly serve as a complete explanation of the Holocaust. Many men killed out of a sincere belief in Nazi racial ideology, and not only because it came from the Leader. Even more important, tens of thousands of highly educated Germans helped Hitler organize and carry out the murders, and very many of these men, perhaps most, were not Nazis. The next chapter explains why anti-Semitism played such a central role in German politics during the first four decades of the twentieth century, making Hitler's theories about Jews acceptable to the country's elite.

CHAPTER 9

WHY THE JEWISH PEOPLE?

If one had at the beginning and during the war held twelve or fifteen thousand of these Hebrew corrupters of the people under poison gas, as hundreds of thousands of our very best German workers from all walks of life had to endure, then the sacrifice of millions at the front would not have been in vain.

—Adolf Hitler, on the socialists, whom he blamed
for Germany's losing World War I[1]

Adolf Hitler ordered the murder of the Jewish people because he embraced the most extreme version of a conspiracy theory that had gained widespread support on the right wing of European politics decades before the Holocaust began. He believed that Jews everywhere were working together to dominate the world, undermining every nation by promoting socialism and communism and by manipulating the financial system. His ferocious hatred toward the Jewish people also stemmed from his belief—shared by very many Germans—that Jewish socialists had made Germany lose World

War I by engineering the democratic revolution of 1918. Like many of his accomplices, Hitler believed that Jews controlled the governments that fought against Germany in World War II—Britain, the United States, and the Soviet Union. His government organized much of its propaganda around the idea that this war was actually not a war against other countries, but rather "a war against the Jews," who supposedly started the war in the first place.[2]

But why the Jewish people? Various ethnic and religious minorities have faced hostility and discrimination throughout recorded history. Why, among all these minorities, were Jews singled out, greatly feared, and presented as a dangerous enemy, even as the embodiment of all evil, at this time in Germany? There is no consensus on this point, but four possible reasons stand out. One is that Jews were a minority not just in one way, but in two: ethnic and religious. Since Jews were a minority in every European country, and minorities were everywhere disliked, Jews encountered hostility throughout the continent.

Second, not only were Jews a religious minority on an overwhelmingly Christian continent, but their faith was both the parent and the rival of the Christian tradition. Consequently, Judaism played an important role in Christian theology, and it became over the centuries the focus of an obsession among the leadership of the Christian churches. In the eyes of millions of devout Christians, the Jews became traitors to their own tradition when, having prophesied the coming of a messiah, they rejected him when he appeared, supposedly causing his death. Today the notion of Jews as "the killers of Christ" seems so ridiculous as to be almost quaint, but not until 1965 did the Catholic Church officially renounce this accusation against the Jewish people. In earlier centuries, including much of the twentieth, this hateful belief was alive and well among numberless millions of practicing Christians. Beginning in the Middle Ages, even more destructive ideas about the Jewish people took root in Europe.

Clergy and laity alike sometimes came to see Jews as the offspring of Satan, or even as the embodiment of Satan and all evil. One often spoke of them not as a group of individuals, but as "the Jew," a frightening abstraction suggesting an impersonal and evil force.[3]

This demonization of the Jewish people paved the way for the secular theories of an international Jewish conspiracy, theories that first emerged in the 1860s and became widely accepted after World War I. Although Hitler, many of his top aides, and the upper ranks of his SS were vehemently hostile to Christianity, the traditional Christian image of "the Jew" as the ultimate enemy, the embodiment of all evil, was echoed in their belief that exterminating the Jews would usher in a better future for humanity.[4]

Jews also differed from other minorities in that they were truly an international minority: almost every European country, and many nations outside of Europe, had Jewish populations. This fact nourished suspicions that French or German or Polish Jews might feel loyalty primarily to Jews in other countries, rather than to the countries of which they were citizens. From such suspicions it was only a short step to theories of an international conspiracy.

Jews also differed from other minorities, and from the majority populations of the countries where they lived, in another crucially important way: by being extraordinarily successful in many occupations. In 1933, the year Hitler took power, Germany's 503,000 Jews represented only 0.76 percent of the population, yet they constituted over 16 percent of Germany's lawyers and notaries public and nearly 11 percent of the doctors. German Jews' contributions to scholarship are harder to quantify, but may have been even more impressive in comparison to their limited numbers. Among the Jewish scientists who left Germany after Hitler took power, six already held the Nobel Prize in their fields, and another sixteen would earn the prize during their later careers. Of the four most important thinkers who emerged in Western civilization during the nineteenth century, one was English: Charles Darwin. The other three—Karl Marx, Sigmund Freud, and Albert Einstein—were German speakers of Jewish ancestry.[5]

Jewish success is important for two reasons. First, it necessarily inspired envy and hatred born from feelings of inferiority. Adolf Hitler might be the most important example of a person whose hatred was nourished by envy of Jewish success, although the documentary record is too thin to properly test this theory. However, his deep-seated (and thoroughly justified) feelings of inferiority are well understood, as is his humiliating failure to make a career as an artist, which might have been all the more galling given the success of many Jewish painters, in numbers far out of proportion to the percentage of Jews in the German population.[6]

Jewish success was also central to anti-Semitism because it nourished theories of a Jewish conspiracy by creating the illusion of "Jewish influence." The prominent Jewish role in newspaper and book publishing was of crucial importance here, since it encouraged the belief that Jews could shape intellectual life and control the political agenda. On the eve of World War I, of the three most important publishers of Germany's national press, two—Mosse and Ullstein—were Jewish. Many editors in chief and leading editorial writers were also Jewish, including Theodor Wolff, editor of the *Berliner Tageblatt*; Georg Bernhard, editor of the renowned *Vossische Zeitung*; and dozens of other political opinion makers and cultural critics. Mosse and Ullstein also played a major role in book publishing, as did Samuel Fischer, whose role in publishing German literature has been compared to that of Random House and Scribner's in the United States.[7]

Shortly before World War I, leading nationalist Heinrich Class claimed that Jews controlled virtually all German newspapers. "Who has the courage to deny," he exclaimed, "that our entire political life stands under Jewish influence?" The "masses," according to Class, were "held by Jewry through its daily newspapers . . . by the reins." There was of course no such thing as "Jewish influence," because German Jews wrote and published as individuals, not as Jews, and did not coordinate their actions with Jews who lived in other European countries. Nonetheless, theories of a Jewish conspiracy had already begun to gain acceptance by the 1890s. Many such theories were centered on the accusation that Jews were the chief instigators of Marxist socialism, and expressed the hope that if "Jewish influence" were eliminated, the socialist parties would die out. The belief that Jews promoted Marxism led more directly to the Holocaust than did any other component of anti-Semitism, yet it had virtually no basis in reality.[8]

The faulty logic leading to this connection between Judaism and Marxism in the minds of so many Germans stemmed from several factors. First, Karl Marx, the chief intellectual father of socialism and communism, was of Jewish ancestry, which made it easier to blame Jews for the rise of these movements. It is also relevant that socialism and communism were both explicitly international movements. It was an article of faith in both movements that "the worker has no country," that the working class of every nation owed its primary loyalty to other workers, no matter where they lived, and that wars were only opportunities for industrialists to make money and to divide the world's workers against each other. In practice, Europe's socialist workers were usually quite patriotic and loyal to the countries in which they lived. However, the socialists' internationalist rhetoric contributed to the illusion that Jews were the instigators of socialism and communism, because the Jewish people were a truly international minority who lived in every European country.

Most German Jews, being middle class in economic status, had no use for socialism, and tended to support the more liberal of the middle-class parties. However, the socialist party took a public stance against anti-Semitism beginning in the 1890s, and unlike many other German parties, did not discriminate against Jews. Free to join, and rise, in the socialist party, some Jews became party leaders, which gave ammunition to right-wing politicians who blamed "Jewish influence" for the rise of socialism, and later for the threat of communism. In Russia as well, Jews played a visible role in socialism and communism and were overrepresented in the leadership of these parties. During the 1920s, Jews were likewise overrepresented in the ranks of the communist party and the Soviet government, although Joseph Stalin, the Soviet dictator, later purged large numbers of them.[9]

Conservative elites in Germany and elsewhere had an additional reason to blame Jews for the rise of socialism and communism. Especially in countries like Russia and Germany that had undemocratic constitutions before World War I, the ruling class firmly rejected democracy and insisted that ordinary citizens were too stupid and irresponsible to govern themselves. Such elites also did not accept that industrial workers had reasonable economic and political grievances. Consequently, elites believed that the masses of ordinary citizens could have embraced socialism only if they had been manipulated by unscrupulous agitators. Who better to accuse of such agitation than Jewish journalists and intellectuals, who already qualified—in the eyes of conservative nationalists—as outsiders? The right-wing German nationalist Heinrich Class made this argument explicit in his popular tract, *If I Were the Emperor*. A great danger to Germany, Class wrote, stemmed from "yielding to mass instincts." He contended that "Jewry is the representative and leader of these mass instincts, working with all methods and possibilities of influence." In the socialist party, Class insisted, "Jews control the leadership and exploit the seduced masses for a battle against the whole established order." Such views were common on the right wing of German politics on the eve of World War I. The powerful pressure group of large landowners, the Agrarian League, together with the main conservative party, promoted anti-Semitism. When the socialists became the largest party in the 1912 elections, the chief conservative newspaper labeled the balloting the "Jewish election" and complained of "Judah's money power" in the socialist party.[10]

The most notorious theory of a Jewish conspiracy found expression in the *Protocols of the Elders of Zion*, a fabricated document usually attributed to the Imperial Russian secret police. The *Protocols*, still sold by anti-Semites in millions of copies today, may have been written in France at the end of the nineteenth century, but were largely unknown outside of Russia before World War I. This document purports to be the transcript of twenty-four meetings of the men who led the conspiracy, spelling out their plans.[11]

According to the *Protocols*, the Jewish conspirators wanted to destroy all religions and all established institutions. Having eliminated all national governments, they would impose a single Jewish world government ruled by an emperor descended from King David. Jews had brought about all earlier revolutions and political crises in history, fostered antagonisms between social classes, instigated all large-scale strikes, and were responsible for all political assassinations. According to this document, Jews promoted social crisis by driving up food prices, spreading infectious diseases, and encouraging workers to become alcoholics.

Monarchist Russian emigrants, fleeing the communist revolution and civil war in their country from 1917 to 1922, seem to have brought the *Protocols* to Western Europe, where they were promptly translated into most of the world's major languages, including Chinese and Japanese. German and British newspapers published them as a series. In the United States, automobile manufacturer Henry Ford sponsored their publication, and hundreds of thousands of copies were sold.[12]

Yet despite all the distinctive features of Europe's Jewish populations, and despite the increasing use of anti-Semitism as a weapon against socialism, conspiracy theories had enjoyed little respectability before World War I. Jews in Western Europe had faced far less discrimination than, for example, African Americans did in the American South. World War I changed European anti-Semitism decisively, demonstrating yet again that without the war, the Holocaust would not have been possible. After the war, the conspiracy theories gained widespread acceptance. The *Protocols of the Elders of Zion* are only the most obvious example of this sea change. Also crucially important was the new respectability of racist anti-Semitism. Classifying Jews as a race, as biologically distinct from the rest of humanity, made it possible to regard them as being less than human. This shift in perspective did much to make the Holocaust possible.[13]

Much of the new anti-Semitism came from using Jews as scapegoats for the war's terrible cost and the dramatic political upheavals that came in its wake. Ten million young men died in combat. The ruling monarchies of four great powers—Germany, Austria-Hungary, Russia, and Ottoman Turkey—fell from power. The Austro-Hungarian Empire broke apart into its constituent ethnic fragments, spawning a group of unstable and often mutually antagonistic successor states: Austria, Czechoslovakia, Hungary, Poland, and Yugoslavia. The need for scapegoats was especially great in Germany, whose citizens suffered not only the loss of the war, but a peace treaty they considered grossly unfair, not to mention runaway inflation that destroyed the life savings of much of the middle class. Scapegoating of Jews for military setbacks began already in 1916, with baseless allegations that the Jews had unscrupulously profited from the war industries and shirked military duty. When it became apparent that the war was lost, right-wing nationalists became positively hysterical in their anti-Semitic tirades. The Pan-German League set up a "Jewish Committee" in September 1918, prompting Heinrich Class to echo the words of an earlier German nationalist: "Kill them; the world court is not asking you for your reasons!"[14]

World War I intensified European anti-Semitism in another, probably more important way as well: it made possible the communist revolution of 1917 in Russia. Going as far back as the 1890s, opponents of socialism had consistently blamed the Jews for the rise of socialist labor unions and political parties. The Russian revolution dramatically intensified this source of anti-Semitism, because communism was so much more frightening than socialism: while socialists had used peaceful methods for achieving their goals, relying mainly on the democratic process, Russian communists imposed social revolution at the point of a gun, setting off four years of bloody civil war that claimed millions of lives. Ultimately, the Russian communists confiscated all businesses and farms and most personal property, directing the country's entire economy from a central planning apparatus in Moscow. Thomas Mann, possibly Germany's greatest living author at the time, recorded a conversation in his diary in May 1918: "We spoke of the type of Russian Jew, the leader of the world revolutionary movement, that explosive mixture of Jewish intellectual radicalism and Slavic Christian enthusiasm." Mann added: "A world that still retains an instinct of self-preservation must act against such people with all the energy that can be mobilized and with the swiftness of martial law."[15]

The ruling elites—and probably much of the middle class—of many European countries surely became more anti-Semitic after Russia's communist revolution in 1917. It is unclear, however, whether Germans reacted more strongly than other nations, and whether the Holocaust originated in Germany, and not in France or Russia, because the Germans were more violently anti-Semitic. There has been almost no research systematically comparing anti-Semitism across national boundaries. Scholars have instead written only national histories, that is, separate studies of France, of Germany, of Poland, and so on. This was a fatal flaw in Daniel Goldhagen's much-criticized 1996 book *Hitler's Willing*

Executioners: he created a sensation by arguing that most Germans had embraced a uniquely dangerous form of anti-Semitism long before Hitler took power, but he did not compare this allegedly unique German anti-Semitism to anti-Semitism in other countries. Even worse for Goldhagen's argument, the history of anti-Semitism in other European countries makes one point quite obvious: anti-Semitism was far more widespread, intense, and violent in Eastern Europe and on the territory of the Soviet Union than it was in any Western European country, Germany included. If someone had asked well-informed Europeans in 1920 or 1930 which country was most likely to perpetrate large-scale massacres of Jews, Germany would probably not even have been mentioned. Poland, Hungary, Romania, and the Soviet Union would have seemed the most likely perpetrators of such a horrific deed.[16]

In Russia, anti-Semitic violence had a long history. A wave of anti-Jewish riots, or pogroms, swept through regions of Jewish settlement in 1881, most beginning after Easter, historically a time of tension between Christians and Jews. In that year alone, the authorities counted 224 such riots, which claimed 16 lives and extensively damaged property. More pogroms followed in 1882, including an upheaval in Balta, where 40 Jews were murdered or seriously wounded. A second wave of pogroms followed between 1903 and 1906, many sparked by the accusation that Jews had instigated the abortive 1905 revolution. All told, as many as 3,000 lost their lives. In 1930s Poland, new laws were established, forcing Jews out of several professions, and mass boycotts were organized against Jewish-owned shops. Jewish students had to be taught in separate lecture halls at universities, and the effort was made to strip Jews of their Polish nationality. Successive Polish governments advocated deporting some 1.5 million Polish Jews (half the Jewish population) to Palestine or to the inhospitable island of Madagascar. In the context of the bloody Russian Civil War, massive pogroms swept through Ukraine in 1918–1919, killing an estimated 150,000 to 200,000 people, a full 10 percent of Ukrainian Jewry. Ferocious anti-Semitism on Soviet territory supplied the Germans with thousands of willing collaborators who helped them murder the Jewish population of the Soviet Union after the invasion of June 1941.[17]

Within Germany, physical violence toward Jews was relatively rare, and seldom lethal, during the decades before Hitler took power in 1933, although it did worsen significantly during the 1920s. When it happened, violence against Jews was condemned in the press, except by publications of the Nazi Party and other groups of the extreme Right. Legal discrimination was also absent during that time: Jews were fully equal with Gentiles before the law, even if informal discrimination continued in certain occupations, such as the military and higher civil service. Before Hitler became prime minister, Germany remained, by any standard, vastly less anti-Semitic than the nations of Eastern Europe and the territories of the Soviet Union. How Germany differed from Western European nations or the United States in this regard is less clear, owing to the lack of comparative research.[18]

In this discussion it is very important to distinguish Germany's elite—a group of perhaps half a million men and a few thousand women—from the rest of the population. Most citizens left few written records of their feelings toward Jews, so any assessment of their anti-Semitism is little more than an educated guess. Some anti-Jewish prejudice was clearly widespread. A large number of civic organizations excluded Jews from membership. Very many Germans subscribed to one or another of certain negative beliefs about Jews: that the Jews were alien, somehow not German; that they had been disloyal during World War I; that they controlled the press and used it to their advantage; or that they had profited from the war and from Germany's economic distress during the 1920s. That said, it seems reasonable to think that actual hatred or sympathy for German Jews was far less common than simply a vague feeling of unease about them. This negative emotion certainly did not translate into a desire to harm Jews, but may have defused objections that Germans might otherwise have had to the Nazis' militant anti-Semitism.[19]

How Germans' vague unease about Jews compared to the typical attitude in France, Britain, or the United States is difficult to say. In fourteen polls conducted between 1938 and 1946, the Opinion Research Corporation (ORC) asked Americans: "Do you think Jews have too much power in the United States?" Those answering yes numbered 41 percent of respondents in 1938, rising steadily thereafter to 47 percent in February 1942, 56 percent in May 1944, and 58 percent in June 1945. In four other ORC surveys from the years 1939 to 1941, about a third of the American people agreed that "the Jews in this country would like to get the United States into the European war." In the 1920s and 1930s, Harvard, Yale, and Princeton established quotas limiting the number of Jews who could study at their institutions, and they then maintained these quotas well into the postwar era. *Washington Post* publisher Katharine Graham recalled driving into Florida in 1940, where she saw an apartment house displaying a sign that read, "No Dogs or Jews Allowed." However, one absolutely crucial difference separated the English-speaking world from France and Germany: anti-Semitism was an important political issue in France and Germany, whereas it played next to no role in party politics in Britain and the United States.[20]

In both France and Germany, anti-Semitism had been a hallmark of the political Right from the 1890s onward. In the depth of their anti-Semitism, the two countries seem to have been more similar to each other than different until World War I broke out in 1914. However, there are good reasons for thinking that after the war began, and especially after the war was lost, German elites became much more dangerously anti-Semitic than did their counterparts in other Western European countries. German elites should have been different because Germany lost the war and then suffered a relentless series of traumatic and disorienting misfortunes: a democratic revolution; a peace treaty they perceived as unfair and humiliating; violent uprisings and political assassinations; and runaway inflation that ruined millions financially.[21]

Of course, traumatic events do not automatically mean that a minority will be treated as scapegoats. But the entire political development of the German Right since 1890 had laid the groundwork for blaming Jews for the lost war and the calamities that followed: Jews were supposedly unpatriotic and responsible for the rise of socialism, itself an internationalist, allegedly unpatriotic movement. When elements of the socialist party turned against the war, attacks on German Jews correspondingly mounted. Adolf Hitler spoke for countless Germans when he blamed Jewish socialists for Germany's defeat, although his language was unusually violent: "If one had at the beginning and during the war held twelve or fifteen thousand of these Hebrew corrupters of the people under poison gas, as hundreds of thousands of our very best German workers from all walks of life had to endure, then the sacrifice of millions at the front would not have been in vain."[22]

German elites had a second reason to become more anti-Semitic than did the elites of other European countries. Although Jews were everywhere blamed for socialism and then communism, Germany's ruling class had more reason to fear both Marxist movements, and thus all the more reason to imagine a dangerous "Jewish threat." Before World War I, the German socialist party was the largest socialist party in Europe. Unlike their counterparts in France, the German socialists demanded not only a change in economic relationships, but also a political revolution. France had been a democracy since 1871, and French socialists supported the democratic constitution, but German elites were fiercely defending an authoritarian political system all the way down to the revolution of 1918. Put another way, Germany's ruling class had a lot more to lose before 1918 than the French elites did, because they could lose not only property, but also their monopoly on political power.

Although Russia's communist revolution in 1917 unnerved the ruling class of every country, Germany's elites had special reason to be frightened. Unlike France and Britain, Germany experienced a political revolution in 1918, and the socialist party took the leading role during the first crucial months thereafter. Socialists led the first government of the newly created Weimar Republic, and seven members of the cabinet were Jewish. Although the socialists pursued very moderate policies while in government, their leading role was terrifying for the country's elite, which had feared socialism for decades. Moreover, if socialists could take over the government, conservatives had to ask themselves, could a communist revolution be that far behind? The entire political situation in Germany right after the war was far more unstable than it was in most of Western Europe. During those years, German political development was extraordinarily violent and unpredictable, and power seemed up for grabs. The possibility that the communists might triumph must have seemed much more real in Germany than it did in most other places. Consequently, anti-Semitism, driven by fear of communism, may have been especially rampant among the top layers of German society. This remains only an educated guess. However, anti-Semitism was extremely virulent at German universities in the 1920s, where the elites of the 1930s and 1940s were earning their professional credentials and forming their political views.[23]

In the early 1920s, students' political activity at German universities was completely dominated by the *Deutscher Hochschulring*, a militantly anti-Semitic organization. Within this organization, the leading anti-Semites explicitly rejected the idea that only cultural differences separated Jews from Gentiles. Rather,

Germans and Jews were biologically distinct "races," they said, and only radical measures could solve the "Jewish problem." Every member of the *Hochschulring* had to declare that he had no Jewish parents or grandparents. Student-organized social life also took on an explicitly anti-Semitic tone. Roughly 60 percent of German students belonged to fraternities, and by 1930 almost no fraternities accepted Jews as members.[24]

After 1926, the student organization of the Nazi Party increasingly replaced the *Hochschulring* at German universities. By the time Hitler took power in 1933, this Nazi association had become the dominant student organization at German institutions of higher learning. Of all occupational groups in German society, only university students belonged in their majority to a Nazi organization. Thousands of them would carry their militant anti-Semitism into careers in the Nazi Party and German government and into the planning offices and shooting squads of the extermination program. The rest would serve the government as it carried out the murders, and look the other way.[25]

To understand the role anti-Semitism played in the Holocaust, one must recognize that there were many different anti-Semitisms in Germany and in Europe as a whole, each playing a different part in this tragedy. At the center of the murder program stood a hard core of Nazi fanatics, perhaps only a few thousand men, who shared Adolf Hitler's belief that the Jews constituted the greatest threat to Germany's survival. Tens of thousands of rank-and-file Nazi Party activists displayed another strain of anti-Semitism, expressed less in racial theories than in recurring violence against their Jewish neighbors, whose lives they made miserable at every opportunity. More widespread, and ultimately more dangerous than the fury of rioting Nazi thugs, was the anti-Semitism of much of Germany's elite, a group raised across three generations since the 1890s to blame Jews for Marxism, and sharing the enthusiasm of educated men nearly everywhere for "scientific" theories about racial difference. In Eastern Europe and on the territory of the Soviet Union, a widespread and ferociously violent anti-Semitism supplied the Germans with tens of thousands of volunteers who helped to identify and capture Jews and carry out the murders.

The anti-Semitism of most Germans—those who belonged neither to the Nazi Party nor to the country's elite—was surely much milder than the violent hatred seen in Poland or Ukraine, or among Nazi Party activists. For most Germans, anti-Semitism may have gone no further than the belief that German Jews were not really German. Even such muted prejudice was enough to let Germans react with indifference as their Jewish neighbors were persecuted in the 1930s, and murdered in the 1940s. However, this brand of anti-Semitism did not *cause* the Holocaust, or provide a major motive for the murder program. The Holocaust did not happen because the German people rose up and demanded it, but rather because a wildly popular dictator and his fanatical followers planned it, because the country's elite shared enough of Nazi anti-Semitism to participate in the killing, and because the rest of the country looked the other way.[26]

The political conflicts that produced Hitler's anti-Semitism and the somewhat less extreme anti-Semitism of Germany's elites tell only part of this story. For the Holocaust to happen, it was not enough that these men blamed Jews for the rise of socialism and communism. Also necessary was that they believed that the Jewish people constituted a *race* that was biologically distinct from the rest of all humanity and genetically predisposed to behave destructively. This way of seeing the Jews could only have happened in the twentieth century, the high-water mark of racist thinking in world history. At that fateful juncture, racism became much more than a social prejudice. It became a widely accepted scientific theory, commanding the unquestioning support that people of that era granted to anything they called "science."

CHAPTER 10

HATRED AS SCIENCE

In general, the brain is larger in mature adults than in the elderly, in men than in women, in eminent men than in men of mediocre talent, in superior races than in inferior races.

—Anthropologist Paul Broca in 1861[1]

Today the word "racism" means dislike for people whose skin is colored differently from ours, usually paired with the suspicion that they are not as intelligent or morally upright as we are. Yet during the years between about 1890 and 1960, and especially in the 1930s and 1940s, racism meant a great deal more. During those years most educated people in Europe and North America believed that racial differences in intelligence and morality were proven scientific fact. Today racism is seen as the kneejerk reflex of the uneducated and socially marginal, of "losers." In Hitler's day it was instead a conviction shared by most of society's leaders, and by millions of people who ranked below them.

Sometimes, but hardly always, racist belief flowed from some understanding of genetics, of the way that people can inherit

153

physical and mental traits from their parents. Racism usually contained the notion that different races, different nationalities, and also specific classes of society, were born to behave in certain ways. Not only were people of African or Asian descent assumed to naturally act differently from white people, but even different white nationalities—Scotch, Swedes, Greeks, or Poles—were described as having different inborn traits. The poorer classes of every society were also said to have been born with inferior moral and intellectual qualities that kept them at the bottom of the social ladder.[2]

Throughout history and also today, inequality has marked the human condition and the powerful have abused their power. Some countries are militarily stronger than others, the wealthy often monopolize the political process, and infants enter the world with drastically unequal life chances. The Western racism of the nineteenth and twentieth centuries did not by itself widen inequality or worsen abuses of power, but it gave the actions of social elites and mighty nations some new and dangerous qualities. Men who started wars, persecuted minorities, or murdered civilians gained a new confidence in the rightness of their actions. Their deeds, no matter how violent, now escaped moral condemnation, because their actions supposedly reflected "the laws of nature," and the natural world, the animal kingdom, knows no morality. Because the new racism enjoyed the tremendous prestige of scientific certainty, it was intellectually respectable. Finally, most human beings were now thought to be prisoners of their heredity, born to act the way they did, unable to change their own behavior even if they wanted to. No amount of education or political pressure could improve a race or nationality; if the behavior of a particular group was considered harmful, its members might therefore have to be eliminated.

Modern racism had several different intellectual sources, and only with difficulty could one say which of these was most important. However, in this chapter I will focus on the "scientific" strand of racism, which drew its inspiration from Charles Darwin's theory of evolution through natural selection. Several factors dictate this emphasis on Darwinian racism. First, Darwinist racism explicitly motivated Hitler and many other leading perpetrators of the Holocaust. Second, Darwin inspired the researchers, most notably in biology and anthropology, who gave racism its aura of scientific certainty. Third, Darwinian thought may well have been more popular in Germany than anywhere else during these years, in part because Germany was the world's leading center of biological research before World War I and the Germans were exceptionally literate. Finally, Darwinist racism was the brand of racism most easily understood by the widest number of people, in part because Darwin's theory was astonishingly simple and easy to explain.[3]

When he published *On the Origin of Species* in November 1859, the English biologist Charles Darwin set the intellectual world on fire. Within the covers of a single book, he convincingly explained the development of every life form on earth, including humankind. For many readers, he also completely discredited the biblical account of the Earth's creation and human origins. Darwin persuasively argued that human beings did not descend from a single pair created in God's image (Adam and Eve), but instead gradually evolved in a process that might have taken millions of years, from lower life forms to apes, then from primitive apes to those of greater intelligence, and finally from intelligent apes to human beings. In so doing, Darwin dealt a devastating blow to the Christian churches, a blow from which—at least in Western Europe—they never recovered. Especially among the educated classes of Western society, Darwin's theory spread like wildfire from the moment of its publication, not so much through sales of his fairly demanding book as through the works of countless popularizers, who quickly reduced his thinking to a few basic formulas. They could do this easily, and Darwin's ideas could sweep all before them, because the gist of his theory was remarkably simple and could be summarized in only a few pages.

Darwin explained that all living beings struggled constantly against each other for survival. Creatures blessed with useful abilities survived more often than did less gifted organisms, and passed their superior abilities on to their offspring. Across many generations of a species, physical or mental traits that enabled survival would therefore become more widespread and more pronounced. The "fit" (capable) members of the species would live longer and produce more offspring, whereas the unfit members would perish earlier and produce fewer offspring. In this way, lower life forms evolved into higher life forms, and weaknesses were weeded out of the population. Darwin called this process "evolution through natural selection," meaning that the challenge of surviving in nature selected those members of a species who were fit to survive, and thereby improved the species over time. This "survival of the fittest" made the violent struggle for life in the wild something to praise, rather than deplore, because it was a means for a species to progress. Most important, natural selection—rather than God—had given birth to man.[4]

According to Darwin's theory, millions of years of evolution through natural selection had let lower animals evolve into apes, seen as the most intelligent of creatures in the animal kingdom. Over time, apes with larger brains and greater intelligence had then crowded out the less gifted members of their species, who became extinct. Across thousands of generations, apes had become more and more intelligent and had acquired certain useful physical traits, such as hands with opposable thumbs, for grasping tools, and the ability to walk on two legs. This process produced early, primitive versions of the human being, and further evolution through natural selection ultimately culminated in the arrival of the modern humans of Darwin's era. The impact of these ideas on millions of readers must have been nothing short of exhilarating. Where did human beings come from? And was everything in the Bible, word for word, literal truth? What questions could have been more important to people of that time, indeed, of any time? Suddenly anyone with a primary school education could feel able to answer these enormous questions after reading nothing more than a short pamphlet written at the level of a children's book.

As Darwin's theory gained widespread acceptance, thinkers of every stripe began to find lessons in it for understanding the politics and society of their time, using Darwinian thought to support their own agendas. This so-called Social Darwinism ran in many different political directions. The right-wing branch of Social Darwinism—which was not necessarily the most popular strand of it—promoted racism, justified social and political inequality, and glorified war. It also inspired Adolf Hitler and his ardent supporters to launch a world war and exterminate the Jews of Europe.[5]

Right-wing Social Darwinism produced several ideas that were attractive and convenient to the ruling classes of Europe and North America, and especially to Germany's warlike and antidemocratic elites. The most important idea may have been "struggle," the notion that all relations between individuals and between nations were defined by a merciless battle for survival. Struggle followed inevitably from the laws of nature as discovered by Darwin, and therefore had no moral significance. The Christian injunctions to "love your neighbor" and "love your enemies" had no place in the animal kingdom; neither should they control the behavior of human beings, who were not made in the image of God, but rather counted as nothing more than an especially clever type of animal.[6]

From these assumptions about struggle followed the argument that extreme social inequality was natural and permanent. The poor were poor because they were less fit than the rich. Charity for the poor blocked humanity from evolving to a higher plane, because it kept unfit members of society alive, allowing them to reproduce and pollute the gene pool with their inferior intelligence and moral weaknesses. The belief in permanent struggle also supported a bias toward violence between nations, a glorification of warfare. "Superior" peoples had every right to conquer, exploit, and even exterminate "inferior" ones. If such aggression let superior peoples expand and become more numerous, the entire human race would improve in the long run; the extinction of lesser races was a cause for celebration rather than pity. In international relations, might made right: by winning a war, the victor showed that he deserved his victory, because his people were more fit to survive than were the losers.[7]

This brand of Social Darwinism fostered a racism that was all the more dangerous because it claimed a basis in scientific fact. Partly inspired by Darwin's own writings, countless writers and politicians argued that each human population, each race or nation, had evolved from the first humans at its own pace, so that some had progressed further than others. Probably almost all educated people in Europe and North America ranked white people of European descent at the top of the evolutionary ladder, with those of African descent on the bottom rung. Perhaps for this reason, racist caricatures of the time typically represented black people with apelike features. The writers of popularized science, and many biologists and anthropologists, carefully ranked races and nationalities from lowest to highest in value, whites always at the top, and among white people in numerous gradations. American elites generally agreed that among people of European descent, those who had emigrated to the United States from Northern and Western Europe—English, Germans, Scandinavians, and others—were born with the highest intelligence, the strongest work ethic, and the best of other moral qualities. In contrast, immigrants from Southern and Eastern Europe—Poles, Greeks, Italians, Russian Jews, and so on—were said to be markedly inferior, and indeed a potential threat to the country's "racial health." Alarmed by this imagined threat, the US Congress enacted an immigration law in 1924 that closed America's borders to all but a limited number of immigrants from the "wrong" parts of Europe. Earlier laws had almost completely eliminated immigration from China and Japan, whose people, not even being white, were wholly unwanted.[8]

Such racist thinking also applied to individuals and social classes within each Western country. Following the common belief that a larger brain meant a higher intelligence, anthropologist Paul Broca wrote in 1861 that, "in general, the brain is larger in mature adults than in the elderly, in men than in women, in eminent men than in men of mediocre talent, in superior races than in inferior races." Similarly, the American paleontologist E. D. Cope identified four groups of lower-quality human beings: women, non-whites, Jews, and "all lower classes of superior races." The German Ernst Haeckel made the influential argument that each person went through the stages of human evolution over the course of his lifetime, and that many people got, in effect, stuck at some level below the highest point. For each individual, one could pinpoint exactly how far he had managed to evolve from the apes. The Italian physician and pioneer of criminology Cesare Lombroso took this idea forward, blaming crime on the failure of individuals to complete their development. As he succinctly put it: "Criminals are apes in our midst." Consequently, Lombroso thought, some criminals were "born for evil" and could not be reformed. Because their depravity "shows us the inefficiency of punishment for born criminals," he concluded, there was no choice but to "eliminate them completely, even by death."[9]

Without meaning to, Lombroso had put his finger on what made modern racism so dangerous: it encouraged violent solutions to political and social problems. "Scientific" racism made it easy to demonize any foreign enemy or rebellious social underclass, to say that "these people are not made the way we are, they are less than human." And since such "inferior" people were born to act dangerously and could not change their behavior even if they wanted to, one could justifiably eliminate them using violent means, a violence legitimized by the Darwinian glorification of struggle.

Social Darwinist racism met the needs and reflected the fears of ruling elites in many countries, and Germany was no exception. In Germany, ideas of inborn superiority could justify social inequality and thereby serve as a weapon against the growing socialist movement. Promoting the idea of German racial superiority, German elites hoped that they could undermine socialism by getting the German lower classes to see themselves not as workers but rather as Germans, distracting them from their conflict with the propertied classes by fostering antagonism toward German Jews and toward allegedly "inferior" nationalities. (Of course, they probably didn't help their cause when they also argued that German workers were inferior to them and should accept their authoritarian rule.) Elites intensified their anti-Semitic propaganda by asserting that Jews were not just a religious minority, but rather a race, with uniquely harmful inborn qualities. The radical nationalist Heinrich Class insisted that Jews were a race, and "the race is the source of the dangers."[10]

After 1900, the most influential of the nationalist pressure groups, the Pan-German League, became a hotbed of racist thinking. The League's journal became the most important public forum for racial theories in Germany. The Pan-Germans warned ceaselessly against the mortal danger posed by Jews, who allegedly threatened to pollute German "blood" through intermarriage, undermine the family by fostering the women's movement, weaken Germany in the struggle against the Slavic "race," and set off violent revolution by instigating the rise of socialism. The Pan-Germans, and much of the rest of the country's elite, also feared and despised the Slavic peoples of Eastern Europe. According to German racists, the Slavic peoples had much higher birthrates than Germans and might overwhelm Germany through sheer force of numbers. A highly influential physician and researcher on heredity, Alfred Ploetz, wrote in 1913: "Poles, Hungarians, Russians, and South Slavs—nationalities with strong Asiatic traits—have an extremely high birthrate such that they are everywhere successfully pushing westward." He warned that "the preservation of the Nordic race is severely threatened as a result."[11]

The retired German cavalry general Friedrich von Bernhardi gave the application of Social Darwinism to foreign policy its best-known expression in his 1912 book, *Germany and the Next War*, a publishing sensation and instant bestseller that quickly ran through several printings. Bernhardi's grim message of inevitable war in the near future was rapidly amplified in the right-wing press through countless reviews, editorial commentaries, and excerpts from his book. Bernhardi had served for three years as a senior officer of the prestigious Army General Staff, which lent his book a quasi-official respectability, although the German government denied that his views reflected policy.[12]

Bernhardi vehemently attacked all peace movements, declaring that war was a "biological necessity" because it made a "selection" between superior individuals who survived and inferior men who perished. The same progress through destruction marked relations between peoples. "Without war, all too easily inferior or degenerate races would overgrow the healthy, vigorous elements, and a general decline would have to result." Bernhardi argued that "vigorous, healthy and thriving peoples increase in population" and needed to acquire more land. Consequently, "the right to conquer is also generally recognized." When two nations went to war, the stronger was automatically in the right, because "strength is the highest law." War, as the ultimate test of strength, decided the question of justice: war "always reaches a biologically just decision, because its decisions come from the nature of things."[13]

Bernhardi counted Germany among the "vigorous, healthy and thriving peoples" who needed to expand their territory. Yet he believed Britain would block any German effort to acquire new colonies. Anticipating the world war that would break out two years later, Bernhardi predicted that Russia and France would fight at Britain's side. This coalition of enemies would be militarily superior to Germany and her ally, Austria-Hungary, but the war was inevitable: "We must fight it out, cost it what it will."[14]

Such application of Darwinian thought to foreign policy may have been especially dangerous in the hands of Germany's paranoid elite, but it was hardly unique to Germany. When the United States took the Philippines from Spain in an unprovoked war of aggression in 1898, and in the much bloodier war against Filipino independence that raged for the next five years, Albert Beveridge rose in the Senate to justify America's dictatorial rule over the Filipinos. Senator Beveridge argued that the United States needed the Philippines in order to dominate the Pacific Ocean. "Most future wars," Beveridge declared, "will be conflicts for commerce. The power that rules the Pacific, therefore, is the power that rules the world." America, implied Beveridge, needed the Philippines in order to prevail in the Darwinian struggle for survival among nations. As for the Filipinos, of whom perhaps 100,000 died fighting against Americans for their freedom, Beveridge dismissed them as "children." "They are not capable of self-government. How could they be? They are not of a self-governing race. They are Orientals, Malays, instructed by the Spaniards." The British prime minister, Lord Robert Cecil, put the matter with unabashed brutality in another context: "One can roughly divide the nations of the world into the living and the dying."[15]

Seeking to improve the populations of their own countries, doctors, biologists, and other academics created a new science in the late nineteenth century that was known as "eugenics." Francis Galton, a geographer, statistician, and cousin of Charles Darwin, coined the name, describing it as "the right to be well-born." His leading American disciple, Charles Davenport, defined eugenics as "the science of human improvement by better breeding." Eugenicists studied the alleged hereditary transmission of diseases, moral traits (especially bad ones), and intelligence. They hoped to solve social problems, such as poverty, crime, and alcoholism, by encouraging citizens with "good" genes to have larger families, and by preventing "inferior" members of society from reproducing. The eugenics movement was prominent in most Western countries during the first four decades of the twentieth century, with scientists from the United States, Britain, and Germany taking the lead.[16]

In the United States, eugenicists advocated for laws, wrote popularized books and pamphlets, promoted exhibits, sponsored fitter family contests and eugenic sermon competitions, and funded eugenic films. Eugenics found its way into most major high-school textbooks from the 1920s to the 1950s. During World War I, the Harvard psychologist Robert Yerkes persuaded the government to administer the first mass intelligence test, which was given to 1.75 million American soldiers. According to Yerkes, this test proved that the "darker peoples of southern Europe and the Slavs of eastern Europe are less intelligent than the fair peoples of western and northern Europe," while "the Negro lies at the bottom of the scale" of intelligence. Eugenicists later played an important role in enacting the 1924 American immigration law, which drastically limited further immigration from southern and eastern Europe. American eugenicists also managed to push through laws that made it possible to forcibly sterilize the inmates of prisons, sanatoriums, and mental hospitals. By 1935, some thirty states had enacted involuntary sterilization laws to improve the genetic health of the population. Grounds for sterilization included "habitual criminality," "sexual perversion," and "low moral sense." More than 21,000 people had been sterilized under such laws by 1935, and a full 64,000 by the early 1960s, by which point eugenics had been thoroughly discredited within the scientific community.[17]

The Nazi government that took power in 1933 applied eugenics in even more radical ways, moving beyond forced sterilization to mass murder. Not only did the regime sterilize 320,000 to 350,000 people against their will, but in the summer of 1939 Hitler set his aides to work on a new program that would replace sterilization as the means for weeding the "unfit" from the gene pool, the goal being to reduce the "burden" imposed on society by its "unproductive" members. In October of that year a secret order from the Leader finalized the so-called euthanasia policy, a nationwide program to murder mental patients. Epileptics, schizophrenics, and even the "feeble-minded" or sufferers from "senile illnesses" were targeted. Buses with darkened windows visited hospitals and asylums on a regular basis, gathering up patients who had been hastily selected for death, and bringing them to centralized killing centers. There they were murdered in sealed rooms using bottled carbon monoxide gas, their bodies burned. Over 70,000 had died this way by August 1941, when Hitler ended the gassing following public protests by prominent Catholic clergy. The protests probably influenced Hitler's decision, but ultimately accomplished little: doctors continued the program in a decentralized fashion, murdering patients at hospitals and asylums all across Germany.[18]

With the euthanasia program, the regime had crossed a critical moral and psychological threshold to mass murder. It had also created and used a technology that would claim the lives of millions of victims in the Holocaust. The men who ran the killing centers of the euthanasia program soon found similar employment elsewhere:

ninety-two of them went on to staff the death camps at Belzec, Sobibor, and Treblinka, where they murdered more than 1.5 million Jews using the carbon monoxide in engine exhaust.[19]

Just as racist thinking radicalized German domestic policies in the 1930s, so, too, did it shape foreign policy in fateful ways. World War I and the ensuing peace settlement had further intensified the anti-Slavic racism and Social Darwinist glorification of war already established on the right wing of German politics. The terror of communism, following the Russian revolution in 1917, worsened racist hostility toward Russians and Jews. When the victorious Allies recreated an independent Poland, they awarded large regions of eastern Germany to the new Polish state, including areas with substantial German populations. No German government accepted the loss of these territories, and for many on the political Right, it was an article of faith that Poland had to disappear altogether. Leaders of the Steel Helmet, a combat veterans' organization, openly called for war against Poland. The Steel Helmet also echoed the right-wing Nationalist party in its vague demands for expanded "living space" for Germany's alleged surplus population. At the Nationalists' 1931 convention, their leader, Alfred Hugenberg, declared that the German people could gain "freedom and space" only through "energetic self-help," and not through a "hypocritical pacifism." Hugenberg demanded a colonial empire for Germany in Africa, as well as new land for settlement of Germany's "vigorous race" in the East, contending that "the reconstruction of the East, far beyond Germany's old borders, is only possible by Germany." "Energetic self-help" was a euphemism for war, praised in unmistakably Darwinian terms.[20]

Adolf Hitler tied the strands of this radicalized thinking together in his manifesto *Mein Kampf* (*My Struggle*, 1925–1926). In a lengthy tirade against pacifism, which he termed "Jewish nonsense," Hitler explained his Darwinian view of international relations: "Whoever would live, let him fight, and he who does not want to do battle in this world of eternal struggle, does not deserve life." To oppose war was to ignore "the laws of race" and to "prevent the victory of the best race," which was "the precondition of all human progress." In Hitler's view, Germany was too small and too lacking in "living space." It faced the danger of "perishing from the Earth" or serving other nations as a "slave people." Consequently, "Germany will either become a world power, or cease to exist altogether."[21]

Hitler fused his fear of communism, his demand for living space, and his beliefs about the racial inferiority of Russians and Jews into a comprehensive vision for Germany's foreign policy. Germany could annex its needed living space from Russia, because that country was "ripe for collapse." The "inferior" Russians had become a great power only because they had been led by a Germanic ruling class, but the communists—who in Hitler's mind were necessarily Jews because he believed that Jews had instigated communism—had "almost completely exterminated" this Germanic element. "The Jew," according to Hitler, "is the eternal parasite, a bloodsucker, which spreads ever more widely like a harmful bacillus," a microbe that kills its host. The Jews who allegedly controlled communist Russia could therefore not maintain a stable government, and Germany could easily conquer the Soviet Union.[22]

In Hitler's mind, Germany needed to destroy the Soviet Union not only in order to gain the land and resources that would make Germany a great power, but also in order to eliminate the threat of Jewish-inspired communism. This threat was "constantly present," because it was "an instinctive process, i.e., the Jewish people's drive for world domination." "The Jew," wrote Hitler, "follows his path, the path of infiltrating other nations and hollowing them out, and he fights with his usual weapons, with lies and slander, pollution and disintegration, escalating the struggle to the bloody extermination of his hated opponent." Hitler insisted that "the Jew" had always, down through the centuries, sought world domination by undermining other peoples from within. Russian communism was only the latest page in this dark history. These beliefs led Hitler to launch a genocidal war against the Soviet Union in which as many as 25 million Soviet citizens died, and they also moved him to order the complete extermination of the Jewish people. The German military would actively support both policies.[23]

Although few officers may have fully accepted Hitler's theories about Jews, very many embraced anti-Semitism, racist beliefs about the Slavic peoples, and militant anticommunism. Almost none registered any dissent as the German Army rolled into the Soviet Union in June 1941, murdering POWs by the millions and ruthlessly confiscating the civilian food supply. Addressing the top commanders of the invasion army in March of that year, Field Marshal Walther von Brauchitsch emphasized that "the troops must understand that this struggle is being fought race against race, and that they must proceed with the necessary harshness." In May 1941, the tank general Erich Hoepner explained the war's meaning to his troops: "The war against Russia is an essential chapter in the German people's battle for survival. It is the old struggle between the Germanic peoples and the Slavs, the defense of European culture against muscovite-Asiatic invasion, the defense against Jewish communism." The war, Hoepner continued, had to be fought "with unheard-of hardness," inspired by "the iron will to achieve complete, merciless annihilation of the enemy."[24]

As German soldiers stood poised to invade the Soviet Union and crush the "Jewish-communist" conspiracy in June 1941, the army's *Bulletin for the Troops* justified the ruthless methods soon to be used against the enemy. The article focused especially on the communist party's political officers in the Soviet army, a high percentage of whom were supposedly Jewish. "It would be an insult to the animals," the author remarked, to describe these Jews as animalistic. "They are the embodiment of the infernal, the personification of insane hatred against all of noble humanity," and "the rebellion of the sub-human against noble blood."[25]

When Hitler subsequently decided to murder not only the Jews of the Soviet Union, but the entire Jewish population of Europe, he found that German civilian elites were willing to join their military counterparts in carrying out his plan. Without the help of tens of thousands of civil servants, university-trained professionals, corporate managers, and some academics, the Holocaust would not have been possible. Many, if not most, of these elites were not Nazis, but they shared enough of the Nazis' racism, anti-Semitism, and paranoid anticommunism to see the murders as morally justifiable, or at least tolerable. What made their participation easier was that they were not asked to dirty their hands with the actual killing; instead, they "murdered from behind a desk." The victims died out of their sight, in Poland and the Soviet Union, and these men could therefore deny their own responsibility, at least in their own minds. However, thousands of men who were neither Nazis nor members of Germany's ruling class were drafted into the shooting squads that ultimately murdered 1.5 million Jews. These men would have to kill in a way that was up close, personal, and very bloody. Unlike the bureaucrats back in Germany, the members of the death squads could not ignore the moral implications of their acts. Very many were family men, with wives and children at home. When asked to murder defenseless civilians, including women and small children, what would they do?[26]

CHAPTER 11

THE ABSENT MORAL COMPASS

No one wants to be thought a coward.

—A member of a German shooting squad,
explaining why he had helped murder
thousands of Jewish civilians[1]

The causes of the Holocaust discussed in the preceding chapters help explain why Hitler ordered the murders and why his immediate subordinates, and countless Nazi true believers, did his bidding. They also explain why many tens of thousands of educated men in the civil service, professions, business world, and military also participated in the murders, if not directly in the killing. However, many murderers were neither members of the Nazi Party nor even, in many cases, especially anti-Semitic. Why did they kill? To answer this question one must look to patterns of behavior that are common to the human condition, and not specific to Germany or even Europe. And after all, the Holocaust has not been the only genocide. The sad fact is, any dictator who wants to murder civilians can easily find men to do the job.

To explain why thousands of ordinary Germans—not to mention ordinary Turks, Cambodians, Rwandans, and a few Americans—have committed mass murder, psychologists and historians have studied a cluster of three closely related human behaviors: automatic obedience to authority; conformity to the behavior of a group; and adaptation to a role and situation. The experiments of social psychologists demonstrate the power of these mechanisms to swiftly and drastically alter people's ideas of what is right and wrong. Put another way, most human beings lack a moral compass and quickly rewrite their moral code to fit their circumstances.

Two examples illustrate these behavioral patterns. The first is Reserve Police Battalion 101, a group of 500 uniformed Germans who helped shoot 38,000 Jews in German-occupied Poland in 1942 and 1943, and who brutally rounded up another 45,000 victims and forced them onto trains headed for the gas chambers of Treblinka. The second is Charlie Company, a group of 105 American soldiers who shot roughly 500 Vietnamese civilians in My Lai, South Vietnam, on March 16, 1968. The American people also reacted to the My Lai massacre in ways that reveal widespread habits of obedience in American society, at least at that time.[2]

Turning first to Reserve Police Battalion 101, we know a great deal about their motivations and attitudes, thanks to Christopher Browning's remarkable study, as well as to Daniel Goldhagen's work. Both scholars studied these men using judicial interrogations of some 210 members of the battalion.[3]

The men of the reserve police battalion were thoroughly "ordinary." Raised to adulthood under the old German Empire (1871–1918) or the democratic Weimar Republic (1919–1933), they had experienced none of the Nazi indoctrination that molded so much of German youth after Hitler's rise to power in 1933. Except for some of their officers, they were not Nazi fanatics like those who volunteered for the SS. Instead, they were drafted into the Order

Police because they were too old for combat duty. Nearly two-thirds of the rank-and-file members came from the working class of Hamburg, a city in which the Nazi Party had made few inroads before Hitler seized power. Based on their socioeconomic backgrounds, and what we know about politics in Hamburg during the 1920s, it is safe to say that very many of these men—perhaps most of them—had voted before 1933 for one of the two political parties that most strongly opposed the Nazis, the communists or the socialists. Judging from their background, these men should have been the last men in Germany who would murder Jews for the Nazi government.[4]

These men were of course not typical of those who filled most of the murder squads in the East. Most shooters came from the SS or had otherwise demonstrated a commitment to Nazism. However, several thousand other killers were, like the members of Reserve Police Battalion 101, middle-aged conscripts with no prior service in Nazi institutions. Therefore, we must find a way to understand their behavior and motives, which probably also resembled the behavior and motives of many other perpetrators who were not Nazis—for example, those who worked in industry and the civil service doing jobs that helped to facilitate the Holocaust.[5]

On June 20, 1942, after completing their training in the Hamburg region, the men of Reserve Police Battalion 101 received orders sending them to Poland. The men were led to believe that they would be performing guard duty; even their officers probably did not know the awful task that awaited them. They arrived in the Lublin region of Poland on June 25 and settled into their base in the town of Bilgoraj. During the next three weeks they moved among a series of small towns, driving the Jewish populations onto trains that took them for resettlement in urban ghettos. In a few cases, some men seem to have murdered Jews who were too frail or sick to be resettled, but they still did not perceive the full scope of their murderous undertaking in Poland. Their initiation into the extermination of European Jewry came on July 13.[6]

The battalion's commander, Major Wilhelm Trapp, called all units of the battalion from outlying regions back to their base in Bilgoraj on July 12. Trapp met with his officers and gave them their orders for the following day. The men learned that they were going into action, but apparently did not know what it entailed. The officers woke their men early on the 13th, and at about 2:00 A.M. they left Bilgoraj in trucks. They carried their firearms and large amounts of extra ammunition. Arriving at the outskirts of the town of Jozefow just before sunrise, the men stepped from their trucks and assembled to take their orders from Major Trapp.[7]

Trapp explained that roughly 1,800 Jews lived in Jozefow. Over the course of the day, his men would separate out approximately 300 men, especially skilled craftsmen, and ship them to a work camp. The remaining 1,500—women, children, and elderly men—the battalion would shoot dead. Trapp spoke haltingly, with tears in his eyes, as he explained that their orders had come from the highest authority, even as he recognized that this would be a terribly difficult task. He briefly tried to justify the murders by blaming Jews for the bombs then raining on German cities and for guerrilla attacks on German troops in Poland. Then he made an offer to the older men of the battalion, because many had wives and children of their own at home: if they did not feel that they could complete this difficult task, they could step forward and he would assign them some other duty. Ten or twelve men stepped out of line to accept Trapp's offer.[8]

Two platoons surrounded the village, while the remaining men drove the Jews of Jozefow to the marketplace, shooting anyone too frail to walk. After separating out the men slated for the work camp, they shuttled their victims to a nearby forest in trucks and began shooting them. The killing continued almost until nightfall, when some 1,500 men, women, and children lay dead and unburied in the forest. Over the next year and a half, these men carried out a series of smaller mass shootings. Small groups from the battalion also participated in what they called the "Jew hunt." This meant combing through the villages and forests of the northern Lublin region, looking for scattered individuals or families who had gone into hiding, many of them in underground bunkers dug out of the forest floor. They shot their victims on sight and ordered nearby Poles to bury them. In early November 1943, the men of Reserve Police Battalion 101, together with several other units, carried out a massacre of over 30,000 Jews at two work camps.[9]

Although no more than a dozen men immediately accepted Trapp's offer to let them avoid killing, many others asked to be relieved of this duty after taking the lives of one or more victims. Over the course of the year and a half that followed the slaughter at Jozefow, a division of labor developed among the men of the battalion. A substantial minority of men emerged who shot willingly and in some cases eagerly. Such men regularly volunteered for the "Jew hunt." When the battalion carried out a massacre, Trapp could rely on them to do the shooting, and often only their help was needed, allowing the others to avoid this task. A larger group, probably the majority of the battalion, shot when so ordered, but with little enthusiasm. The smallest group—no more than 10 to 20 percent of the battalion—consistently avoided shooting.

How can we understand why an overwhelming majority of the men in Reserve Police Battalion 101 committed murder when asked? None of these murderers would have faced punishment—or any other serious adverse consequences—if they had refused to kill. In all the postwar trials of men who perpetrated the Holocaust, not once could any defense attorney provide an example of punishment for failure to follow such orders. Conversely, in many cases the officers who ordered the killings, acting as Major Trapp had, explicitly offered their men the chance to opt out, acknowledging that the men might find it emotionally difficult to shoot unarmed civilians, especially women and children.[10]

If the killers faced no punishment for refusal to kill, this does not mean that obedience to authority did not play a powerful role in determining their behavior. The reflexive tendency to obey authority figures pervades every functioning society. Without some automatic obedience, civilization would dissolve into chaos. In a celebrated series of experiments conducted in the 1960s, Yale psychologist Stanley Milgram showed just how far such obedience could go, even in a peacetime setting where the authority figure was an unimposing psychology researcher, as opposed to a superior officer in wartime.[11]

Milgram did not tell the subjects of the experiment that they were its focus. Rather, they would "assist" him in a "learning experiment" by administering electric shocks to other people (played by actors) whenever the actors gave wrong answers to questions. The actors pretended to react sharply to the nonexistent shocks. Goaded by the researcher, the true subjects would dial up the voltage of the shocks after each wrong answer. In turn, the actors would complain with increasing vehemence about the pain and cry for help. On the voltage dial, the subjects saw a red zone of high voltage marked "Danger." Responding to instructions from the researchers, many volunteers repeatedly administered shocks at "Danger" levels, even after the actors had fallen silent, presumably passed out from pain or stricken by heart failure. All told, two-thirds of the subjects obeyed the researchers' instructions to the point of causing extreme pain.[12]

In an even more dramatic example of obedience to authority, members of an American infantry company shot roughly 500 unarmed, unresisting Vietnamese civilians at My Lai on March 16, 1968. While the circumstances surrounding the My Lai massacre differed dramatically from those confronting Reserve Police Battalion 101 in Poland, there were enough similarities to warrant including the American soldiers in this discussion. The most obvious difference between the two groups of men is that, unlike the German police unit, Charlie Company had seen combat and had suffered grievous losses during the three months that the men had fought in Vietnam before the massacre. Twenty-three members of the company had been wounded, some maimed for life, and five of their comrades had died. What is more, they had experienced the uniquely frustrating type of combat that characterized the American soldier's lot in Vietnam. During these three months, they had almost never seen their communist enemies, who struck at times and places of their own choosing, only to retreat into the jungle before the Americans could engage them.[13]

Two days before the My Lai massacre, on March 14, Charlie Company lost one its most popular sergeants, George Cox. A booby trap tore him into pieces. Another soldier lost his legs, while a third lost an arm and a leg and was blinded. The following day, the men of the company attended an emotional funeral for Cox and then received their orders for the 16th from Captain Ernest Medina. Medina made clear that now Charlie Company would have a chance to "get even," and claimed that the villagers in My Lai were communist sympathizers. At a subsequent trial, twenty-one witnesses testified that Medina gave an unambiguous order to kill everyone in My Lai the next day, armed or unarmed, man, woman, or child. On March 16, numerous members of Charlie Company did exactly that, although not a single shot was fired in their direction.[14]

The My Lai massacre thus differed markedly from the murders committed by Reserve Police Battalion 101 in Poland. American policy in Vietnam, although terribly careless of civilian lives, did not constitute genocide. Unlike the German policemen, the Americans had recently taken heavy casualties and were motivated in large part by a desire for revenge. And yet, other factors should have caused the American soldiers to be less willing than the German policemen to shoot civilians. The soldiers of Charlie Company had grown up in a democratic society in which prevailing expectations of obedient behavior could not have been as strong as they were in Nazi Germany. Unlike the policemen at Jozefow, who had to commence shooting very shortly after receiving their instructions and had no opportunity to discuss the situation with their comrades, Charlie Company got its murderous orders a good twelve hours before going into action. Any man who disliked the idea of killing civilians had ample time to discuss the matter with his comrades, to seek out those who might support him in refusing to kill, and to rally opposition. Although many of the men did refuse to shoot, despite a direct order on the ground from Lieutenant William Calley, no one seems to have registered any dissent the night before the massacre.[15]

Further insight into Americans' views on obedience to authority comes from examining how the public reacted to the trial of Lieutenant Calley. Convicted of murder at a court martial, Calley was sentenced to life in prison at the end of March 1971. A Gallup poll taken shortly thereafter revealed that 79 percent of Americans disapproved of the verdict, while only 9 percent approved. Two months later, the psychologist Herbert Kelman and the sociologist Lee Hamilton conducted a detailed survey of 990 randomly selected Americans. The survey described a situation identical to that faced by Charlie Company and posed two questions. First, "Do you think *most* people in this situation would follow orders and shoot [the civilians], or do you think most people would refuse to shoot them?" Second, "What do you think you would do in this situation—follow orders and shoot them, or refuse to shoot them?" A full 67 percent said that most people in this situation would kill the civilians, while only 19 percent thought that most people would refuse. In addition, 51 percent said that they themselves would shoot, while 33 percent said they would refuse. However, as Kelman and Hamilton pointed out, refusal was clearly the "right" or desired answer in this survey, so that 33 percent likely overstates the percentage who would refuse; presumably, 51 percent understates the percentage of those who would shoot.[16]

This survey does not necessarily predict how the respondents would actually have behaved if they had found themselves in uniform in a combat zone. However, it does show that a majority of the American people thought murdering civilians under orders was normal, expected, and perhaps even morally right. This finding seems all the more remarkable when one considers that the court martial, by its verdict, had clearly laid down a moral and legal standard sharply opposed to this prevailing sentiment. The court had rendered its judgment: Calley's order to shoot was illegal, and killing these civilians was murder. Moreover, the Vietnam War had for years inspired profound controversy among the American people. Millions had demonstrated against the war, calling it both immoral and futile. The survey's respondents had every reason to see Calley's murderous order as highly controversial and, at a minimum, morally problematic. Nonetheless, a full two-thirds of them thought that most people would kill civilians if ordered, and over half admitted that they would commit murder if told to do so.[17]

Milgram's experiments, the My Lai massacre, and Kelman and Hamilton's survey make it easy to grasp why Reserve Police Battalion 101 committed so many murders with so little dissent. The universal habit of obedience to authority would have operated with doubled effect in the wartime German context. These killers had already lived nine years under the heel of a repressive dictatorship, and their tendency to obey any order must have been massively reinforced by prevailing expectations. They were also committing these murders during a war in which over 5 million German soldiers would lose their lives. Amid this massive cheapening of human life and intense pressure to support the war effort, few men would refuse to kill people whom the regime had branded "enemies of the Reich."[18]

These killers also yielded to a second kind of pressure, namely, the need to conform to the behavior of the group that sheltered them. Loyalty to one's comrades in a military unit has long been recognized as a powerful motive driving soldiers' behavior. It is probably the main reason why almost all soldiers fight when commanded to do so. The men of Reserve Police Battalion 101 were a small, close-knit unit, almost all recruited from the same city and most coming from the same social background. Operating far from home and living in Poland among a hostile population, these men depended entirely upon each other for companionship and moral support. Since the battalion had to shoot even if an individual did not, any man who refused to kill was leaving the "dirty work" to his buddies and faced the risk of being ostracized. Moreover, refusing to shoot might appear as a moral reproach to one's comrades. Consequently, the minority who did avoid shooting (roughly 10 to 20 percent) usually pleaded that they were too "weak" for the task, thereby reaffirming the majority view that murdering civilians was a sign of "toughness." Explaining his actions during a postwar interrogation, one shooter observed that "no one wants to be thought a coward." A policeman who avoided shooting during the battalion's first massacre found that his comrades "showered me with remarks such as 'shithead' and 'weakling' to express their disgust."[19]

Michael Bernhardt, a member of Charlie Company who refused to murder civilians at My Lai, later recalled the men's loyalty to each other and the acceptance of perverted moral norms that came to be shared by most members of the unit:

When you're in an infantry company, in an isolated environment like this, the rules of that company are foremost. They're the things that really count. The laws back home don't make any difference. . . . Killing a bunch of civilians in this way—babies, women, old men, people who were unarmed, helpless—was wrong. Every American would know that. And yet this company sitting out here isolated in this one place didn't see it that way. I'm sure they didn't. This group of people was all that mattered. It was the whole world. What they thought was right was right. . . . The definitions for things were turned around. Courage was seen as stupidity. Cowardice was cunning and wariness, and cruelty and brutality were seen sometimes as heroic.[20]

Bernhardt had joined Charlie Company later than the other men and had remained an outsider. Not fully belonging may have made it easier for him to refuse to kill, to violate a group norm.

Bernhardt also put his finger on a third mechanism that helps explain why men kill under orders: the tendency people have to adapt to any role that they must fulfill and to adjust their notions of morality to the situation that faces them. As he put it, although "every American" would know that killing civilians was wrong, in their role as soldiers and in the terrifying circumstances that confronted them, "the definitions of things were turned around," so that "cruelty and brutality were sometimes seen as heroic." A remarkable experiment, conducted on the Stanford University campus in 1971, further illustrates this inclination to adapt to a prescribed role. A psychology professor, Philip Zimbardo, constructed a mock prison in the basement of a campus building, filling it with "prisoners" and "guards" drawn from a pool of volunteer subjects. Zimbardo put the subjects through a battery of tests, weeding out those who displayed an "authoritarian" personality or who otherwise scored

outside the normal range in various dimensions of their psychological makeup.[21]

Planning the experiment to last two weeks, Zimbardo had to
halt it after only six days because the guards had become so abusive
toward the prisoners. Quickly assuming their assigned roles, many
of the guards engaged in escalating brutality toward the prisoners, subjecting them to increasingly severe humiliation, although
stopping short of physical violence. Zimbardo observed that "most
dramatic and distressing to us was the observation of the ease with
which sadistic behavior could be elicited in individuals who were
not 'sadistic types.'"[22]

Just like the men of Reserve Police Battalion 101, the guards in
Zimbardo's experiment did not all behave in exactly the same way,
but rather fell into three different groups. A minority (fewer than
20 percent) resisted treating the prisoners harshly and sought to do
small favors for them. The majority were "tough but fair," adhering
to the prescribed rules, but not becoming abusive. Roughly one-
third, however, became actively sadistic, eagerly humiliating the
prisoners. This range of behavior, in roughly the same percentages,
also characterized the men of Reserve Police Battalion 101. A small
minority, between 10 and 20 percent, sought ways to avoid shooting. The majority of the men complied with the order to shoot, but
grudgingly and without enthusiasm, often finding themselves de-
pressed and abusing alcohol. About one-third, however, shot their
victims willingly and enthusiastically; they became the battalion's
specialists in shooting whenever the unit perpetrated a massacre
and often went out of their way to torment their victims before killing them. Rudolf Höss, the Auschwitz commandant, found a similar three-part division among concentration camp guards, although
he did not specify what percentages corresponded to each group.[23]

The acts of Zimbardo's guards seem all the more remarkable
when one remembers that they knew their situation was not real

and that it was supposed to last only two weeks. If only six days in a mock prison playing make-believe could profoundly change men's behavior, the changes wrought among the men of Reserve Police Battalion 101, as they made their way to their ghastly assignment in Poland, must have been enormous. They underwent months of training together, reinforcing their adhesion to the group and their identification with their role as agents of Germany's racial policies. They donned a uniform, took gun in hand, and received at least some indoctrination that explained their role in Hitler's demonic plan. The same is true of Charlie Company as it approached its rendezvous with destiny at My Lai. Their role was clearly defined, steeped in tradition, and anchored in training. They were American soldiers, defending the free world against communism. Whatever sense of morality these men may have had at home, whether in Hamburg or in America, it no longer applied in their changed circumstances. Very quickly, and often without reflection, they rewrote their moral codes to fit the new reality. In both groups of men, some measure of racism, the violent wartime context, and the basic human lack of a moral compass combined to produce horrifying results.[24]

CHAPTER 12

WHAT THEY KNEW

We swear, we will not give up the struggle until the last
Jew in Europe is annihilated and is dead.

—Prominent Nazi Party leader Robert Ley, in a
widely broadcast radio speech, May 1943[1]

Psychological mechanisms, combined with the violent wartime
context and widespread anti-Semitism, can explain the behavior
of the many killers who were not fanatical Nazis. But to explain
the Holocaust, we also need to understand a much larger group of
participants: the tens of millions of Germans who belonged neither
to the Nazi Party nor to the country's ruling elite, who did not kill
anyone, but whose silence during the Holocaust made the killers'
task easier. The following pages address three closely related questions. First, what did most Germans know about the Holocaust
while it was happening, that is, from the summer of 1941 until the
end of the war? Second, how did they react to this terrible knowledge? Finally, if they knew of the killings—and very many did—
what responsibility did they bear for this unprecedented crime?[2]

Any German who chose to think about it could know that the German government was murdering Jews in massive numbers. Wartime Germany was positively awash in information about the Holocaust; the only way to avoid absorbing this information was to repress it. In the first place, over 18 million German men served in the military during World War II, the majority of them in Poland or the Soviet Union. Many of these soldiers, especially those who filled support roles behind the lines, could easily have seen for themselves or heard from comrades how the regime's death squads rounded up Jews and shot them by the tens of thousands; regular army units also murdered large numbers of Jews in this manner. The killers did their grisly work in the open, and shootings regularly drew large crowds of spectators, both German soldiers and civilian contractors. Many of these voyeurs took photographs of the murders, a practice that has been called "execution tourism," and which the army forbade in vain. In at least one case, spectators made home movies of a shooting and showed them to friends at home in Germany.[3]

Hundreds of thousands of German soldiers participated in the mass shootings, whether as killers, spectators, or both. The evidence shows that virtually every German soldier knew about these shootings and understood that they were being carried out on a massive scale. Not only could they learn of shootings either first-hand or from comrades, but the German Army High Command acknowledged to its troops that mass murder was in full swing. The military newspaper *Die Front* made this abundantly clear, with the issue of January 21, 1942, for example, declaring that "at the end of this war stands the extermination of the Jews."[4]

Sooner or later, soldiers conveyed this knowledge to their friends and families back home. Few did so by mail, which was subject to review by military censors, but many clearly told of the shootings when home on leave. However, there is some reason to think that many other soldiers did not talk about the murders, since they did not seem to consider the topic very important. British and American intelligence officers secretly recorded conversations among captured German soldiers, producing more than 88,000 pages of word-for-word transcripts. Only in 0.2 percent of these conversations was the mass murder of Jews mentioned, although in those instances the killing was discussed in ways that show it was common knowledge within the military.[5]

Foreign radio broadcasts also informed Germans about the fate of the Jews, often in considerable detail. Listening to "enemy radio" was a punishable offense, but Germans knew they could get more accurate information from foreign radio than from their own government. Millions of Germans listened to the British Broadcasting Corporation's German-language programming from time to time, knowing that it provided accurate news of the military situation. At many points throughout the war, but beginning already in 1941, the BBC reported explicitly on mass shootings, deportations, death through slave labor, and murder by poison gas, identifying several death camps by name, including Auschwitz. In a December 30, 1942, broadcast, entitled "The War Against the Jews," the BBC explained to Germans that their government was systematically murdering every Jew in Europe. The newsreader stated how many Jews from Germany, Austria, Holland, Belgium, and France had already been murdered, and how few remained alive in these countries. The BBC also broadcast the December 17, 1942, declaration by the Allied powers that they would punish guilty Germans for the extermination of the Jews.[6]

Although the BBC was clearly the most popular "enemy radio" in Germany, both the Soviets and the Americans had their own German-language radio programs with large audiences, and both broadcast information about the murder of the Jewish people. Questioning of German POWs in Italy revealed that about

10 percent of them had listened to the American programs. On July 9, 1944, an American radio program, quoting the *New York Times*, announced that "since April 1942, the German government has murdered nearly one and a half million Jews in two [Polish] camps. . . . Millions of Jews have already met their deaths in gas chambers, through hanging, and poisonous injections."[7]

The British and the Americans reinforced their broadcasts about the Holocaust by dropping leaflets from bomber planes over Germany. The Allies scattered literally billions of leaflets across Germany during the course of the war. Most of these gave the Germans information on the military situation, but many millions directly addressed the destruction of the Jewish people. In December 1942, the BBC devoted an entire week to broadcasts about the systematic murder of the Jews of Europe. Then, in January 1943, Allied planes dropped a leaflet that again summarized the extermination process. It said, in part: "One has to assume that far more than a million European Jews have already been exterminated. . . . From all German-occupied countries, the Jews are deported to Eastern Europe under the most brutal and ghastly conditions. In Poland, which the Nazis have turned into their greatest slaughterhouse, the Jews are pulled out of the ghettos established by the invaders, with the exception of the few skilled workers useful to the arms industry. The deportees were never heard from again."[8]

Another flyer from 1943 announced that the Nazi leadership was "now going yet a step further. They are now in the act of killing an entire people: the Jews." It explicitly underscored the unprecedented character of the Holocaust: "At this moment the world looks in suspense, as never before, at the entire German nation. Is there among these 80 millions no one who will stand up and call halt, when in the name of his people the most terrible crime in world history is being committed?" Though no one can know how many Germans picked up such leaflets and read them, some clearly did, since doing so was a crime and quite a few got caught. Germans also gained information from the "deportation" of German Jews to their deaths in the East.[9]

At the beginning of October 1941, some 164,000 Jews still lived in Germany. On the fifteenth of that month, the German government began rounding up German Jews and "deporting" them to "the East," initially to ghettos, but later, in 1942, directly to death camps. Officials typically selected part of a town's Jewish population for a specific transport and gave the victims one week's notice. The government told them that they were being "resettled" and would find paid work in their new homes. At the appointed date and hour, these unfortunates would gather at some central location, permitted only one suitcase for a few belongings, and be herded onto the trains that took them to their fatal destination. The deportations continued until late June 1943, leaving roughly 30,000 Jews in Germany who enjoyed a temporary reprieve because they were married to Gentiles.[10]

The deportations gave Germans many opportunities to think about the fate of their Jewish neighbors—and in many cases to act in ways that were shockingly brutal and opportunistic. Although the government maintained silence in the press about the deportations, word quickly got out, setting off an unseemly scramble for the Jews' apartments and possessions, often before they had even left. Germans sometimes placed requests with the authorities, in advance of a deportation, for this or that prized piece of furniture or other possession belonging to some unfortunate Jewish acquaintance. Others had the gall to approach the doomed Jews directly and ask for their belongings. Regional Nazi Party leaders often promised that the Jews' confiscated apartments would ease the local housing shortage, further calling attention to the deportations. After a deportation, the authorities would sell the victims' possessions at public auction; in some cities, such goods also appeared for sale in special "Jew markets." Roughly 100,000 Germans from the Hamburg region are believed to have purchased the possessions of deported Jews.[11]

When Jews gathered to board the fatal trains, large crowds often came together to watch. Germans surely connected these deportations with the reports from many soldiers of mass shootings in the East; very many must have known early on that deportation was a death sentence. Reports by two foreign observers suggest that such knowledge was widespread. Howard K. Smith, an American journalist who worked in Germany until the end of 1941, described the first deportations. He correctly stated that the unfortunate Jews were shipped to Poland and occupied Soviet territory, where they would die of hunger and other deprivations. Edwin van d'Elden, former secretary of the US Chamber of Commerce in Frankfurt, spent some months in Germany even after Hitler declared war on the United States (December 11, 1941). Interned at the end of that year, he was released because of poor health in February 1942, and he could move freely about Frankfurt until he was expelled in May. Van d'Elden later accurately reported that five trains of deportees had left Frankfurt during his time there. One had arrived in the Lodz ghetto in Poland; the Jews on three of the other trains were shot beside the train tracks en route. This last bit of information was not strictly accurate, but it was close enough to the truth: the Germans shot thousands of Jews upon their arrival at the eastern ghettos (as at Kovno), or shortly thereafter (as at Riga).[12]

An especially poignant kind of evidence helped to confirm this terrible knowledge. When the authorities selected German Jews for their impending deportation, a wave of suicides would often sweep through the Jewish community. Between October 1941 and the summer of 1943, an estimated 3,000 to 4,000 of the Jews slated for deportation took their own lives. At the middle range of this estimate, this amounted to over 2 percent of the remaining Jewish population, more than 1,000 times the rate of suicide among American males in today's statistics.[13]

Especially during the latter part of the deportation process, after German Jews had received more information about the Holocaust, suicide claimed up to 10 percent of the Berlin Jews who were slated for some transports. In one boardinghouse where forty Jews lived, fifteen took their own lives during a six-week period at the beginning of 1942. Walter Schindler, who later went into hiding to escape deportation, described their passing in a letter: "They said their goodbyes after dinner, as if they were going on a trip, went back to their rooms, and in the early morning we would hear the ambulance drive up." Although suicides may have become more frequent during the latter part of the deportation period, they began in large numbers already with the first deportations in the fall of 1941. According to police records, 243 Berlin Jews killed themselves during the last three months of that year.[14]

The waves of Jewish suicides provide two kinds of evidence. First, many Germans must have heard this grim news and drawn the most terrible conclusion about the fate of the deportees. Second, the suicides demonstrate—as does much other documentary evidence—that many German Jews, although forbidden to own radios and cut off from many other sources of information, nonetheless came to know that deportation meant death.[15]

Germans thus received information about the Holocaust from many sources: foreign radio; leaflets dropped by Allied planes; the deportations and the Jewish suicides that accompanied them; and, above all, soldiers home on leave, who knew of the mass shootings behind the front lines. But could not this information be rationalized, minimized, explained away? Enemy radio and leaflets might lie or exaggerate. After all, the British had made grossly exaggerated claims about German atrocities in Belgium during World War I. A reported shooting might have been an isolated incident, its scale overstated. Countless Germans doubtless used such rational-izations to avert their eyes from an unpleasant truth, but millions could not, because their own government treated the Holocaust as an open secret.[16]

Although the German government struggled to conceal the precise details of the killing, Nazi leaders very frequently told the public, in general terms, that they were "exterminating" or "annihilating" the Jews of Europe. Hitler anticipated this remarkable practice, two years before the killing began, in his speech of January 30, 1939, commemorating the sixth anniversary of his becoming prime minister: "I want today to be a prophet . . . : if international finance Jewry inside and outside Europe should succeed in plunging the nations once more into a world war, the result will not be the bolshevization of the earth, and thereby the victory of Jewry, but the annihilation of the Jewish race in Europe." All across Germany, every movie theater featured Hitler's "prophecy" in the weekly newsreel. In eight radio broadcasts during the war, Hitler declared his intention to "exterminate" or "annihilate" the Jews, often explicitly referring back to his prophecy of January 1939. The German press announced every Hitler speech prominently in advance, and government radio often broadcast each speech more than once, to give every German the chance to hear the Leader. The newspapers printed his speeches the next day. Other Nazi leaders—notably Hermann Göring, Joseph Goebbels, and Robert Ley—broadcast similar death threats against the Jewish people. Still other prominent Nazis made countless speeches of this kind across Germany, their remarks quoted in the press. The press itself called on numerous occasions for the "extermination" or "annihilation" of the Jewish people.[17]

It seems strange that the regime would advertise its crimes to the German people, and indeed to the world, but several explanations seem plausible. Hitler may have wished to reaffirm his quasi-religious status as a prophet, which was part of the myth of his personal connection with Providence. Since he had "prophesied" the extermination of the Jews, he needed to tell his people that his prophecy was being fulfilled. The regime also recognized that news of the killing would leak out, and therefore felt the need to justify its murderous policy. Finally, as Germany's defeat in the war seemed increasingly likely, the government may have hoped to bind its citizens to it through shared guilt: having committed terrible crimes, the German people must give their utmost to the military effort, if only to avoid the punishment that would follow a defeat.[18]

Although these death threats never identified the means by which the Jews were to be murdered, they left no doubt as to the victims' fate. There was nothing ambiguous in the language the German authorities used. As early as the summer of 1941, as the shooting squads began their deadly work, the Nazi Party newspaper *Der Angriff* printed a statement by German Labor Front leader Robert Ley, who declared that "This war is the Jew's war. . . . It is a struggle for life and death, to be or not to be. There is no more compromise, no way back. We have crossed the Rubicon. . . . The God of the Jews is the God of revenge. Jehova never forgives, never forgets, he makes no peace, he annihilates and exterminates."[19]

Ley's remarks sounded the keynotes of an intense anti-Semitic propaganda campaign that began in Germany during the second half of 1941 and continued for at least two years thereafter. Echoing Hitler's fantasy of a Jewish conspiracy that controlled the Soviet, British, and American governments, the Nazi regime blamed the war on the Jews, who must now suffer dire consequences.[20]

This propaganda campaign was as massive in scale as it was bloodthirsty in its language. The claim that "the Jews" had caused the war and must perish because of it confronted the German people at every turn, not only in speeches by Hitler and other leading

Nazis, but also in thousands of newspapers and periodicals that repeated the messages dictated to them on a daily basis by Hitler's press chief, Otto Dietrich. Death threats against the Jews also screamed from "wall newspapers," large posters featuring lurid headlines, eye-catching illustrations, and brief texts in large type. Entitled "Word of the Week," no fewer than 125,000 of these wall newspapers were posted every week all across Germany from 1937 until the spring of 1943. Prominently displayed in locations as diverse as market squares, bus stops, hospital waiting rooms, and schools, these placards could hardly be avoided, and so every German must have encountered on many occasions the government's death threats against the Jewish people. From 1940 to early 1943, roughly one-third of these wall newspapers accused the Jews of causing the war or used other radically anti-Semitic language.[21]

In countless ways this propaganda made it clear that "extermination" and "annihilation" were not vague metaphors for military defeat, but meant complete biological extinction: the Jews intended to exterminate the Germans, so Germans were forced to kill or be killed. For example, in August 1941 the regime began a propaganda initiative organized around the pamphlet *Germany Must Perish*, published in the United States in early 1941 by a certain Theodore Kaufman. Kaufman, an obscure crank, called for all Germans to be sterilized. German propaganda represented Kaufman's rant as the policy of the American government. A German pamphlet released in September asked: "Who should die, the Germans or the Jews?" This pamphlet claimed that 20 million Jews lived around the world and suggested that they should be sterilized, rather than 80 million Germans, as Kaufman had proposed. "Then peace would be secured." In November, every German family received with their ration cards a leaflet about Kaufman which proclaimed that "80 million cultured, industrious, decent German women, men, and children are to be exterminated." In April 1943

German troops made a grisly find near the Russian city of Smolensk: the mass graves of more than 10,000 Polish officers who had been shot on Stalin's orders in 1940. Gruesome newsreel footage of exhumed corpses underscored the recurring theme of German propaganda: if Germany were to lose the war, "Jewish Bolsheviks" would exterminate the German people.[22]

On January 30, 1942, the ninth anniversary of his taking power, Hitler invoked his "prophecy" of January 1939 that a world war would lead to the "annihilation of the Jewish race." He promised "the disappearance of the Jews from Europe" and "the annihilation of Jewry." Hinting at the unprecedented nature of the genocide that was by then well underway, Hitler declared: "For the first time, the genuine old-Jewish law will be applied: An eye for an eye, a tooth for a tooth!" He further promised his listeners that "the *most evil world enemy of all time at least in the last thousand years* will be finished off." In May 1943 Robert Ley gave a speech to armaments workers that was broadcast by radio and also much commented upon in the press. "We swear," Ley declared, "we will not give up the struggle until the last Jew in Europe is annihilated and is dead."[23]

Though it is difficult to know how literally Germans interpreted such threats, there are several reasons why they should have taken them very seriously. The nationwide "Crystal Night" riots of November 1938, in which synagogues were burned in every German town that had one, had shown Germans something of the regime's capacity for violence toward Jews. Second, Hitler and his minions had proclaimed, on countless occasions since 1933, that the presence of Jews constituted a "Jewish problem," and that solving this "problem" was one of the regime's highest priorities. By plunging his nation into a war that would claim the lives of more than 7 million Germans and tens of millions of other people, Hitler had shown that he would never hesitate to pursue the most violent solution available to anything he perceived as a problem. Finally, by constantly blaming the Jews for the war, by portraying Jews everywhere as Germany's ultimate enemy and as the controlling power behind all other enemies, the regime marked them for death. After all, what does one do to one's enemies in wartime, if not kill them?

Given how much information was available concerning the Holocaust, and in view of the regime's constant death threats against the Jews, how could anyone not know about the Holocaust? The diary of Karl Dürkefälden, a worker in Lower Saxony, shows us how easily even a German who lacked government connections could learn about the murders. In February 1942, having read in the local press Hitler's recent reference to his "prophecy" of the Jews' annihilation, Dürkefälden noted that he thought such threats should be taken seriously. A few days earlier, he had heard the famed German author Thomas Mann on the BBC. Mann had reported that four hundred young Dutch Jews had been murdered with poison gas. Dürkefälden connected this report with Hitler having publicly threatened the Jewish people with extermination. In July a Dutch truck driver told Dürkefälden about the deportation of Dutch Jews, and a few months later he learned from the BBC that French Jews were being deported. In the fall of 1942 he recorded the accurate news from the BBC that the Germans had gassed Jews in vans. In January 1943, a soldier told him that Jews from France and other countries were being shot and gassed in Poland, and that only a tenth of the Jewish population in the Lithuanian city of Vilna was still alive. In June 1942, his brother-in-law, an engineer who had helped build a bridge near Kiev, described a mass shooting in graphic detail to him. Somewhat inflating the actual numbers, he told of 50,000 Jews buried on one occasion and 80,000 on another. On a later trip home from the front, he told Dürkefälden that no more Jews lived in Ukraine—they "were now all dead."[24]

If Dürkefälden demonstrated how much a German could know, receiving information does not automatically mean that someone has knowledge. To truly gain knowledge, a person has to choose to think about the information he or she has encountered. Very many Germans, perhaps most, repressed information they received about the killing. We are all very good at not knowing something we do not want to know, at not thinking about something that troubles us but which we may feel powerless to change. For example, Ursula von Kardorff, an opponent of the regime, confided to her diary in January 1944 the news of a Jewish girl who had poisoned her mother to save her from deportation. "If only one knew what is happening to the Jews who have been deported," she mused. Yet six months earlier she had written in her diary that someone who had been in the East had told her that Jews were being shot in front of mass graves. Helmuth James von Moltke, a leader of opposition to the Nazi regime, who later would pay for his courage with his life, gives us another example of repressed knowledge. Writing to his wife in October 1942, he told of a lunchtime conversation with a man who had come directly from occupied Poland, and who "told us on good authority about the 'SS furnace.' Until then I had not believed it, but he assured me that it was true: in this furnace 6,000 human beings are 'processed' daily." Nonetheless, in March 1943, Moltke gave a different account in a letter he mailed in Sweden to a British agent. He described a camp for 40,000 to 50,000 people in Upper Silesia (where Auschwitz was located), and said that 3,000 to 4,000 people a month (as opposed to the 6,000 daily mentioned in his earlier letter) "are supposedly killed there. But this information reaches me, yes me, who is searching for such facts, in a rather vague, hazy and imprecise form."[25]

Given the human capacity for repressing or ignoring unpleasant information, a German who lived during the war and who claims to have known nothing is not necessarily lying. Moreover, even the many Germans who did know something probably did not understand the radical scope of the Holocaust: the murder of every Jew in Europe. Only seldom can one find a diary entry comparable to one by Victor Klemperer, in which he concluded that the regime was indeed aiming at "the complete extermination of the Jews." Klemperer was a former professor of romance languages and an unusually perceptive observer of the regime. Even Karl Dürkefälden, discussed above, who carefully recorded information about the murders, could not discern the policy's unprecedented nature.[26]

Although rumors of murder by poison gas were widespread, very few people seem to have formed a picture of the death camps. This should surprise no one. Even today, after all that we have learned about the Holocaust, we find that places like Auschwitz and Treblinka stretch our imagination to its limits. Helmuth James von Moltke, whose militant opposition to the Nazis should have helped him see the depth of their depravity, could not accept a reliable account of the "SS furnace" burning 6,000 bodies a day. Therefore, those Germans who did not ignore the information they received probably knew of mass shootings, but not of death camps. Almost certainly they also recognized (or strongly suspected) that deportation meant death for their Jewish neighbors. How many Germans had this level of knowledge?[27]

Postwar surveys give at least a rough idea of how many Germans received information about the Holocaust while it was happening *and* who thought about it seriously enough that many years later they could remember hearing it. Professional polling organizations have conducted five surveys of representative samples of the German population. These surveys took place in 1961, 1988, 1991, 1995, and 1996. Every German questioned was at least fifteen years old when the war ended in 1945.[28]

In the first three surveys, polltakers interviewed their subjects face to face and asked them this question: "When did you hear, for the first time, something about the extermination. I don't mean details, but rather just generally: that it was happening?" The 1995 survey, conducted over the phone, asked a more general question that is not so useful for our purposes: "When did you learn of the crimes of the Nazis?" This question thus did not refer directly to the Holocaust. The 1996 survey, likewise done over the phone, referred to the murder of the Jewish people and then asked, "Did you yourself learn something, did you, back then, hear something from others about it, or did you first learn of it after the war?"[29]

Despite the problem with the 1995 survey question, these five polls produced remarkably consistent results across a space of thirty-five years: about one-third of the respondents said they had heard about mass murder of Jews (or, in 1995, "Nazi crimes") before World War II ended. A phone survey conducted by academic researchers in 2000 likewise suggested that about one-third had heard about the killing, as did a carefully constructed mail survey taken in the 1990s. If anything, this fraction understates the extent of Germans' knowledge, because some respondents may have forgotten, while many others surely lied when they said that they had not known.[30]

People lie in surveys, concealing actions that might invite criticism, and overstating their tendency to engage in virtuous behavior. In surveys taken from the 1970s to the 1990s, for instance, Americans consistently underreported racist attitudes, use of illicit drugs and alcohol, smoking, abortion, energy consumption, and criminal acts. In turn, they consistently over-reported socially desirable behaviors such as voting and going to church. That said, one cannot simply assume that a large fraction of the survey respondents were unwilling to admit that they had known about the Holocaust while it was happening. One early postwar survey showed that Germans honestly reported their earlier membership in the Nazi Party, while a good half of respondents to a poll in the 1980s admitted their enthusiastic support for Nazism during at least some years of the Third Reich. Comparing the answers to the polls on knowledge of the Holocaust from different groups of respondents, one can argue that a significant number lied when they denied having known, though the evidence for this conclusion is far from dramatic. In any case, a third of the population or somewhat less still translates to 20 million or 25 million adult Germans who had substantial knowledge of the murders; nearly all of the rest could have known if they had chosen to think about the information they received.[31]

How did the German people react to this terrible knowledge? The most reasonable conclusion is that they were coldly indifferent to the fate of the Jewish people. Given how much information was available about the Holocaust during the war, the postwar surveys, which prove knowledge for only a third of the population, suggest that most Germans deliberately avoided thinking about the information they received, deciding to turn a blind eye and never processing the information into actual knowledge. As for those who thought about it enough to recognize that Jews were being murdered in great numbers, they, too, demonstrated their indifference, not only by not commenting negatively on the murders, but by not talking about the killing at all. Agents of the Nazi Party and German government reported constantly on public opinion and the main topics of discussion among the people, eavesdropping on conversations in bars or train stations and taking informal soundings from those whom they trusted. Amid the immense volume of these reports on public opinion, there is almost total silence about the Jews during the war years.[32]

Fear of the dreaded secret police (Gestapo) must account for the silence of some Germans. Postwar memoirs and testimony suggest that fear of the Gestapo was pervasive; in a mail survey from the 1990s, over a quarter of the respondents remembered having personally known someone who had been arrested or interrogated for political reasons, which also suggests that nearly everyone else must have at least heard rumors. By aggressively pursuing even the slightest signs of dissent from anti-Semitic policy, the Gestapo had made it abundantly clear that criticizing the persecution of the Jews would not be tolerated. Yet fear can hardly account for all of the silence, and probably not even for most of it. After all, since Nazi leaders loudly and frequently boasted that they were exterminating the Jewish people, it is difficult to see that Germans would regard the topic as taboo, as long as they did not openly criticize the regime. Since the government routinely blamed Jews for the suffering and privations Germans endured because of the war, Germans could have discussed the killing and blamed the victims for their own suffering, to insulate themselves from accusations of disloyalty to the regime. What is more, Germans frequently criticized other government policies in unvarnished terms. In Bavaria, for example, farmers openly rejected the continuation of the war and characterized the regime's economic policy as a "swindle," as deliberate exploitation for the benefit of Nazi Party bosses, who were seen as parasitic drones. Industrial workers in Bavaria likewise called Nazi economic policy a "swindle," frequently complained of government corruption, and sharply criticized the Nazi Party leadership. Since fear of punishment cannot explain most Germans' silence about the murders, the more likely explanation is that they did not care.[33]

Michael Müller-Claudius's wartime survey of sixty-one Nazi Party members provides further evidence of German indifference toward the fate of Europe's Jews. Müller-Claudius was a psychologist and carried out his poll in the fall of 1942. Without telling his subjects that he was conducting a survey, Müller-Claudius asked them their opinion of the regime's Jewish policy. He prefaced his questions by stating that "the Jewish problem still hasn't been cleared up," and "we hear nothing at all about what sort of solution is imagined." Müller-Claudius found that forty-two of these

Nazis (69 percent of the sample) gave responses that he classified as "indifference of conscience." Typical was one man who stated, "To be frank, I've heard some very unpleasant things, but are they true? How much can you believe of rumors, anyway? Nobody can test them, so it's best to keep out of it." Another advised Müller-Claudius to "have a cigarette instead. I'm busy 12 hours a day, and can't be concerned with that as well. I need to keep all my thoughts on my work, and the rest of the time for relaxation." Of the rest of his sample, three people expressed open approval of the extermination program, while only three revealed what Müller-Claudius termed a "clear detachment from anti-Semitism." Finally, thirteen showed some moral qualms, despite their patently anti-Semitic attitudes. These Nazis argued that the Jewish people should be given their own country; they agreed that the Jews had to be expelled from Germany, but said that they should not be killed.[34]

If tens of millions of adult Germans knew a good deal about the Holocaust while it was happening, could they have done anything to stop it? Put another way, if they had felt outrage, rather than indifference, at this monstrous crime, could their moral indignation have changed the course of history?

Hitler was obsessed with his own popularity and sometimes changed course when he was confronted with widespread dissent and unrest. The regime backtracked as a result of public opinion, for example, in its attacks on religious schooling and Catholic organizations, and in the "euthanasia" program to kill the frail and the disabled. However, as new research by Nathan Stoltzfus has shown, dissent that erupted into mass unrest could be most effective when it was rooted in the long-established traditions of family life and religious practice. Protest against the murder of the Jews could not rely on these advantages, however, except when it concerned German Jews who were married to Gentiles. What is more, given how aggressively the regime had intimidated and punished Germans who criticized the Jews' persecution during the 1930s or showed them sympathy, it is easy to see why few Germans would have felt safe openly criticizing the killing. Finally, even massive unrest may not have been able to help the Jews, because in contrast to the euthanasia program, murdering the Jews of Europe was one of Adolf Hitler's highest priorities. Indeed, after it dawned upon him that he would lose the war against his military enemies, winning his war against the defenseless Jews may well have been his most important goal.[35]

If there was a chance to stop the Holocaust, it probably lay not in protest but rather in shaming the tens of thousands of elites who participated in the murders, and the hundreds of thousands of others who served and supported the Nazi regime in other ways. If the great majority of Germans had been horrified at the killing, instead of coldly indifferent, might elites have acted differently? This seems possible but on balance unlikely, given German elites' social arrogance and belief in their own superiority. The opinions of the middle and lower classes probably interested them little. Ultimately, the German people's indifference may be most important, not as a cause of the Holocaust, but as a moral wrong in its own right, a wrong that we need to condemn.

Is such indifference uniquely—or even especially—German? Our own country's history gives the lie to such a comforting illusion. During the Rwandan genocide of 1994, at least one military expert argued that 5,000 well-armed American or European troops could have halted the killing. Armed intervention is of course always risky. Perhaps such risks fully justified the inaction of our government and the equal passivity of several European states, any one of which could have mounted a military expedition. Significantly, however, intervention was never even seriously discussed, and neither our Congress nor the American people called for action to stop the killing. During the entire three months of the frenetic killing in Rwanda, during which some 500,000 people were murdered, not once did President Bill Clinton meet with his top advisers to discuss the genocide. Nor did the cabinet-level foreign policy team gather to consider the problem.[36]

This hardly means that American inaction in Rwanda is on a moral plane with German crimes in World War II. For one thing, Germans continued to support Adolf Hitler even as he boasted of annihilating and exterminating the Jews of Europe. Germans knew that their government, and often their own family members, perpetrated these crimes, whereas Americans had no hand in the Rwandan genocide. And yet, while Germans had to be careful about criticizing their government, Americans did not even face inconvenience if they wanted to raise their voices in protest. After all, it takes all of a minute to call one's representative in Congress to express an opinion. My point is of course not to diminish Germans' guilt by showing that Americans have also cared little for the sufferings of others. The indifference of the German people toward the Jews' cruel fate was morally disgusting. Yet American indifference, including that of this author, was also disgusting, and both peoples must strive to learn from their moral failures. What explains this seemingly universal lack of concern for the suffering of others?

Several factors must have contributed to Germans' fundamental lack of interest in the Holocaust. Anti-Semitism was widespread in German society before Hitler took power in 1933, and thereafter the government segregated Jews from Gentiles and subjected Germans to a steady drumbeat of anti-Semitic propaganda, which surely intensified anti-Semitism among millions of Germans. Segregation also contributed to Germans' indifference. Jews had in a very real sense ceased to be their neighbors, and friendships between Jews and Gentiles had withered. Many Germans also probably felt that they had too many problems of their own to concern themselves with the fate of strangers. American and British planes rained bombs on German cities, killing half a million civilians, and more than 5 million German men died in combat. "I've had it up to here with this war," one Nazi remarked to Michael Müller-Claudius. "I want [to live in] normal conditions. What role the Jews play in this is not my concern." Many others saw no need to think about something that they felt powerless to change. "It is risky to talk about it," another man told Müller-Claudius, "and no one has any influence on these things." Another remarked that "I didn't make Jewish policy and I know as little as you do about how it is developing. Ultimately we have an all-powerful government. It alone bears the responsibility." Finally, Hitler's enormous popularity, and the fact that "annihilating" the Jews was obviously one of his highest priorities, must have gone a long way toward overcoming any dismay that Germans may have felt about the murders. Yet none of these factors played a role in Americans' indifference to the Rwandan genocide, so it seems that there must be sociological or psychological mechanisms, common to many human societies, which explain our lack of concern for much of the world's suffering.[37]

One such mechanism is the diffusion of the sense of responsibility that comes when a large number of people know about some kind of harm. Each person can easily feel that if many people know, then one's own share of the collective responsibility is small. If the entire nation has knowledge, each individual's responsibility is insignificant: if all are responsible, no one is responsible. A second mechanism is distancing of the self from the crime or its victim. The further away people feel they are from the victims—whether geographically remote or psychologically distant from people they dislike or simply consider different from themselves—the less they care about the unfortunates' fate. Stanley Milgram demonstrated the effect of distance in his obedience experiments. When his subjects had to administer the shocks by forcing the victim's hand down on a metal plate that was supposedly electrified, only 30 percent of them obeyed instructions and escalated the shocks all the way to the end of the experiment. But when the victim was put out of sight behind a wall, a full 62.5 percent obeyed commands all the way to the maximum shock, even though they could hear the victim's screams on an intercom system. Distance played an obvious role in the Holocaust as well as in the American people's lack of reaction to the Rwandan genocide. In both cases, the murders took place far away, out of sight and out of mind. In both genocides, the victims seemed different from the bystanders who ignored their fate: the Rwandans because their skin color differed from that of most Americans, and because Americans think of Africa as an exotic and violent place; the Jews because widespread anti-Semitism, incessant Nazi propaganda, and the segregation of Jews and Gentiles created enormous distance between Germans and Jews, including even German Jews, who had rightfully considered themselves to be German.[38]

Distancing also bears on a final mechanism, namely, the way that most people draw a circle around a part of humanity, and feel moral obligation only to those who fall within this circle. For some, this "universe of obligation" might include only their family and friends, but for most it is some larger group: a clan or tribe, a religious community, or, most broadly of all, their fellow citizens in the country in which they live. By and large, people feel little concern for that great majority of the human species that falls outside their chosen universe of obligation, and no duty to protect them from harm. We have not yet learned to be our brother's keeper, and until we do, genocide will remain part of the human condition.[39]

CONCLUSION

The Holocaust terrifies everyone who chooses to think about it, in large part because, until now, no one has really tried to explain why it happened. Not understanding its causes, we fall back on the absurd notion that human beings are evil, and that, despite all the economic and technological progress we have made, we are morally still in the Stone Age. Yet even a cursory look at history shows us that human beings have been both persistently idealistic and astonishingly resourceful. In view of humanity's idealism and creativity, it seems almost grotesque to argue that our collective future could be anything but bright and full of promise. Nonetheless, the Holocaust might appear to defeat our hope for progress. But this is only if we do not understand why it happened. As the preceding chapters have shown, it took an almost impossible combination of dangerous ideas, ruined people, and unimaginably bad luck to make this catastrophe possible. Putting all the pieces of the puzzle together, we can now answer the question with which this book began: Why did the Holocaust happen?

The Holocaust happened above all because Germany did not become a democracy before the 1918 revolution. This delay in democratization gave Germany's ruling elites the motive and the opportunity to fight a long battle, between the 1880s and 1918, against democratic reform and social change. In this battle they used anti-Semitism and extreme nationalism as their weapons: they accused Jews of creating the socialist movement, and they tried to overcome class conflict by uniting all Germans against alleged "enemies"—Jews at home and other countries abroad. In so doing they prepared themselves and much of the German middle class to support Hitler, the most extreme nationalist and anti-Semite of all. In addition, because democracy came so late to Germany, this form of government did not have enough time to establish its legitimacy among the German people before the Great Depression struck their country with unprecedented fury. Not having learned to value democracy, having been encouraged since the 1880s to fear Jews and hate Germany's neighbors, desperate amid 30 percent unemployment and the paralysis of their government, a full third of Germany's voters gave their ballots to the Nazis in the last free elections of November 1932. Yet even after this long evolution which paved Hitler's road to power, only several blunders by Germany's government allowed him to take office, while dumb luck on Hitler's part then gave him the triumphs that convinced countless Germans of his genius and rendered his authority almost immune to challenge.[1]

In an anarchic political system in which Hitler became the sole source of power and legitimacy, his subordinates pushed constantly to radicalize German policy toward the Jewish people, building their careers by fulfilling what they claimed Hitler wanted, based on his violent and threatening statements about Jews. This mechanism of "working towards the Leader" created pressure for ever more violent policies toward Jews, while showing Hitler that he could count on active help for the most extreme policy he might choose. In turn, Germany's military victories pushed the thinking of Hitler and his subordinates toward genocide by bringing ever larger numbers of Jews under Germany's control: they could now imagine eliminating all the Jews of Europe, while less violent methods, such as forced emigration, were no longer feasible. Hitler's decision to invade the Soviet Union in 1941, and thereby destroy an imaginary "Jewish-communist conspiracy," made the Holocaust not only conceivable, but perhaps inevitable. In a war that would take the lives of millions, it was unlikely that the lives of Jews, whom Hitler blamed for the war, would be spared.

The decades-long use of anti-Semitism as a weapon against socialism and democracy made the Jews targets of oppression and violence, but it was not enough to mark them all for death. Two further historical developments robbed them of their humanity in the eyes of their killers and made their murder possible. During the decades leading up to the Holocaust, racism reached its high water mark in the history of Western civilization: inborn differences in value between different ethnic groups were now assumed to be scientific facts. Now it was possible to define the Jewish people as a separate species, genetically hardwired to behave destructively and therefore undeserving of life. Equally important, the vast and senseless slaughter of young men in World War I deprived human life of much of its value, creating a generation of killers who prided themselves on the "toughness" which they demonstrated by committing mass murder.

The foregoing causes of the Holocaust explain how Hitler could come to power, why he came to seek the extinction of the Jewish people, and how racism, anti-Semitism, and worship of Hitler motivated most of the murderers: not only the SS and other Nazis, but also tens of thousands of men and women from the educated elite of German society. Yet countless murderers were neither Nazi Party members nor members of the elite, nor were the tens of millions of Germans who had substantial knowledge of the killing but did not seem to care about it. These killers and bystanders may have been much less anti-Semitic than the country's elite, indeed, perhaps no more so than the average citizen of France or the United States at that time. While some degree of anti-Semitism, and the violent wartime context, provides a partial explanation, psychological factors—common in many societies besides Germany—also played a crucial role: automatic deference to authority, conformity to group behavior, and adaptation to a role, in the case of the killers; distancing from the victims and diffusion of responsibility, in the case of the bystanders. Put another way, most human beings lack a moral compass and feel no moral obligation toward those who fall outside some group with which they identify.

Some causes of the Holocaust were psychological and therefore perhaps universally human. Others—"scientific" racism, political anti-Semitism, the cheapening of life in World War I—were common throughout Western civilization in the first half of the twentieth century. Yet some causes were unique to Germany. Although the Germans found willing collaborators all across Europe, the Holocaust was a German project, instigated and organized by a German government, led by Germans at every level of the vast machinery of death. Why did Germany's rulers, and not the leaders of France, Britain, or Russia, perpetrate what may rank as the most terrible crime in history? What was different about the Germans?

Germany's failure to become a democracy before 1918 produced most of the political problems that set Germany apart from other Western societies. This failure can in turn be traced back to two very specific facts that had momentous consequences: Otto von Bismarck's genius, and the mutual antagonisms between Germany's political parties. Only Bismarck's boldness and political skill, combined with the Prussian armies' luck at the Battle of Sadowa and a brief window of opportunity in international politics, had made possible the creation of a united Germany in the first place. Partisan divisions, more than any other factor, prevented this German Empire from evolving into a parliamentary democracy.

As a consequence, German politics from the 1880s all the way down to the end of the Third Reich in 1945 was dominated by a single recurring dynamic: as class and partisan divisions intensified, attempts to overcome these divisions by the demagogic use of anti-Semitism and aggressive nationalism became ever more extreme. By the time the Great Depression struck in 1929, German politics had developed in such a destructive fashion that an authoritarian outcome was probable and discrimination against German Jews almost inevitable. Yet most of the fatal weaknesses in Germany's political system can be blamed on only two causes: Bismarck's genius and the intensity of partisan strife. We must also recognize that happenstance played an indispensable role in this tragedy.[2]

Had Bismarck not arrived on the scene in 1862, or if Prussia had lost the 1866 war against Austria as informed observers had expected, the German Empire would not have been created at the time that it was, nor with Bismarck's authoritarian constitution, if it were even created at all. If so, Germans could have learned the democratic process long before 1918. The German voter would not have been indoctrinated with rabid nationalism and anti-Semitism, and German foreign policy would not have provoked the tensions that led to World War I. Furthermore, absent terrible blunders by the German government after the Depression began, Hitler would not have gotten into power. Only astonishing luck on Hitler's part gave him a spectacular run of domestic and foreign policy triumphs between 1933 and 1941. These triumphs convinced millions of his genius, neutralizing opposition and moving his followers to commit unspeakable crimes at his behest. Only Germany's lightning-fast conquest of France in 1940—a victory won almost in spite of Hitler rather than because of him—made possible Hitler's invasion of the Soviet Union and the Holocaust. And if Hitler had died in World War I, as did 2 million of his countrymen, or in the assassination attempt that nearly claimed his life in November 1939, all of world history in the twentieth century would have taken a very different course, and the Holocaust would not have happened.

Seen in this light, the specifically German causes of the Holocaust, although they were indispensable to making it happen, don't make the Germans seem terribly different from other peoples, which is precisely the point: they weren't and they aren't. Not some deep and widespread flaw in German "national psychology," but rather accidents of history and partisan strife, combined to make possible Hitler's rise to power and the loyalty of millions to him. The crucial problem of partisan divisions should also remind us how pointless it is to generalize about the Germans as if they were all alike. If anything, their worst problem was that they differed too much from each other, that they were too diverse.

To argue against theories of German national pathology is certainly not to argue for German innocence. True, it makes no sense to speak of collective guilt, to blame "the German people" for Nazi crimes. Nonetheless, during the twelve years of the Third Reich, tens of millions of individual Germans made terrible moral choices. The worst offenders were the country's elite, perhaps half a million men and several thousand women, the leaders of German society in all of its institutions and contexts. Beyond the many tens of thousands who led the Nazi Party at its upper levels, tens of thousands more helped to carry out the extermination of European Jewry. Army officers of all ranks supported the shooting squads that raged behind the lines of the eastern front; many ordered their men to help with the killing. Hundreds of corporations used half a million Jews as slave labor, showing little concern as these workers perished at horrific rates from malnutrition and abuse. Civil servants organized and legalized the Jews' discrimination, deportation, and murder. Very seldom did any of these soldiers, managers, or bureaucrats opt out of their ghastly assignment, although they could have done so easily and without serious penalty.[3]

Most of Germany's elite did not participate in murder, although this may be only because they weren't given the opportunity. Unlike the volunteers in the SS, killers from the professions, the civil service, the military, and the business community were largely selected at random. They differed not at all from the rest of the elite—in background, outlook, or moral character. Therefore, their conduct tells us how most others of their class would have acted if asked to participate. Moreover, even those elites who did not participate bore a much greater responsibility than did most citizens. Without them, the Nazi regime could not have functioned, and so they must bear some guilt for its criminal acts. Unlike most Germans, these men and women had opportunities to influence policy, if only by remonstrating with friends and colleagues who were directly involved. Finally, as the leaders of their society, they were more engaged politically than most citizens and necessarily better informed. They read newspapers and listened to radio, and the murderers were their friends and lovers, fathers and sons, husbands and wives. Each of these men and women encountered plentiful and varied information about mass murder, information that was available to every German, but especially to them. If they did not actually know about the killing—and postwar surveys suggest a majority did not—this was only because they refused to know, because they chose to ignore terrible truths that they, more than anyone else, had a moral obligation to confront.[4]

As for the rest of the country, Germans of that era can hardly claim to have come away from this tragedy with clean hands. A full third of German voters gave their ballots to the Nazi Party in the last free elections, in November 1932. To be sure, they did not vote for World War II or the Holocaust when they chose Hitler. Foreign policy played little role in the election campaigns of 1930–1932, beyond the standard denunciations of the Versailles Treaty. Given that much of the treaty had been unfair to Germany, condemning it certainly did not mean enthusiasm for war. Everything known about German public opinion during the 1930s indicates that the German people did not want another war, much less the horrifically costly war that they got. As for the Holocaust, even Hitler had no inkling in 1932 that he would later try to exterminate the Jewish people, so the voters can hardly be faulted for not discerning this possibility. However, Hitler's voters knew full well that the Nazis were violently anti-Semitic, and they chose to accept this ugly reality when they marked their ballots. Once Hitler took power, tens of thousands of Nazi Party activists tormented their Jewish neighbors, while millions of Germans looked on approvingly, and most of the rest showed little solidarity with German Jews, who, in their overwhelming majority, were ardent German patriots who fully identified themselves with German culture. And when their government proceeded to "deport" their Jewish neighbors to certain death, when they learned of mass shootings in the East, when their beloved Leader and his henchmen loudly boasted of exterminating and annihilating the Jews of Europe, tens of millions of Germans not only registered no sign of disapproval, but did not even care enough to gossip about it.[5]

The French have a lovely saying that nonetheless is deeply troubling in its implications: "To understand all is to forgive all." If we understand why psychologically normal people, people just like us, commit terrible crimes, do we surrender our right to judge them in moral terms? Surely we do not. Every killer, every accomplice, every passive bystander in this tragedy had free will and made free choices. No German who pulled a trigger or signed an order had reason to fear punishment if he refused to become a murderer. At the same time, understanding them should make us think twice before assuming that we would have done better had we stood in their shoes. Surely most of us would not, for we share with the Germans the same human nature and the same weaknesses. People often wonder how they would have behaved had they lived in Nazi Germany. Such speculation is pointless: if we had lived in that time and in that place, we would not be the people we are today, but rather someone entirely different. Demonizing the Germans is unworthy of us because it denies both their humanity and ours. We are the Germans and they are we.

ACKNOWLEDGMENTS

I wish first to thank the many people who gave generously of their time by reading part or all of one of the over twenty drafts that this book has gone through, and by giving me countless valuable comments: Myriam Abramowicz, Soledad Arias, Prof. Shelley Baranowski, Susan Bernofsky, Peter R. Black, John K. Cameron, Noah Cliff, Russ Clune, Prof. John Cox, Susan Dalsimer, Prof. Istvan Deak, Manuela Del Prete, Michael Denneny, Paul DeRienzo, Paul Dippolito, Joseph P. Feely, Mike Friedman, Christopher Geering, Lisa Geering-Tomoff, David I. Graber, R. J. Hanson, Charles Heller, Elaine Heller, Joe Hopkins, Luna Kaufmann, Prof. Ian Kershaw, Paul Keye, Prof. Thomas Kühne, Janet Lee, Gerard Luisi, Ron Maimon, Daniel Maoz, Paul Margulies, Victoria Margulies, Deborah McMillan, Eirlys Mow, Dawn Muniz, Peter M. Paulino, Prof. Robert O. Paxton, Jacqueline Plavier, Michaelyn Plavier, Julianne Rainbolt, Alessandra Seggi, Karina Shaw, Prof. Allan Silver, Renate Soybel, Prof. Kevin Spicer, David Sternlieb, Prof. Kiril Tomoff, Jon Vanden Heuvel, Mark A. Walsh, Prof. Gerhard L. Weinberg, Prof. S. Jonathan Wiesen, Clive Williams, Helmut Zerbes, Joachim Zerbes, and Reinhilde Zerbes. My readers deserve considerable credit for the book's strengths, while the responsibility for its faults is necessarily mine.

Heartfelt thanks go also to my agent, William Clark, who always believed in the project and found the ideal publisher for my book. My editors at Basic Books, Lara Heimert and Katy O'Donnell, provided valuable assistance with the writing through the last two stages of revision. Last but hardly least, my publicists, Angela Baggetta and Lynn Goldberg of Goldberg McDuffie Communications, worked tirelessly and effectively to help me reach my audience.

Special thanks go, finally, to Soledad Arias, John K. Cameron, Istvan Deak, Mike Friedman, Ian Kershaw, Janet Lee, Robert O. Paxton, S. Jonathan Wiesen, and, above all, to my mother, Deborah McMillan, who sustained me with her love and support from the beginning of this journey to the very end.

NOTES

INTRODUCTION

1. Elie Wiesel, "Plea for the Dead," in *Legends of Our Time* (New York: Holt, Rinehart and Winston, 1968), 181–182. The second and third sentences of the quoted passage are separated by roughly a page of text. Emphasis in original.

2. Primo Levi, quoted in Inga Clendinnen, *Reading the Holocaust* (New York: Cambridge University Press, 1999), 88; Elie Wiesel, "Plea for the Dead," 180–181. At 181 Wiesel also asked: "We dare interpret the agony and anguish, the self-sacrifice before faith and faith itself of six million human beings, all named Job? Who are we to judge them?"

3. With Himmler I have departed slightly from a literal translation to make this passage more readable. I have also left out a significant (but in my view misleading) comment on the nature of the Nazi belief system. The complete passage was as follows: "Mit dem Antisemitismus ist es genauso wie mit der Entlausung. Es ist keine Weltanschauungsfrage, daß man die Läuse entfernt. Das ist eine Reinlichkeitsangelegenheit. Genauso ist der Antisemitismus für uns keine Weltanschauungsfrage gewesen, sondern eine Reinlichkeitsangelegenheit, die jetzt bald ausgestanden ist. Wir sind bald entlaust. Wir haben nur noch 20,000 Läuse, dann ist es vorbei damit in ganz Deutschland." Excerpt from Himmler's speech to SS-Korpsführer, April 24, 1943, in Heinrich Himmler, *Geheimreden 1933 bis 1945*, Bradley F. Smith and Agnes Peterson, eds., with an introduction by Joachim C. Fest (Frankfurt: Propyläen, 1974), 200. On the complete extermination and other unique features of the Holocaust, see Chapter 2.

4. Historians and psychologists generally agree that most perpetrators of the Holocaust were psychologically normal, at least before they began committing mass murder. See, for example, Victoria Barnett, *Bystanders: Conscience and Complicity During the Holocaust* (Westport, CT: Greenwood Press, 1999), 23; Zygmunt Bauman, *Modernity and the Holocaust* (Cambridge, UK: Polity Press, 1989), 19;

Ervin Staub, *The Roots of Evil: The Origins of Genocide and Other Group Vi-olence* (New York: Cambridge University Press, 1989), 91; Harald Welzer, *Täter: Wie aus ganz normalen Menschen Massenmörder werden* (Frankfurt: S. Fischer, 2005), esp. 7–17; James Waller, *Becoming Evil: How Ordinary People Commit Genocide and Mass Murder*, 2nd ed. (New York: Oxford University Press, 2007).

5. Simon Wiesenthal, *The Murderers Among Us: The Memoirs of the World's Most Relentless Nazi-Hunter*, Joseph Wechsberg, ed. (New York: Bantam Books, 1967).

CHAPTER 1

1. Quoted in Jeremy Noakes and Geoffrey Pridham, eds., *Nazism 1919–1945: A Documentary Reader*, vol. 3, *Foreign Policy, War and Racial Extermination* (Exeter: University of Exeter Press, 1988), 1199–1200; Peter Longerich, *Heinrich Himmler*, trans. Jeremy Noakes and Lesley Sharpe (New York: Oxford University Press, 2012), 689ff.

2. The figure of 11 million was discussed during the Wannsee Conference, January 20, 1942. Noakes and Pridham, eds., *Nazism 1919–1945*, 3:1127–1135, esp. 1130. *On worldwide extermination*: Yehuda Bauer, *Rethinking the Holocaust* (New Haven, CT: Yale University Press, 2001), 49. Gerhard Weinberg goes further, arguing that exterminating all Jewish populations on Earth was an explicit goal of Hitler and his accomplices. Weinberg provides extensive evidence that Hitler took concrete steps toward this goal, for example (as revealed in recent research by Klaus-Michael Mallmann), by attaching an *Einsatzkommando* shooting squad to General Erwin Rommel's army. Had Rommel not been defeated at El Alamein, this shooting squad would have embarked on the murder of Jews throughout the Mid-dle East. Gerhard Weinberg, "A World Wide Holocaust Project," paper delivered at the conference "Global Perspectives on the Holocaust," Middle Tennessee State University, October 21, 2011, cited with the author's permission.

I remain agnostic on Weinberg's thesis because I haven't done research in the primary sources concerning the decision for the Final Solution, and, in addition, because an explicit goal of worldwide extermination does not appear in any of the scholarly literature on the topic. I also see a problem for Weinberg's thesis in the actions of the *Einsatzkommando* that was detailed to the German Army, which occupied Tunisia from late 1942 until May 1943. Rather than setting out to mur-der the 85,000 Jews of Tunisia, the *Einsatzkommando* subjected them to forced labor, deporting only roughly 20 to death camps. These actions do not seem con-sistent with a decision for worldwide extermination. See Longerich, *Heinrich Himmler*, 662–663.

Estimates of the death toll among Roma have varied widely. For Peter Lon-gerich's careful reconstruction of Himmler's inconsistent policy toward this mi-nority, see ibid., 668–672, where he suggests a toll in the low tens of thousands. Longerich's account makes clear that the Nazis never aimed at complete extermi-nation of the Roma. At the upper extreme is Doris L. Bergen's estimate; she puts the figure at somewhere between 250,000 and 500,000 Roma dead, in her *War and Genocide: A Concise History of the Holocaust*, 2nd ed. (New York: Rowman and Littlefield, 2009), 200. The estimate of 220,000 comes from the United States Memorial Holocaust Museum, "Genocide of European Roma (Gypsies), 1939–1945," www.ushmm.org/wlc/en/article.php?ModuleId=10005219, accessed July 1, 2013.

3. Specifically concerning the war against the Soviet Union, see, for example, Steven G. Fritz, *Ostkrieg: Hitler's War of Extermination in the East* (Lexington: University of Kentucky Press, 2011), 1–76, esp. 4–8, 75–76. The German government also made this accusation a central theme of its propaganda after 1941. See the excellent study by Jeffrey Herf, *The Jewish Enemy: Nazi Propaganda During World War II and the Holocaust* (Cambridge, MA: Harvard University Press, 2006). By "indirectly" I mean the handicapped, Sinti and Roma, homosexual men, and other categories of people who, consistent with Nazi racial ideology, were thought to impair Germany's strength and efficiency during wartime.

4. The following discussion of Hitler's worldview is based primarily on Eberhard Jäckel, *Hitler's World View: A Blueprint for Power*, trans. Herbert Arnold (Cambridge, MA: Harvard University Press, 1981), and on Ian Kershaw, *Hitler*, 2 vols. (New York: W. W. Norton, 1998–2000). Kershaw sees Hitler's worldview as a rationalization of his "burning thirst for revenge" upon the people, Jews foremost among them, whom he blamed for Germany's humiliating defeat in World War I. Ian Kershaw, "Hitler's Role in the Final Solution," in *Hitler, the Germans, and the Final Solution* (New Haven, CT: Yale University Press, 2008), 90–91.

5. Alan E. Steinweis, *Kristallnacht 1938* (Cambridge, MA: Harvard University Press, 2009); Noakes and Pridham, *Nazism 1919–1945*, vol. 2, *State, Economy and Society* (Exeter: University of Exeter Press, 1984), 553–554. *On the number who died in concentration camps:* Peter Longerich, *Holocaust: The Nazi Persecution and Murder of the Jews* (New York: Oxford University Press), 112–113.

6. A partial catalog of the regime's countless anti-Jewish measures is found in Joseph Walk, ed., *Das Sonderrecht für die Juden im NS-Staat: Eine Sammlung der gesetzlichen Maßnahmen und Richtlinien-Inhalt und Bedeutung*, 2nd ed. (Heidelberg: C. F. Müller Wissenschaft, 2013 [reprint of 1996 2nd ed.]). The secret police (Gestapo) and local Nazi Party activists worked relentlessly to intimidate people who maintained even the most casual personal or business contact with Jews, as Robert Gellately has demonstrated in his study of the Gestapo in Würzburg and Lower Franconia in his book *The Gestapo and German Society: Enforcing Racial Policy, 1933–1945* (New York: Oxford University Press, 1990), 160, 174–204. One man was investigated for shaking a Jew's hand on the street; a woman who visited an elderly Jewish woman, for whom she had worked as a servant for ten years, spent three weeks in jail for this "offense." Ibid., 174, 177. The Gestapo's case files were deliberately destroyed in every jurisdiction except Düsseldorf and Würzburg–Lower Franconia, but Gellately persuasively argues that the pressure to avoid contact with Jews would have been, if anything, more severe in other parts of

Germany, as Würzburg lay in a Catholic region that had shown little sympathy for Nazism before Hitler took power in 1933. Regions with large Jewish populations and a history of Nazi voting would have seen larger numbers of people willing to report their neighbors for "Jew-friendly" behavior. Ibid., 185–186.

7. *On Jewish policy as a tool to expand the Nazi Party's power, and Jews' exclusion from different spheres:* see Longerich, *Holocaust*, 31–32, 72–85.

8. A vivid example of the dilemma created by moral compromises is the path taken by German big business as it collaborated in the persecution and murder of the Jews, a subject analyzed by Peter Hayes in "State Policy and Corporate Involvement in the Holocaust," in Michael Berenbaum and Abraham J. Peck, eds., *The Holocaust and History: The Known, the Unknown, the Disputed, and the Reexamined* (Bloomington: Indiana University Press, 1998), 197–218.

9. Ian Kershaw locates the decision in late November or early December 1941 in his *Fateful Choices: Ten Decisions That Changed the World, 1940–1941* (New York: Penguin, 2007), 464. Christopher R. Browning locates the decision to exterminate the Jews of Europe in mid-October in *The Origins of the Final Solution: The Evolution of Nazi Jewish Policy, September 1939–March 1942*, with contributions by Jürgen Matthäus (Lincoln: University of Nebraska Press, 2004), 370–372. In contrast, Himmler's biographer, Peter Longerich, sees no single point at which a decision was made, but rather an accretion of smaller steps leading to a point, not until late April or early May 1942, at which total extermination was now the policy. Longerich, *Heinrich Himmler*, 541–574, esp. 563–564. Longerich's thesis is problematic for several reasons: Hitler is almost absent from Longerich's discussion of the decision-making process, although his active involvement at every step is well documented; Longerich fails to adequately explore the implications of Himmler's order on October 23, 1941, blocking all further emigration from German-controlled Europe; Longerich's account tends to understate the important role that death camps had assumed in the Nazi leadership's thinking by the end of 1941; and the minutes of the Wannsee Conference (January 20, 1942) explicitly announce a plan to murder 11 million European Jews. Saul Friedländer argues that Hitler was compelled by his "prophecy" of January 1939 to commit himself, in the presence of the higher ranks of the Nazi Party, to total extermination of the Jews no later than the second week of December 1941: now that the United States was at war with Germany (December 11), the world war of Hitler's prophecy had begun, so that the Jews of Europe would have to be "annihilated." Saul Friedländer, *Nazi Germany and the Jews, 1933–1945*, vol. 2, *The Years of Extermination* (New York: HarperCollins, 2007), 286–288. However, Kershaw has argued persuasively that Hitler would not have made anything like a formal announcement of such a policy to such a large number of players. Kershaw, *Hitler, the Germans, and the Final Solution*, 99.

10. *On Hitler as an indispensable cause of the Holocaust:* see, for example, Ian Kershaw, "Hitler and the Holocaust," in *Hitler, the Germans, and the Final Solution*, 237–281. Raul Hilberg finds that "without him," the Holocaust would

have been "inconceivable." Raul Hilberg, *Perpetrators Victims Bystanders: The Jewish Catastrophe, 1933–1945* (New York: HarperCollins, 1992), ix. *On Hitler's "historic mission" against the Jews:* see Saul Friedländer, *Nazi Germany and the Jews, 1933–1945*, vol. 1, *The Years of Persecution* (New York: HarperCollins, 1997), 73–112; Friedländer, *Years of Extermination*, 286–288.

11. A prime example is Himmler's pushing the shooting squads to expand their killing to entire Jewish communities, in a bid to expand his own power, and in the (correct) expectation that Hitler would approve. Longerich, *Heinrich Himmler*, 530–540.

12. *On the early expulsion plans:* see Browning, *Origins of the Final Solution*, 36–71, and the summary table at 109. *On the planners' acceptance that very many Jews would die:* see Longerich, *Holocaust*, 153–155. *On the Madagascar Plan:* see Browning, *Origins of the Final Solution*, 88–89; Michael Wildt, *An Uncompromising Generation: The Nazi Leadership of the Reich Security Main Office*, trans. Tom Lampert (Madison: University of Wisconsin Press, 2009), 303.

13. Kershaw, *Fateful Choices*, 54–90; Fritz, *Ostkrieg*, 1–76. Kershaw emphasizes that Hitler had always been skeptical of the prospects of successfully invading Britain and announced his decision to invade the Soviet Union to his generals on July 31, 1940, long before the decisive weeks of the Battle of Britain. However, Hitler's decision was not finalized in military directives until December, and no one can say what course he would have chosen had the Luftwaffe defeated the Royal Air Force in the fall of 1940.

14. *On the German Army's enthusiasm for the shootings:* see, for example, Fritz, *Ostkrieg*, 97–104.

15. Christopher Browning has documented a clear correlation between military victory and the radicalization of Hitler's thinking at several points between September 1939 and October 1941 in Browning, *Origins of the Final Solution*, esp. 314–330, 370–372, 425–427; both Hitler quotes at 370. Peter Longerich and others have contended that Hitler never made an identifiable decision, and that the policy of complete extermination instead evolved in numerous small increments until one day (in Longerich's account, in April or May 1942) it happened to be the policy. This interpretation makes little sense: attempting to exterminate 11 million people (by Heydrich's calculation) isn't something that people just fall into doing. This interpretation is also not easily reconciled with the overriding importance that Jews had in Hitler's thinking, the way that the magnitude of the threat they posed defined his own greatness as the hero who vanquished them, the very active role Hitler played at every step in the radicalization of anti-Jewish policy, and Hitler's role as the sole source of power and legitimacy in the Nazi political system.

16. Citing an unpublished manuscript by Ray Brandon, Timothy Snyder puts the total of shooting victims in 1941 at 1 million, in *Bloodlands: Europe Between Hitler and Stalin* (New York: Basic Books, 2010), 218. Not having seen Brandon's manuscript, I am sticking with the lower figure given in Friedländer, *Years of Extermination*, 209.

On the total number shot: Raul Hilberg, *The Destruction of the European Jews,* 3rd ed., 3 vols. (New Haven, CT: Yale University Press, 2003), 3:1320; Peter Black, "Foot Soldiers of the Final Solution: The Trawniki Training Camp and Operation Reinhard," *Holocaust and Genocide Studies* 25, no. 1 (2011): 2. *On the "problems" involved in shooting:* Richard Rhodes, *Masters of Death: The SS-Einsatzgruppen and the Invention of the Holocaust* (New York: Random House, 2002), 215–228; Rudolph [Rudolf] Höss, *Death Dealer: The Memoirs of the SS Kommandant in Auschwitz,* ed. Steven Paskuly, fwd. Primo Levi, trans. Andrew Pollinger (New York: Da Capo Press, 1996), 156–157.

There is some disagreement among historians over whether Majdanek was truly an extermination camp. The Majdanek gas chamber was used only episodically, and at least one estimate of its death toll has been revised downward to 24,000. Black, "Foot Soldiers of the Final Solution," 21, 38 n. 285.

17. Murder by carbon monoxide began at Chelmno on December 8, 1941. Browning, *Origins of the Final Solution,* 418.

Auschwitz murdered Jews at all times of day and night, around the clock in some peak periods, but at Treblinka, any death trains that arrived at night were left standing until morning, so that the killing could begin at daybreak. Yitzhak Arad, *Belzec, Sobibor, Treblinka: The Operation Reinhard Death Camps* (Bloomington: Indiana University Press, 1987), 66. *On Auschwitz:* see the testimony of Rudolf Vrba in Claude Lanzmann, *Shoah: The Complete Text of the Acclaimed Holocaust Film* (New York: Da Capo Press, 1995), 34.

18. See, for example, Filip Müller, *Eyewitness Auschwitz: Three Years in the Gas Chambers,* ed. and trans. Susanne Flatauer (Chicago: Ivan R. Dee, 1979).

19. At Belzec, the guards would briefly turn the lights on in the gas chambers, to see through peepholes how many of their victims had died. See Kurt Gerstein's observations in Noakes and Pridham, *Nazism 1919–1945,* 3:1149–1153, esp. 1152. At Auschwitz, the guards likewise turned the lights off to gas their victims. Leni Yahil, *The Holocaust: The Fate of European Jewry, 1932–1945,* trans. Ina Friedman and Haya Galai (New York: Oxford University Press, 1990), 366.

At Belzec, Chelmno, Sobibor, and Treblinka, the Germans initially buried their victims, but later exhumed and burned their bodies to destroy the evidence and switched over to burning all subsequent victims who arrived at the camps.

20. *On ghetto inhabitants' knowledge of their fate:* Friedländer, *Years of Extermination,* 441–442; "Notes by a Jewish Observer in the Lodz Ghetto Following the Deportation of the Children," dated September 16, 1942, in Yitzhak Arad, Israel Gutman, and Abraham Margaliot, eds., *Documents on the Holocaust,* 8th ed., trans. Lea Ben Dor (Lincoln: University of Nebraska Press, 1999), 284–286; Christopher R. Browning, *Remembering Survival: Inside a Nazi Slave-Labor Camp* (New York: W. W. Norton, 2010), 69–71. The most thorough and analytical memoir by an Auschwitz survivor is Primo Levi, *Survival in Auschwitz,* trans. Stuart Woolf (New York: Touchstone, 1996).

21. Black, "Foot Soldiers of the Final Solution," 93 n. 285; Friedländer, *Years of Extermination*, 662.

22. Alon Confino sees "consensus" among historians about why the Holocaust happened, centered on Nazi ideology, institutional pressures, and the radicalizing context of World War II, in his *Foundational Pasts: The Holocaust as Historical Understanding* (New York: Cambridge University Press, 2012), 37–39.

23. Ben Kiernan puts the Cambodian death toll at 1,671,000 in *The Pol Pot Regime: Race, Power, and Genocide in Cambodia Under the Khmer Rouge, 1975–1979* (New Haven, CT: Yale University Press, 1996), 458. Journalists and the United Nations usually put the Rwandan death toll at 800,000; there were only 660,000 Tutsi in the country per the 1991 census. Triangulating from three sets of sources, Alison Des Forges, in *"Leave None to Tell the Story": Genocide in Rwanda* (New York: Human Rights Watch, 1999), estimated a figure somewhat above 500,000 Tutsi and about 10,000 Hutu. Scott Straus adopted these figures in *The Order of Genocide: Race, Power, and War in Rwanda* (Ithaca, NY: Cornell University Press, 2006), 51.

I base the claim that people put the Holocaust in a class by itself mainly on the evidence in the paragraphs that follow, but partly also on my experience of talking and teaching about the Holocaust for four decades, and partly on the fact that so much more has been published, and so many more films have been produced, about the Holocaust than about other genocides. This volume of cultural production serves at least as indirect evidence of the special fascination the Holocaust holds for the public. On books, a rough indicator of the public's interest is the number of entries gained by searching the Amazon website for books on "Holocaust" (12,921), "Rwanda genocide" (1,091), "Armenian genocide" (670), and "Cambodian genocide" (177) (figures as of June 12, 2011). A search on Amazon for films (both feature and made-for-TV movies) turned up 646 entries on the Holocaust, 35 on "Rwanda genocide," 22 on "Armenian genocide," and 5 on "Cambodian genocide" (as of June 12, 2011). A public opinion poll taken in the United States in 1992 is inconclusive because it did not ask whether the Holocaust was "unique," but rather whether there were other historical events to which it could be "compared." Katherine Bischoping and Andrea Kelmin, "Public Opinion About Comparisons to the Holocaust," *Public Opinion Quarterly* 63, no. 4 (1999): 485–507.

The "Gorgon" quotation is from Inga Clendinnen, *Reading the Holocaust* (New York: Cambridge University Press, 1999), 4, also quoted in John K. Roth, "The Ethics of Uniqueness," in Alan S. Rosenbaum, ed., *Is the Holocaust Unique? Perspectives on Comparative Genocide*, 2nd ed. (Boulder: Westview Press, 2001), 28.

24. See, for example, Alan S. Rosenbaum, ed., *Is the Holocaust Unique? Perspectives on Comparative Genocide*, 2nd ed. (Boulder: Westview Press, 2001); Gavriel D. Rosenfeld, "The Politics of Uniqueness: Reflections on the Recent Polemical Turn in Holocaust Scholarship," *Holocaust and Genocide Studies* 13, no. 1 (1999): 28–61. The quotation is from Taner Akçam, *The Young Turks' Crime Against Humanity: The Armenian Genocide and Ethnic Cleansing in the*

Ottoman Empire (Princeton, NJ: Princeton University Press, 2012), xxix. In the case of the Armenian genocide, Akçam finds that "the struggle to prove similarities [to the Holocaust] reached such ludicrous lengths that some of the most significant structural components of the Armenian Genocide, such as religious conversions or the assimilation of Armenian children into Muslim households, were almost completely omitted from analyses of the events of 1915 because such elements played no role in the annihilation of the Jewish people." Ibid., xxx.

25. Saul Friedländer, in "The 'Final Solution': On the Unease in Historical Interpretation," in *Lessons and Legacies*, vol. 1, *The Meaning of the Holocaust in a Changing World*, ed. Peter Hayes (Evanston, IL: Northwestern University Press, 1991), 23–35, writes at 31–32: "We should be dealing with this epoch and these events as with any other epoch and events, considering them from all possible angles, suggesting all possible hypotheses and linkages. But, as we know, this is not the case and, implicitly, for most, this cannot be the case." And at 35: "Paradoxically, the 'Final Solution,' as a result of its apparent historical exceptionalism, could well be inaccessible to all attempts at a significant representation and interpretation." Without referring to Friedländer, Alon Confino suggests that "most historians today" (as opposed to "several decades ago" when this view was "dominant") would not subscribe to the view that the Holocaust "was unimaginable and is unrepresentable," although he finds that "a self-imposed methodological and interpretive constraint still exists," in "Forum: Cultural History and the Holocaust," *German History* 31, no. 1 (2013): 61–85, esp. 65; see also 68 and remarks by Amos Goldberg at 69–70.

On Auschwitz being incomprehensible: Charles S. Maier, *The Unmasterable Past: History, Holocaust, and German National Identity* (Cambridge, MA: Harvard University Press, 1988), 92, quoted in Friedländer, "The 'Final Solution,'" 24. *On bafflement after five years of study:* Friedländer, "The 'Final Solution,'" 24, paraphrasing Arno J. Mayer in the preface to Mayer's *Why Did the Heavens Not Darken? The "Final Solution" in History* (New York: Pantheon, 1988); Bergen, *War and Genocide*, viii. See also Confino, *Foundational Pasts*, 3.

26. See, for example, Deborah E. Lipstadt, *Denying the Holocaust: The Growing Assault on Truth and Memory* (New York: Free Press, 1993); John C. Zimmerman, *Holocaust Denial: Demographics, Testimonies and Ideologies* (Lanham, MD: University Press of America, 2000); Steven E. Atkins, *Holocaust Denial as an International Movement* (Westport, CT: Praeger, 2009). On the existence of deniers of other genocides besides the Holocaust and the Armenian genocide, I am indebted to Professor Steven Jacobs of the University of Alabama.

CHAPTER 2

1. Claude Lanzmann, *Shoah: The Complete Text of the Acclaimed Holocaust Film* (New York: Da Capo Press, 1995), 182.

2. I have seen references to a population of around 1,000 prisoners at Treblinka, but Yitzhak Arad's overview of the squads of prisoners who did different

kinds of work in the camp suggests a total number closer to 500. Yitzhak Arad, *Belzec, Sobibor, Treblinka: The Operation Reinhard Death Camps* (Bloomington: Indiana University Press, 1987), 108–113.

3. Gitta Sereny, *Into That Darkness: An Examination of Conscience* (New York: Vintage, 1974), 207–208.

4. Testimony of Richard Glazar, in Lanzmann, *Shoah: The Complete Text*, 111–112; Arad, *Belzec, Sobibor, Treblinka*, 121–122, 194–195. Glazar remembered the prisoners who escorted victims into the infirmary as belonging to the "blue squad," but Arad (at 108) said they wore red armbands and were known as the "reds" and "the burial society."

5. Sereny, *Into That Darkness*, 207–208.

6. *On the burning and drowning of Armenians:* Vahakan N. Dadrian, "Patterns of Twentieth Century Genocide: The Armenian, Jewish, and Rwandan Cases, *Journal of Genocide Research* 6, no. 4 (2004): 490–491. *On the Armenian genocide generally:* Taner Akçam, *The Young Turks' Crime Against Humanity: The Armenian Genocide and Ethnic Cleansing in the Ottoman Empire* (Princeton, NJ: Princeton University Press, 2012); Vahakn N. Dadrian, *The History of the Armenian Genocide: Ethnic Conflict from the Balkans to Anatolia to the Caucasus*, 6th ed. (New York: Berghahn Books, 2004); Raymond Kévorkian, *The Armenian Genocide: A Complete History* (New York: I. B. Tauris, 2011). *On Cambodia:* Ben Kiernan, *The Pol Pot Regime: Race, Power, and Genocide in Cambodia Under the Khmer Rouge, 1975–1979* (New Haven, CT: Yale University Press, 1996). *On Rwanda:* Scott Straus, *The Order of Genocide: Race, Power, and War in Rwanda* (Ithaca, NY: Cornell University Press, 2006); Phillip Gourevitch, *We Wish to Inform You That Tomorrow We Will Be Killed with Our Families: Stories from Rwanda* (New York: Farrar, Straus and Giroux, 1998).

7. *On the uniqueness of the Nazi assault on moral values:* see also Jonathan Glover, *Humanity: A Moral History of the Twentieth Century* (New Haven, CT: Yale University Press, 2000), 327, 343–344, 356.

In the literature on other genocides, there are scattered references to the victims being described as vermin or bacteria, but this language was used metaphorically, rather than as an expression of a theory of biological difference, as seen in the Holocaust. This is the case, for example, with the leaders of the Khmer Rouge, who labeled their political enemies as "diseased elements" and "microbes." Ben Kiernan, *Blood and Soil: A World History of Genocide and Extermination from Sparta to Darfur* (New Haven, CT: Yale University Press, 2007), 401, 406, 549–550. Yet almost all the victims of the Pol Pot regime were ethnic Khmers, so biological racism played a role only in the extermination of the 20,000 Vietnamese who remained in the country, and perhaps in the less thorough assault on the Cham minority.

Biological racism played little role in the Armenian genocide, as shown by the adoption of as many as 200,000 Armenian children into Turkish homes; the large numbers of Turkish men who took Armenian women as wives or concubines after their forced conversion to Islam; and the regime's assimilationist policies toward non-Turkic Muslims. Akçam, *Young Turks' Crime*, xv–xviii, 40–41, 287–339, esp. 334–339. See also Robert F. Melson, *Revolution and Genocide: On the Origins of the Armenian Genocide and the Holocaust* (Chicago: University of Chicago Press, 1992), 251–252. *On Turkey and Cambodia:* see also Rowan Savage, "'Disease Incarnate': Biopolitical Discourse and Genocidal Dehumanization in the Age of Modernity," *Journal of Historical Sociology* 20, no. 3 (2007): 404–440, esp. 410, 417, 419, 421. Significantly, Savage's examples of Armenians being described as "microbes" came from the pens of Turkish nationalists who were medical doctors, so such statements cannot be taken as representative of the CUP leadership. Savage's Cambodian examples are clearly metaphorical rather than literally biological—for example, Pol Pot's references to "sickness of consciousness" among politically unreliable elements within the Khmer Rouge.

On Rwanda, Scott Straus's interviews with 210 convicted killers show that racist ideas or even ethnic antipathy provided a motive for only a minority, while 70 percent of his sample had had at least one Tutsi family member, and almost none of them voiced any objection to the idea of themselves or one of their children marrying a Tutsi. While racist ideas may have been prominent in some of the radio propaganda emanating from Kigali, killers at the local level said racism played little role in their actions, although nationalist and racist ideas do seem to have influenced the most violent killers. Straus, *Order of Genocide*, 9, 124–135. Much has been made of the use of the term "cockroaches" (*inyenzi*), supposedly as a derogatory term for Tutsi. However, the term may have been used chiefly with a more narrow meaning, signifying only Kagame's invasion force. The term *inyenzi* had been applied to armed Tutsi rebels since the civil strife of the early 1960s, apparently because they, like roaches, were active mainly at night. Only 0.6 percent of the killers Straus interviewed described the violence as "killing *inyenzi*." Ibid., 157–160. See also Gérard Prunier, *The Rwanda Crisis: History of a Genocide* (New York: Columbia University Press, 1997), 402. Throughout his treatment, Prunier uses this word, and quotes others using it, solely to signify Kagame's fighters. See Alison Des Forges, *Leave None to Tell the Story: Genocide in Rwanda* (New York: Human Rights Watch, 1999), 51 n. 34, and *passim*.

8. *On the Jews of Norway, Kos, and Finland:* see Saul Friedländer, *Nazi Germany and the Jews, 1933–1945*, vol. 2, *The Years of Extermination* (New York: HarperCollins, 2007), 449, 454, 613.

Vahakn Dadrian, a distinguished historian of the Armenian genocide, contends that the Ittihadist government sought to completely exterminate Turkey's Armenian population. Dadrian, "Patterns of Twentieth Century Genocide," 494. In addition to the fact that the Turks left so many alive whom they could have killed, other facts defeat Dadrian's claim: tens of thousands, or even hundreds of thousands, of Armenians saved their lives by accepting forced conversion to Islam; the Armenian children who were spared and adopted into Turkish homes numbered in at least the tens of thousands, with estimates running as high as 200,000; the regime effectively subcontracted the killing to all manner of irregular and undisciplined groups who operated beyond the government's control, including Kurdish and Chechen tribesmen, mobs of Turkish villagers, and the infamous Special Organization, consisting of violent felons recruited directly from prison and set upon the hapless Armenian caravans after only a week's training. Had complete extermination been the goal, they would have relied on disciplined formations subject to centralized control, for example, the army. *On conversions and adoptions:* see Akçam, *Young Turks' Crime,* 287–339; Kévorkian, *Armenian Genocide,* 295–296, 809–810. *On the lack of central control over the killing process:* Dadrian, "Patterns of Twentieth Century Genocide," 490, 505; Kévorkian, *Armenian Genocide,* 294–296, 630, 652, 665.

On the intention to exterminate the entire Tutsi population of Rwanda: see Straus, *Order of Genocide,* 49, 53–55, 89, 163–165. However, Straus's work concerns mainly the killing at the local level, rather than the plans of Hutu leaders in Kigali.

9. *On Turkey:* see Akçam, *Young Turks' Crime,* xvii–xviii, 130–202, esp. 130–134; Dadrian, *History of the Armenian Genocide,* 185–199. *On Rwanda:* see Straus, *Order of Genocide,* 7, 9, 12, 44–49, 135–157.

On Hitler's euphoric mood when he finalized his decision for complete extermination: see the quotations in Christopher R. Browning, *The Origins of the Final Solution: The Evolution of Nazi Jewish Policy, September 1939–March 1942,* with contributions by Jürgen Matthäus (Lincoln: University of Nebraska Press, 2004), 370. The leadership cadres of the Reich Security Main Office, which constituted the "nerve center" of the Final Solution, shared Hitler's enthusiasm and exciting sense of unlimited possibilities. Michael Wildt, *An Uncompromising Generation: The Nazi Leadership of the Reich Security Main Office,* trans. Tom Lampert (Madison: University of Wisconsin Press, 2009), 443–444.

10. Andrzej Strzelecki, "The Plunder of Victims and Their Corpses," in Yisrael Gutman and Michael Berenbaum, eds., *Anatomy of the Auschwitz Death Camp* (Indianapolis: Indiana University Press, 1994), 246–266; "From the Final Report by Katzmann, Commander of the SS and Police in the District of Galicia, on 'The Solution of the Jewish Problem' in Galicia," in Yitzhak Arad, Israel Gutman, and Abraham Margaliot, eds., *Documents on the Holocaust,* 8th ed., trans. Lea Ben Dor (Lincoln: University of Nebraska Press, 1999), 335–341; Raul Hilberg, *The Destruction of the European Jews,* 3rd ed., 3 vols. (New Haven, CT: Yale University Press, 2003), 3:1049.

11. Quoted in Hilberg, *Destruction of the European Jews,* 3:1029–1030, n. 12.

12. Arad, *Belzec, Sobibor, Treblinka,* 109, 160; Friedländer, *Years of Extermination,* 503, 591–592.

13. Friedländer, *Years of Extermination,* 296–297, 592–593; Arad et al., *Documents on the Holocaust,* 353. From the context it is unclear whether the photographers were Ukrainian, German, or both.

14. The famine that directly or indirectly carried off most of the Cambodian victims resulted from economic dislocation and a shortfall in rice imports, as opposed

to the Germans' deliberate policy of murder by malnutrition. Although urban dwellers or peasants living outside of zones previously controlled by the Khmer Rouge were clearly disfavored in the Cambodian genocide (Kiernan estimates that 33 percent of them perished, versus 15 percent of the "old people" from KR-controlled rural areas), they were not condemned to death at the outset, whereas every Jew, without exception, would inevitably be murdered, and both victims and killers understood this awful truth. See Kiernan, *Pol Pot Regime*, 163–164, 456–458.

The "transit camps" in present-day Syria and Iraq, where upward of 600,000 Armenian deportees perished from hunger and disease, have been described as "death camps," and were clearly used as part of a deliberate effort to decimate the Armenian population. However, they were largely administered and guarded (to keep out hostile tribes) by the Armenians, and produced almost no interaction between Armenians and Turks. They therefore do not represent a parallel to the phenomenon of killers living among their victims in the Holocaust. Kévorkian, *Armenian Genocide*, 632–670, esp. 632–637 and 670–672.

15. Quoted in Sereny, *Into That Darkness*, 131, 189. Yitzhak Arad sees in Stangl the "outlook, that Jews are not within the realm of humanity . . . a complete identification with Nazi racial ideology," demonstrated by a "withdrawal from any contact with the prisoners, even with regard to the most cruel acts." Arad, *Belzec, Sobibor, Treblinka*, 186. However, Stangl did not in fact avoid all contact with prisoners, as discussed at the beginning of this chapter.

16. Robert Jay Lifton, *The Nazi Doctors: Medical Killing and the Psychology of Genocide*, rev. ed. (New York: Basic Books, 2000), 363; Rudolph [Rudolf] Höss, *Death Dealer: The Memoirs of the SS Kommandant in Auschwitz*, ed. Steven Paskuly, fwd. Primo Levi, trans. Andrew Pollinger (New York: Da Capo Press, 1996), 239.

17. Friedländer, *Years of Extermination*, 209.

18. See, especially, the memoir of Fania Fenelon, who played in a separate women's orchestra in Auschwitz, *Playing for Time* (Syracuse: Syracuse University Press, 1976); Arad, *Belzec, Sobibor, Treblinka*, 227–233.

19. Lanzmann, *Shoah: The Complete Text*, 2–3, 84, 91–92; Arad, *Belzec, Sobibor, Treblinka*, 231–232.

20. *On anger at victims:* Herbert C. Kelman and V. Lee Hamilton, *Crimes of Obedience: Toward a Social Psychology of Authority and Responsibility* (New Haven, CT: Yale University Press, 1989), 19–20. Kelman and Hamilton write: "Those who participate in the massacre directly . . . are reinforced in their perception of the victims as less than human by observing their very victimization. The only way they can justify what is being done to these people—both by others and by themselves—and the only way they can extract some degree of meaning out of the absurd events in which they find themselves participating, is by coming to believe that the victims are subhuman and deserve to be rooted out."

21. Daniel Jonah Goldhagen, *Hitler's Willing Executioners: Ordinary Germans and the Holocaust* (New York: Knopf, 1996), 263–292; Friedländer, *Years of*

Extermination, 509–510; Ernst Klee, Willi Dressen, and Volker Riess, eds., *"The Good Old Days": The Holocaust as Seen by Its Perpetrators and Bystanders*, trans. Deborah Burnstone (Old Saybrook, CT: Konecky and Konecky, 1991), 104; Christopher R. Browning, *Ordinary Men: Reserve Police Battalion 101 and the Final Solution in Poland*, rev. ed. (New York: HarperCollins, 1998), 90–95. Some 11,000 Miedzyrzec Jews were targeted for deportation; the surviving Jews in the town counted 960 who had been killed during the roundup, so I have given a figure of 10,000 who were deported and died at Treblinka. Captain Julius Wohlauf's men were outraged that Wohlauf had let his bride witness their actions, although it has been argued that their main concern was for the health of a woman who was four months pregnant. Ibid., 93; Goldhagen, *Hitler's Willing Executioners*, 242–243.

22. Klee et al., eds., *"Good Old Days,"* 259–261, 264.

23. Ibid., 262, and *passim*.

24. Primo Levi, *Survival in Auschwitz*, trans. Stuart Woolf (New York: Touchstone, 1996), 105–106.

25. Again, Cambodia's lethal agricultural projects under the Khmer Rouge form a partial exception, but unlike the situation in the Holocaust, the Cambodian victims were not condemned to death in advance, which necessarily meant a very different kind of relationship between guards and prisoners than the type seen in the Holocaust.

26. Höss, *Death Dealer*, 35.

27. *On the initial selection at Auschwitz:* a good overview is in Lifton, *Nazi Doctors*, 163–179. *On the survivors' perspective:* Levi, *Survival in Auschwitz*, 19–21; Fenelon, *Playing for Time*, 16–18.

28. Klee et al., eds., *"Good Old Days,"* 178–179.

29. Arad, *Belzec, Sobibor, Treblinka*, 202; Levi, *Survival in Auschwitz*, 128.

30. Raul Hilberg, *Perpetrators Victims Bystanders: The Jewish Catastrophe, 1933–1945* (New York: HarperCollins, 1992), 103.

31. Former SS officer Franz Suchomel stated that the men always died first. Lanzmann, *Shoah: The Complete Text*, 108–109. *On the organization of laborers in the camp:* Arad, *Belzec, Sobibor, Treblinka*, 108–113.

32. Arad, *Belzec, Sobibor, Treblinka*, 120–121. This estimate of the number killed refers to the new gas chambers, constructed in September and October 1942. Arad suggests that these chambers could absorb a maximum of 2,300 victims. The SS officer Heinrich Matthes testified that each chamber could hold about 300 people, so that 1,800 could be murdered at one blow. Other sources say that there were ten chambers rather than six, so that, according to Arad's estimate, 3,800 could be killed in one batch.

33. For a broad spectrum of beliefs within a ghetto about the fate of deportees, see Christopher R. Browning, *Remembering Survival: Inside a Nazi Slave-Labor Camp* (New York: W. W. Norton, 2010), 69–71.

34. Arad et al., eds., *Documents on the Holocaust*, 283–284.

35. Shlomo Venezia, *Inside the Gas Chambers: Eight Months in the*

Sonderkommando of Auschwitz, in collaboration with Beatrice Prasquier, trans. Andrew Brown (Malden, MA, 2009), 67–68. "Special squad" refers to the *Sonderkommando.*

36. Arad, *Belzec, Sobibor, Treblinka,* 108.

37. Filip Müller, *Eyewitness Auschwitz. Three Years in the Gas Chambers,* Susanne Flatauer, ed. and trans. (Chicago, 1979); Arad, *Belzec, Sobibor, Treblinka,* 209–214; Venezia, *Inside the Gas Chambers,* 74.

38. Quoted in Lanzmann, *Shoah: The Complete Text,* 105, 107.

39. Ibid., 108.

CHAPTER 3

1. Primo Levi, *Survival in Auschwitz,* trans. Stuart Woolf (New York: Touchstone, 1996), 141.

2. See Hans-Ulrich Wehler, *Deutsche Gesellschaftsgeschichte,* vol. 3, *1849–1914* (Munich: C. H. Beck, 1995), 459–486; David Blackbourn and Geoff Eley, *The Peculiarities of German History: Bourgeois Society and Politics in Nineteenth-Century Germany* (New York: Oxford University Press, 1984); Jürgen Kocka, ed., *Bürgertum im 19: Jahrhundert. Deutschland im europäischen Vergleich,* 3 vols. (Munich: Deutscher Taschenbuch Verlag, 1988); and the useful summary in Matthew Jefferies, *Contesting the German Empire, 1871–1918* (Malden, MA: Blackwell, 2008), 33–46.

3. Saul Friedländer, *Nazi Germany and the Jews, 1933–1945,* vol. 2, *The Years of Extermination* (New York: HarperCollins, 2007), 213, 221–223, 225; Report of October 15, 1941, from Einsatzgruppe A, in Yitzhak Arad, Israel Gutman, and Abraham Margaliot, eds., *Documents on the Holocaust,* 8th ed., trans. Lea Ben Dor (Lincoln: University of Nebraska Press, 1999), 389–393. *On willing collaborators throughout Europe more generally:* see Raul Hilberg, *Perpetrators Victims Bystanders: The Jewish Catastrophe, 1933–1945* (New York: HarperCollins, 1992). Recent research shows that many early massacres following the German invasion were less spontaneous efforts by the local population than had previously been thought and that the Germans played an important but concealed role in instigating the killings. Peter Longerich, *Holocaust: The Nazi Persecution and Murder of the Jews* (New York: Oxford University Press, 2010), 192–196.

4. The best survey of German history during the nineteenth century and first two decades of the twentieth is David Blackbourn, *History of Germany, 1780–1918: The Long Nineteenth Century,* 2nd ed. (Malden, MA: Blackwell, 2003); older, but still useful, is William Carr, *A History of Germany, 1815–1990,* 4th ed. (New York: Arnold, 1991). *On the empire:* see, especially, Hans-Ulrich Wehler, *The German Empire, 1871–1918,* trans. Kim Traynor (New York: Berg, 1985); also useful is Wolfgang J. Mommsen, *Imperial Germany, 1867–1918: Politics, Culture, and Society in an Authoritarian State,* trans. Richard Deveson (New York: Arnold, 1995).

5. Christopher R. Browning, *Ordinary Men: Reserve Police Battalion 101 and the Final Solution in Poland,* rev. ed. (New York: HarperCollins, 1998), 217–218.

On a tendency to obedience during the empire: see the thoughtful discussion in David Blackbourn, *The Long Nineteenth Century: A History of Germany, 1780–1918* (New York: Oxford University Press, 1998) (hereafter Blackbourn, *Long Nineteenth Century*, 1st ed.), 372–375, but qualified at 41, with respect to the early nineteenth century; more generally, see Gordon A. Craig, *The Germans* (New York: Putnam, 1982), 22–23 and *passim*. Note, however, that no less an observer than Carl von Clausewitz, writing in 1807, characterized the French as especially militaristic and obedient to authority, while the Germans, in his opinion, had too critical an attitude to blindly submit to tyranny. Blackbourn, *Long Nineteenth Century*, 1st ed., xiii.

On the radicalism of the "second revolution" of 1849: see Blackbourn, *Long Nineteenth Century*, 1st ed.,162, and Blackbourn's list of episodes of protest at 171; Jonathan Sperber, *Rhineland Radicals: The Democratic Movement and the Revolution of 1848–1849* (Princeton, NJ: Princeton University Press, 1991). *On voting in Germany:* Blackbourn, *Long Nineteenth Century*, 1st ed., 411. In 1909–1910, the German socialist party had 720,000 members, more than the socialist parties of Austria, Belgium, Denmark, France, Italy, Holland, Norway, Sweden, and Great Britain combined. Ibid., 412.

On the United States: see, for example, William Greider, *Who Will Tell the People: The Betrayal of American Democracy*, with a new introduction (New York: Simon and Schuster, 2009 [1992]); Jacob S. Hacker and Paul Pierson, *Winner-Take-All Politics: How Washington Made the Rich Richer—and Turned Its Back on the Middle Class* (New York: Simon and Schuster, 2010); Robert G. Kaiser, *So Damn Much Money: The Triumph of Lobbying and the Corrosion of American Government*, with a new epilogue (New York: Vintage, 2010); Lawrence Lessig, *Republic, Lost: How Money Corrupts Congress—and a Plan to Stop It* (New York: Hachette, 2011).

6. The best introduction to German liberalism remains James J. Sheehan, *German Liberalism in the Nineteenth Century* (Chicago: University of Chicago Press, 1978); for a more recent review of the literature, see Dieter Langewiesche, *Liberalism in Germany*, trans. Christiane Banerji (Princeton, NJ: Princeton University Press, 2000).

7. Blackbourn, *Long Nineteenth Century,* 1st ed., 240ff.

8. Most historians would characterize Bismarck as a political genius whose role in German unification was indispensable. See Jefferies, *Contesting the German Empire*, 50–61. The best biography is Lothar Gall, *Bismarck, the White Revolutionary*, trans. J. A. Underwood, 2 vols. (Boston: Allen and Unwin, 1986); also useful is Otto Pflanze, *Bismarck and the Development of Germany*, 3 vols. (Princeton, NJ: Princeton University Press, 1990).

9. Blackbourn, *Long Nineteenth Century*, 1st ed., xvi, 249; Carr, *History of Germany*, 100; quotation and account of the battle in James J. Sheehan, *German History, 1770–1866* (New York: Oxford University Press, 1989), 908–909.

10. See the amusing examples of Bismarck worship in Blackbourn, *Long*

Nineteenth Century, 1st ed., 257–258. Many historians argue that Bismarck was able to unify Germany in part because he acted within "a unique window of opportunity in European affairs" that opened in the 1860s, which was caused by, among other factors, the impetus given to German unification by the unification of Italy, Russia's turning away from European politics after its defeat in the Crimean War, Britain's preoccupation with "domestic and imperial issues," and Napoleon III's desperate search for foreign policy successes to enhance his regime's legitimacy in France. Jefferies, *Contesting the German Empire*, 58.

11. This argument has been made by, among others, Hagen Schulze, in *Weimar: Deutschland, 1917–1933* (Berlin: Severin und Siedler, 1982), 67ff. For the most recent thorough treatment of this thesis, see Christoph Schönberger, "Die überholte Parlamentarisierung: Einflußgewinn und fehlende Herrschaftsfähigkeit des Reichstages im sich demokratisierenden Kaiserreich," *Historische Zeitschrift* 272, no. 3 (2001): 623–666. As David Blackbourn points out, a potential reformist coalition of socialists, center, and left liberals had a permanent majority of seats in parliament from 1890 onward, but were divided by the mutual hostility of liberals and Catholics as well as the antagonism between socialists and both of the other parties. Blackbourn adds other factors that militated against a transition to parliamentary control: electoral districts that favored the conservative countryside over the cities, the executive's ability to dissolve parliament and call new elections, the parties' cooperation with the executive in exchange for favors, the popularity of the monarchy as an institution, and the tendency of economic-interest pressure groups to divide the parties internally and from each other. However, Blackbourn also points out that the first two problems were hardly decisive, while the parties' cooperation in exchange for favors and the power of economic interests strike me as functions of parliament's weakness. Pressure groups flourished in part because the lack of parliamentary control privileged economic interests that could lobby the executive branch directly. See Blackbourn, *Long Nineteenth Century*, 1st ed., 417–424.

12. *On France's lack of homogeneity:* Eugen Weber, *Peasants into Frenchmen: The Modernization of Rural France, 1870–1914* (Palo Alto, CA: Stanford University Press, 1976).

13. The seminal work is Rainer Lepsius, "Parteiensystem und Sozialstruktur: Zum Problem der Demokratisierung der deutschen Gesellschaft," in Wilhelm Abel, ed., *Wirtschaft, Geschichte und Wirtschaftsgeschichte: Festschrift zum 65. Geburtstag von Friedrich Lütge* (Stuttgart: G. Fischer, 1966), 371ff. Research since the 1980s has somewhat diminished the appeal of this explanatory model, as scholars have demonstrated unexpected overlapping of constituencies (for example, middle-class voters for the socialist party) as well as greater fluidity between the parties as voters shifted back and forth between them. Jefferies, *Contesting the German Empire*, 120–125. However, Brett Fairbairn has concluded that the transition to mass mobilization of voters by the parties circa 1900 "reinforced the roots of certain parties in particular social structures and groupings. It did not substitute for social affiliations, but rather strengthened them." Brett Fairbairn,

Democracy in the Undemocratic State: The Reichstag Elections of 1898 and 1903 (Toronto: University of Toronto Press, 1997), 242–243. Similarly, Christoph Schönberger finds that the transition to mass politics only intensified the divisions between the German parties as represented in the Reichstag, so that "they were therefore hardly capable of [forming] coalitions and [exercising] power." Schönberger, "Die überholte Parlamentarisierung," 656.

Fairbairn has questioned the thesis that party antagonisms prevented the transition to parliamentary rule, but unfortunately he measures the fragmentation of the political spectrum not by the incompatibility of the parties' programs and the mutual hostility expressed in their rhetoric, but rather by such mechanical criteria as the average share of the vote per party and the "effective number of parties," which leads to, among other problems, the absurd contention that fragmentation had decreased by 1912 because the socialists had attracted such a large fraction of the electorate. In fact, as will be seen below, the socialist victory in 1912 only heightened a sense of crisis in German politics. Fairbairn, *Democracy in the Undemocratic State*, 256–257.

On the socialist milieu: Vernon L. Lidtke, *The Alternative Culture: Socialist Labor in Imperial Germany* (New York: Oxford University Press, 1985), esp. 22–23.

14. See the Socialists' Erfurt Program (1891), the party's official dogma until revisions were made in 1921, in Karl Kautsky, *Das Erfurter Programm: In seinem grundsätzlichen Teil erläutert*, intro. Susanne Miller (Berlin: J. H. W. Dietz, 1980), 253–258, and Kautsky's comments at 146. This volume is a reprint of the 17th ed., originally published in 1922, and largely unchanged since the first edition in 1892, although the party had adopted a new program the preceding year.

15. Gerhard A. Ritter, ed., *Das deutsche Kaiserreich, 1871–1914: Ein historisches Lesebuch* (Göttingen: Vandenhoeck und Ruprecht, 1992), 366–367.

16. Theodore Abel, *Why Hitler Came into Power*, fwd. Thomas Childers (Cambridge, MA: Harvard University Press, 1986 [1938]), 137–146.

CHAPTER 4

1. Daniel Frymann [Heinrich Claß], *Wenn ich der Kaiser wär': Politische Wahrheiten und Notwendigkeiten* (Leipzig, Dieterich, 1912), 50 ("Class 1912" hereafter). The 5th edition, published before the outbreak of war in 1914, also published by Dieterich in Leipzig, was expanded by two chapters at the end, at 236–270, and hereafter will be referred to as "Class 1914." I have rendered Claß's name as "Class" so as not to confuse English-language readers. The ß symbol is pronounced the same as "ss."

2. Indirect evidence comes in the form of the markedly populist quality of German radical nationalism, as explored by Geoff Eley in *Reshaping the German Right: Radical Nationalism and Political Change After Bismarck* (New Haven, CT: Yale University Press, 1980), 188, 193–194, 201–205, 356. Radical nationalists frequently claimed to express the "free will of the people," said to be ignored

by the parliament, the government, and implicitly even the emperor. One piece of circumstantial evidence might be the qualitatively greater force and intensity of German radical nationalism before World War I in comparison to its counterpart in Great Britain. I contend that this difference supports my thesis: since Britain was a democracy, the British had no need of nationalism in its role as a substitute for democracy. Of course, historians have offered other explanations for the differences between British and German nationalism. See Paul Kennedy and Anthony Nicholls, eds., *Nationalist and Racialist Movements in Britain and Germany Before 1914* (London: Macmillan, 1981), essays by Kennedy (esp. 16), Summers (esp. 73), Fest (esp. 171), and Eley (esp. 57 and n. 23). Similarly, Hans-Ulrich Wehler concludes that domestic political pressures for imperialist expansion were stronger in Germany than anywhere else in the Western world. Hans-Ulrich Wehler, *Deutsche Gesellschaftsgeschichte*, vol. 3, *1849–1914* (Munich: C. H. Beck, 1995), 1291.

On nationalism as a weapon against socialism: see, for example, Eley, *Reshaping the German Right*, 167–176; Wehler, *Deutsche Gesellschaftsgeschichte*, 3:985–990, 1129–1141.

3. See, for example, Ernst Graf zu Reventlow, *Die deutsche Flotte: Ihre Entwickelung und Organisation* (Zwiebrücken i. Pfalz: Lehmann, 1901), 53: "Alle die verschiedenen Elemente, die für das Flottengesetz vereint kämpften, haben sich dadurch überhaupt einander genähert und vor allem das gemeinsame Gefühl, Deutsche zu sein, empfunden." See also Eley, *Reshaping the German Right*, 200.

4. Wehler, *Deutsche Gesellschaftsgeschichte*, 3:1071–1081; Eley, *Reshaping the German Right*, especially concerning the Navy League.

5. Wehler, *Deutsche Gesellschaftsgeschichte*, 3:1068–1071, 1075–1077.

6. See, especially, Roger Chickering, *We Men Who Feel Most German: A Cultural Study of the Pan-German League, 1890–1914* (Boston: Allen and Unwin, 1984).

7. Class 1912 (see n. 1 above).

8. Class 1914, 235–237.

9. Class 1912, 53.

10. Ibid., 68–69, 74–78.

11. Ibid., 34–38, esp. 38; Class 1914, 253. Most of these quotations are emphasized in the original by wider spacing between the letters, but I have chosen not to italicize them. I have translated the word *Erreger* as "virus."

12. Class 1914, 255–260. Class refers not directly to armed force, but to a "coup" (*Staatsstreich*), which he and others assumed would require that the military suppress protest by the socialists and labor unions. The first sentence quoted in this paragraph was emphasized in the original.

13. Class 1912, 53, 183, 185. The first phrase quoted in this paragraph was emphasized in the original.

14. By "university" I mean all institutions of higher learning, including Technische Hochschulen. The percentage of each age cohort of nineteen- to

twenty-four-year-olds reached 3.4 percent in 1911, having risen sharply since 1871, so less than 3 percent is a rough average over the entire history of the empire. The number of students at all German institutions of higher learning rose from 17,800 in 1870 to 79,305 in 1914, and thus almost quintupled, whereas the country's population rose by only about 60 percent. Wehler, *Deutsche Gesellschaftsgeschichte*, vol. 3, 1211, vol. 4, *1914–1949*, 463.

CHAPTER 5

1. Adolf Hitler, *Mein Kampf* (Munich: Franz Eher Nachfolger, 1943), 179. The edition cited in this book is the 805–809th printing, which is an unaltered reprint of the 1925–1926 first edition.

2. John Keegan, *The Face of Battle* (New York: Penguin, 1976), 207–289. The image of a fatal race is Keegan's.

3. On the eastern front, where Germany and Austria-Hungary fought Russia, the fighting was much more mobile, as major offensives moved the front lines great distances back and forth. However, just as on the western front, the fighting was enormously costly in materiel, munitions, and human lives.

4. John Keegan, *The First World War* (New York: Vintage Books, 1998), 278–279; Bernd Hüppauf, "Schlachtenmythen und die Konstruktion des 'Neuen Menschen,'" in Gerhard Hirschfeld, Gerd Krumeich, and Irina Renz, eds., *Keiner fühlt sich hier mehr als Mensch . . . Erlebnis und Wirkung des Ersten Weltkriegs* (Essen: Klartext, 1993), 43–84, esp. 61.

5. Keegan, *First World War*, 278–286.

6. "Battle of materiel" translates *Materialschlacht*.

7. Ernst Jünger, *In Stahlgewittern* (Stuttgart: E. Klett, 1961 [1920]), 193; Otto Germar, "Trommelfeuer," in Ernst Jünger, ed., *Das Antlitz des Weltkrieges. Fronterlebnisse deutscher Soldaten* (Berlin: Neufeld und Henius, 1930), 27–35, esp. 35 ("Jünger, ed., *Antlitz*," hereafter); Friedrich Bethge, "Offensive," in Jünger, ed., *Antlitz*, 55–71, esp. 56.

8. Jünger, *Stahlgewittern*, 106–107.

9. Germar, "Trommelfeuer," 32–33. According to Germar, being buried alive was a common fate and probably the one most greatly feared. See also his "Verwundet," in Jünger, ed., *Antlitz*, 72–86; Jünger, *Stahlgewittern*, 109.

10. Germar, "Trommelfeuer," 28; Grote, "Bilder aus der Sommesschlacht," in Jünger, ed., *Antlitz*, 163–183, esp. 180–181.

11. Quoted in Peter Knoch, "Erleben und Nacherleben: Das Kriegserlebnis in Augenzeugenberichten und im Geschichtsunterricht," in Hirschfeld et al., eds., *Keiner fühlt sich hier mehr als Mensch*, 199–219, esp. 205.

12. On the "war youth generation" born between 1900 and 1910, too young to be drafted but old enough to be caught up in the wartime nationalist fervor: see, especially, Michael Wildt, *An Uncompromising Generation: The Nazi Leadership of the Reich Security Main Office*, trans. Tom Lampert (Madison: University of Wisconsin Press, 2009).

13. *On Jünger's importance:* Ulrich Herbert, *Best: Biographische Studien über Radikalismus, Weltanschauung und Vernunft, 1903–1989* (Bonn: J. H. W. Dietz, 1996), 95; Jünger, *Stahlgewittern*, 104.

14. Jünger, *Stahlgewittern*, 195–197, esp. 197.

15. Grote, "Bilder aus der Sommesschlacht," 181–182; Germar, "Trommelfeuer," 32–33.

16. Quoted in Hüppauf, "Schlachtenmythen und die Konstruktion des 'Neuen Menschen,'" in Hirschfeld et al., eds., *Keiner fühlt sich hier mehr als Mensch*, 43–84, esp. 64; Germar, "Trommelfeuer," 27.

17. Beingolf, "Das Grauen," in Jünger, ed., *Antlitz*, 12–15, esp. 13.

18. Hitler, *Mein Kampf*, 181–182.

19. Jünger, *Stahlgewittern*, 103.

20. Peter Longerich, *Heinrich Himmler*, trans. Jeremy Noakes and Lesley Sharpe (New York: Oxford University Press, 2012), 26, 315–351, 738–739.

21. Jeremy Noakes and Geoffrey Pridham, eds., *Nazism 1919–1945: A Documentary Reader*, vol. 3, *Foreign Policy, War, and Racial Extermination* (Exeter: University of Exeter Press, 1988), 1199–1200; Longerich, *Heinrich Himmler*, 689ff.

22. Mark Mazower, *Hitler's Empire: How the Nazis Ruled Europe* (New York: Penguin, 2008), 28. Of 221 leaders of the Reich Security Main Office studied by Michael Wildt, over 10 percent had belonged to the Free Corps or other right-wing paramilitary formations. Wildt, *Uncompromising Generation*, 29. The early, pre-1933 leadership of the SS was recruited, above all, from men born during the years 1890 to 1900 who had fought in World War I, usually as officers, and who often joined Free Corps and found it difficult to adjust to civilian life. Longerich, *Heinrich Himmler*, 128ff.

CHAPTER 6

1. General Friedrich von Bernhardi, *Deutschland und der nächste Krieg* (Berlin: J. G. Cotta, 1912), 53. I have used some poetic license in the translation: "So wird sich die Auffassung nicht bestreiten lassen, daß es unter Umständen die sittliche und politische Pflicht des Staates ist, den Krieg als politisches Mittel zu verwenden."

2. The emperor made this statement on July 31, 1914. Rudolf H. Lutz, *The Fall of the German Empire: Documents, 1914–1918*, 2 vols. (Palo Alto, CA: Stanford University Press, 1932), 1:9.

3. Slightly modified from Barbara Henderson's translation, which appeared in the *New York Times*, October 15, 1914. Lissauer wrote the poem on August 24, 1914; it can be found in Ernst Lissauer, *Der brennende Tag: Ausgewählte Gedichte* (Berlin: Schuster und Loeffler, 1916), 40–42.

4. Quoted in Roger Chickering, *Imperial Germany and the Great War, 1914–1918* (New York: Cambridge University Press, 1998), 161.

5. A brief summary of Bethmann-Hollweg's September Program is in David Blackbourn, *The Long Nineteenth Century: A History of Germany, 1780–1918*, 1st ed. (New York: Oxford University Press, 1998), 480.

6. Chickering, *Imperial Germany and the Great War*, 168–172.

7. The revolution came during October by the calendar then in use in Russia, but in November by the calendar used in Germany and other Western societies.

8. The voting percentages are from Thomas Childers, *The Nazi Voter: The Social Foundations of Fascism in Germany, 1919–1933* (Chapel Hill: University of North Carolina Press, 1983), 58, 211. The French Communist Party enjoyed comparable support, polling 8 percent of the vote in 1924 and 9.3 percent in 1928: Philippe Bernard and Henri Dubief, *The Decline of the Third Republic, 1914–1938* (New York: Cambridge University Press, 1985), 155.

9. The most recent one-volume history of the Weimar Republic is the engaging and readable work by Eric D. Weitz, *Weimar Germany: Promise and Tragedy* (Princeton, NJ: Princeton University Press, 2007); see also the seminal work of Detlev J. K. Peukert, *The Weimar Republic: The Crisis of Classical Modernity*, trans. Richard Deveson (New York: Hill and Wang, 1989); also useful is Mary Fulbrook, *Divided Nation: A History of Germany, 1918–1990* (New York: Oxford University Press, 1992).

10. These voting percentages are from Peukert, *Weimar Republic*, 33.

11. The troop numbers are from Alexander Watson, *Enduring the Great War: Combat, Morale and Collapse in the German and British Armies, 1914–1918* (New York: Cambridge University Press, 2008), 188–189.

12. Hagen Schulze, *Weimar: Deutschland, 1917–1933* (Berlin: Severin und Siedler, 1982), 206–207; Ian Kershaw, "Hitler's Role in the 'Final Solution,'" in Kershaw, *Hitler, the Germans, and the Final Solution* (New Haven, CT: Yale University Press, 2008), 90.

13. For a balanced assessment of the Versailles Treaty, see Peukert, *Weimar Republic*, 42–46. But cf. John Maynard Keynes, *The Economic Consequences of the Peace* (New York: Harcourt Brace and Howe, 1920).

14. Schulze, *Weimar*, 193–201; speech by Schiffer in *Verhandlungen der Verfassunggebenden deutschen Nationalversammlung: Stenographische Berichte* (Berlin: Druck und Verlag der norddeutschen Buchdruckerei, 1920), 1118–1120 (June 22, 1919). The German People's Party (Deutsche Volkspartei, or DVP) was the successor to the National Liberal Party of the empire; the German Nationalist People's Party (Deutschnationale Volkspartei, or DNVP) was the successor to the two conservative parties and, arguably, the radical nationalist pressure groups of the empire. See the speeches of Wehner-Posadowsky (DNVP) in ibid., 1120ff, and Kahl (DVP) in ibid., 1129ff.

15. Schulze, *Weimar*, 222. Schulze rounded the vote percentages to the nearest single digit. Of the parties of the Weimar Coalition, the Social Democratic Party polled 21 percent, the Center Party 18 percent, and the German Democratic Party 8 percent, down from 37.9 percent, 19.7 percent, and 18.5 percent, respectively, in January 1919.

16. See, for example, Hagen Schulze, *Freikorps und Republik, 1918–1920* (Boppard: H. Boldt, 1969), 54–68.

17. Ibid., 80. *On Munich:* Ian Kershaw, *Hitler,* vol. 1, *1889–1936: Hubris* (New York: W. W. Norton, 1999), 112–115. *On the Ruhr:* Schulze, *Freikorps und Republik,* 304–318, death toll at 316.

18. Kershaw, *Hitler,* 1:171; Schulze, *Weimar,* 210–211, 240. Nominally Erzberger won his lawsuit, but he lost in the court of public opinion; some of Helfferich's less damning accusations stuck. Erzberger was murdered on June 26, 1921.

19. Schulze, *Weimar,* 238–243, verse at 242. In the original: "Haut immer feste auf den Wirth / Haut seinen Schädel, daß es klirrt / Auch Rathenau, der Walther / Erreicht kein hohes Alter / Knallt ab den Walther Rathenau / Die gott-verfluchte Judensau!"

20. Chickering, *Imperial Germany and the Great War,* 103–107. A war bond that sold for 1,000 marks at the beginning of the war was worth only about 300 prewar marks by the summer of 1918. Ibid., 107. Taking the cost of living in 1913 as 1, it had reached 20.41 by January 1922, and 1,120.27 by January 1923. Hans-Ulrich Wehler, *Deutsche Gesellschaftsgeschichte,* vol. 4, *1914–1949* (Munich: C. H. Beck, 2003), 246.

21. Childers, *Nazi Voter,* 50; Schulze, *Weimar,* 261.

22. Childers, *Nazi Voter,* 61, 125, 263.

23. Kershaw, *Hitler,* 1:24, 39–43, 48.

24. Ibid., 52–54, 83–85.

25. Quoted in ibid., 88.

26. Adolf Hitler, *Mein Kampf* (Munich: Franz Eher Nachfolger, 1943), 225; Kershaw, *Hitler,* 1:104.

CHAPTER 7

1. Quoted in Theodore Abel, *Why Hitler Came into Power* (Cambridge, MA: Harvard University Press, 1986 [1938]), 152–153.

2. See, for example, Ian Kershaw, "Hitler and the Holocaust," in *Hitler, the Germans, and the Final Solution* (New Haven, CT: Yale University Press, 2008), 237–281. Raul Hilberg finds that "without him," the Holocaust would have been "inconceivable." Raul Hilberg, *Perpetrators Bystanders Victims: The Jewish Catastrophe, 1933–1945* (New York: HarperCollins, 1992), ix.

3. One might see his companion of his teen years, August Kubizek, as a kind of friend, although Kubizek seems for Hitler to have fulfilled the role of syco-phant, feeding Hitler's narcissism by listening to his endless self-aggrandizing talk. When Hitler failed for a second time (October 1908) to gain admission to the Viennese Academy of Fine Arts, he moved out of their shared apartment and left no forwarding address, probably unable to face Kubizek after this humiliating failure. Ian Kershaw, *Hitler,* vol. 1, *1889–1936: Hubris* (New York: W. W. Norton, 1999), 20–21, 48.

4. Hitler's leading biographer posed the central question of why "highly skilled 'professionals' and clever minds in all walks of life were ready to pay uncritical

obeisance to an autodidact whose only indisputable talent was one for stirring up the base emotions of the masses." Ibid., xii.

5. Ibid., 123–127, 131–133, 195–196.

6. Examples of incompetence include his resignation from the party in 1921 in a tantrum, furious at his inability to block a merger with another party; his provocation of a confrontation with the Reichswehr in the spring of 1923, which led to a great loss of face on his part; and his failure to provide any leadership for the party during his imprisonment. Ibid., 163–164, 196, 200, 227–230. *On the putsch:* ibid., 206–211.

7. Ibid., 214–217, 235–239.

8. Ibid., 259–311, esp. 259–261, 280, 299–300.

9. Kershaw describes the Nazis as a "fringe irritant on the political scene," in ibid., 302. Vote totals in Thomas Childers, *The Nazi Voter: The Social Foundations of Fascism in Germany, 1919–1933* (Chapel Hill: University of North Carolina Press, 1983), 61, 125. The figure of 3 percent in 1924 includes votes for smaller radical right groups allied with the Nazis.

10. For this discussion of Hitler's path to power, 1930–1933, I have relied primarily on Kershaw, *Hitler*, vol. 1; Martin Broszat, *Hitler and the Collapse of Weimar Germany* (Providence, RI: Berg, 1987); Hagen Schulze, *Weimar: Deutschland, 1917–1933* (Berlin: Severin und Siedler 1982); and Hans-Ulrich Wehler, *Deutsche Gesellschaftsgeschichte*, vol. 4, *1914–1949* (Munich: C. H. Beck, 1995), 512–588.

11. Kershaw suggests that Hindenburg could have given the prime minister, Hermann Müller, an emergency decree that would have resolved the impasse over the unemployment insurance fund. Kershaw, *Hitler*, 1:322–324.

12. Ibid., 333; Childers, *Nazi Voter*, 192.

13. Kershaw, *Hitler*, 1:367. A succinct summary of Brüning's policies and their disastrous consequences is in Wehler, *Deutsche Gesellschaftsgeschichte*, 4:516–520. See also Broszat, *Hitler and the Collapse of Weimar Germany*, 95–96, 104–105.

14. The coalition of moderate parties included the Socialists (SPD), with 24.5 percent; the Catholic Center Party, with 14.8 percent; and the Democrats (DDP), with 3.5 percent. If the People's Party (DVP), with 4.9 percent, had joined this hypothetical coalition, it would have garnered 47.7 percent of the 1930 vote. Broszat goes so far as to suggest that a government could still be formed on the basis of a parliamentary majority, in *Hitler and the Collapse of Weimar Germany*, 109. However, it is unclear whether the Center Party, which by then had drifted to the right and begun to openly criticize the system of parliamentary government, would have considered joining such a coalition. In any case, Hindenburg never considered such a course of action.

15. Kershaw, *Hitler*, 1:369.

16. Partly for this reason, Hans-Ulrich Wehler argues that a military dictatorship was not a realistic option, so that after the elections of July and November

1932, appointing Hitler prime minister was the only solution to the crisis of governance. Wehler, *Deutsche Gesellschaftsgeschichte*, 4:587.

17. Kershaw, *Hitler*, 1:384–385, 395–396.

18. Abel, *Why Hitler Came into Power*, 1–4. A total of 683 people submitted essays, but Abel excluded from his analysis the forty-eight submissions by women, since he felt this sample was too small to be meaningful, as well as a large number of essays that were only one or two pages in length, so that his analysis is based on six hundred essays. He limited participation in the contest to people who had joined the Nazi Party, or had been "in sympathy" with it, by January 1, 1933, to exclude party members who may have joined for opportunistic reasons after Hitler took power on January 30 of that year.

19. Ibid., 137–165, esp. 137, 139. Abel adds a fourth element, national socialism, which gave the party its name, but I have collapsed it into the ideal of the national community for the sake of brevity and simplicity, because it simply expresses the notion of national community in other words. "Community" translates *Gemeinschaft*; "national community" translates *Volksgemeinschaft*, although this can also be rendered as "racial community," depending on context.

20. Ibid., 142.

21. Ibid., 138.

22. Ibid., 146–154, esp. 147, 151, 152–153.

23. Ibid., 154–165, esp. 155, 159, 160.

24. Kershaw, *Hitler*, 1:332, 471. Kershaw bases his analysis on Peter H. Merkl's examination of the essays that Abel collected in *Political Violence Under the Swastika: 581 Early Nazis* (Princeton, NJ: Princeton University Press, 1975), esp. 33, 453, 522.

25. The best expert on the Nazi voter, Thomas Childers, describes the Nazi Party in 1932 as "a catch-all party of protest." Childers, *Nazi Voter*, 176–177, 225–226, 231–232, 268–269.

26. *On anti-Marxism as a theme:* Childers, *Nazi Voter*, 268. *On party divisions:* Kershaw, *Hitler*, 1:329–330; Childers, *Nazi Voter*, 139. Paradoxically, the Nazis also shrewdly targeted each occupational interest group with appeals tailored to its economic interests. Kershaw, *Hitler*, 1:333; Childers, *Nazi Voter*, 11–12, 198–201. The quotation by Luise Solmitz is from Kershaw, *Hitler*, 1:364. *On the failure of other parties:* ibid., 369.

27. The Democrats (DDP) were heir to the left-liberal parties of the empire; the People's Party (DVP) was heir to the National Liberal Party; and the Nationalists (DNVP) were heir to the conservative parties of the empire. The vote totals are from Childers, *Nazi Voter*, 61, 125, 141.

28. Ibid., 141, 209, 262–263. In December 1924, the DNVP polled 20.5 percent of the electorate, the DVP 10.1 percent, and the DDP 6.3 percent; for July 1932, the corresponding percentages were 5.9, 1.2, and 1.0. Ibid., 61, 209.

29. Ibid., 209, 260–261.

30. Michael Mann has argued that "settler democracies" in parts of North America and Australia perpetrated genocide against native peoples. Mann, *The Dark Side of Democracy: Explaining Ethnic Cleansing* (New York: Cambridge University Press, 2005), 70–110, esp. 85–98. Mann's argument is problematic for two main reasons: (1) the settler societies were far from being fully democratic, nor was the United States as a whole during this period, and it is an open question whether political conditions on the violent frontier should be better characterized as anarchy than as democracy; (2) characterizing the fate of the native peoples as genocide badly stretches the definition of that crime, as there was no clear intention to wipe out the Amerindians on the part of the national government. Mann tries to evade this problem by describing massacres as "local genocide," in my view a contradiction in terms. Ibid., 96–98.

CHAPTER 8

1. Jeremy Noakes and Geoffrey Pridham, eds., *Nazism 1919–1945: A Documentary Reader*, vol. 2, *State, Economy and Society, 1933–1939* (Exeter: University of Exeter Press, 1984), 572. I have slightly altered the translation from the British English of this collection, substituting "workplace" for "work room" and "living room" for "parlour." Hitler was speaking to his secretaries about having just occupied the remainder of Czechoslovakia. Quoted in Ian Kershaw, *Hitler*, vol. 2, *1936–1945: Nemesis* (New York: W. W. Norton, 2000), 155.

2. For the origins and nature of Hitler's charisma, the definitive study remains Ian Kershaw, *The "Hitler Myth": Image and Reality in the Third Reich* (New York: Oxford University Press, 1987).

3. As Max Weber explained, a charismatic leader "gains and retains [his charisma] solely by proving his powers in practice. He must work miracles, if he wants to be a prophet. He must perform heroic deeds, if he wants to be a warlord." Max Weber, *Economy and Society: An Outline of Interpretive Sociology*, ed. Guenther Roth and Claus Wittich, vol. 2 (Berkeley: University of California Press, 1978), 1114.

4. Kershaw, *"Hitler Myth,"* 8; Weber, *Economy and Society*, 1:242, 2:1111–1112.

5. *On Bismarck's dominance:* see David Blackbourn, *The Long Nineteenth Century: A History of Germany, 1780–1918*, 1st ed. (New York: Oxford University Press, 1998), 400–402; Matthew Jefferies, *Contesting the German Empire, 1871–1918* (Malden, MA: Blackwell, 2008), 101. *On "Bismarck towers":* Kershaw, *"Hitler Myth,"* 15–16.

6. Kershaw, *"Hitler Myth,"* 20–21.

7. Theodore Abel, *Why Hitler Came into Power* (Cambridge, MA: Harvard University Press, 1986 [1938]), 153.

8. Kershaw, *"Hitler Myth,"* esp. 3, 72–73, 79–80; Lawrence W. Levine and Cornelia R. Levine, *The People and the President: America's Conversation with FDR* (Boston: Beacon Press, 2002), ix, xi. The authors also note that some 15

million letters to FDR are housed in the Franklin D. Roosevelt Presidential Library and Museum, while the National Archives contain "millions more." *On Hitler:* see Henrik Eberle, ed., *Briefe an Hitler: Ein Volk schreibt seinem Führer. Unbekannte Dokumente aus Moskauer Archiven—zum ersten Mal veröffentlicht* (Bergisch Gladbach: Bastei Lübbe, 2007), 9.

9. Ian Kershaw demonstrates that the fire took Hitler by surprise and that he saw a communist uprising as a real possibility. Kershaw, *Hitler,* 1:457–458, 460. *On the suppression of communism as a source of Hitler's popularity:* Kershaw, *"Hitler Myth,"* 253–254. Despite repeated attempts to show that the Nazis actually set the fire, there remains a consensus among historians that the Dutch communist, Marinus van der Lubbe, acted alone. Anson Rabinbach, "Staging Antifascism: The Brown Book of the Reichstag Fire and Hitler Terror," *New German Critique* 103, vol. 35, no. 1 (2008): 97–126, esp. 97–99. Further evidence that no one working for Hitler set the fire comes from an entry in Joseph Goebbels's diary dated August 9, 1941. Goebbels records a conversation with Hitler in which they speculated on who stood behind Georg Elser's assassination attempt of November 1939, and Hitler then mused that the communist Ernst Torgler may have instigated the Reichstag fire: "Bei Reichstagsbrand tippt er auf Torgler als Urheber." Joseph Goebbels, *Tagebücher, 1924–1945,* ed. Ralf Georg Reuth (Munich: Piper, 1992), 4:1559.

10. *On Hitler's ignorance of economics:* Kershaw, *Hitler,* 1:448–449. Kershaw concludes that by the summer of 1936, "most Germans, whatever their grumbles, were at least in some respects Hitler supporters," in part because unemployment had practically been wiped out. Kershaw, *Hitler,* 2:xxxix–xl. More than 6 million Germans were unemployed when Hitler took power in January 1933, a number that fell to slightly more than 1 million in September 1936, and, after a rise to 1.8 million in January 1937, to under half a million in September of that year. Noakes and Pridham, eds., *Nazism 1919–1945,* 2:359.

11. Kershaw, *Hitler,* 2:283.

12. *On the Austrians' wishes:* see plebiscites conducted during the 1920s. Ibid., 65. The Austrians' early interest in fusion with Germany was deflected during the 1919 peace negotiations when the victorious Allies promised them better terms if they agreed to remain a separate country. Richard M. Watt, *The Kings Depart: The Tragedy of Germany, Versailles, and the German Revolution* (New York: Simon and Schuster, 1968), 435–436. *On British opinion regarding the Treaty of Versailles:* Kershaw, *Hitler,* 1:555, 558. *On appeasement:* A. J. P. Taylor, *Origins of the Second World War* (New York: Simon and Schuster, 1996). Taylor's argument overstates the case but is still useful.

13. *On German public opinion:* see, for example, Kershaw, *Hitler,* 2:107, 118, concerning the diplomatic crisis over Germany's designs on the Sudetenland.

14. Ibid., 549–556, esp. 550, 552.

15. Ibid., 584, 590. "Demoralization" is Kershaw's translation of *Zersetzung.* Kershaw, *"Hitler Myth,"* 125–131.

16. Kershaw, *Hitler*, 2:79–81. Austrian support is seen also in the 99.75 percent yes vote to annexation and in support of "the list of the Leader" in the April plebiscite in Austria. Ibid., 83; Kershaw, *"Hitler Myth,"* 130.

17. In mid-November 1937, Lord Halifax, Lord Privy Seal and President of the Council in the British government, who soon thereafter became foreign secretary, told Hitler that Austria, Czechoslovakia, and the city of Danzig (disputed between Germany and Poland) "fell into the category of possible alterations in the European order which might be destined to come about with the passage of time." Quoted in Kershaw, *Hitler*, 2:66; see also 91.

18. Casualty figures from Kershaw, *Hitler*, 2:297.

19. Ibid., 284; Gerhard L. Weinberg, *A World at Arms: A Global History of World War II* (New York: Cambridge University Press, 1994), 108, 111.

20. Kershaw, *Hitler*, 2:285; Weinberg, *World at Arms*, 111–112, 122–123. The planned German invasion was postponed twenty-nine times because of bad weather and disagreements over strategy.

21. Kershaw, *Hitler*, 2:290–291. Other factors besides Manstein's plan contributed to the stunning German victory, including the French failure to adapt to the new tank tactics pioneered by the Germans; lack of a combined Allied command, along with a chaotic French command structure; and the French commander Maurice Gamelin's failure to hold significant forces in reserve. As Gerhard Weinberg said, "the basic factor was surely that a poorly led and badly coordinated Allied force was pierced at a critical point by concentrated German armor and was never able to regain even its balance, to say nothing of the initiative." Weinberg, *World at Arms*, 113–114, 123, 126–129.

22. Making the problem worse, the Dutch and Belgian governments, trying to preserve their neutrality in the vain hope of not giving the Germans an excuse to invade, refused to coordinate their defense with the French and British. Thus the Allies had to commit their forces immediately, rushing them northward toward Holland. Weinberg, *World at Arms*, 113–114.

23. Kershaw, *"Hitler Myth,"* 155.

24. Ibid., 66, 81. In Kershaw, the woman is quoted as referring to the prayer as "the Our Father" (*Vaterunser*), which is known to most Americans as the Lord's Prayer.

25. Noakes and Pridham, eds., *Nazism 1919–1945*, 2:199–200. See also Ernst Rudolf Huber at 199.

26. Noakes and Pridham, eds., *Nazism 1919–1945*, 2:496. Himmler is quoted in Peter Longerich, *Heinrich Himmler*, trans. Jeremy Noakes and Lesley Sharpe (New York: Oxford University Press, 2012), 305.

27. For example, Jürgen Förster shows that the conquest of France overcame the reservations of generals who had objected to SS atrocities in Poland the preceding fall and prepared them to accept the genocidal quality of the forthcoming Russian campaign. Jürgen Förster, "Complicity or Entanglement? Wehrmacht, War and Holocaust," in Michael Berenbaum and Abraham J. Peck, eds., *The*

Holocaust and History: The Known, the Unknown, the Disputed, and the Re-examined (Bloomington: Indiana University Press, 1998), 266–283, esp. 272. *On the impact of the "Hitler cult" on bureaucrats:* Mary Fulbrook, *A Small Town Near Auschwitz: Ordinary Nazis and the Holocaust* (New York: Oxford University Press, 2012), 67.

28. Richard Rhodes, *Masters of Death: The SS-Einsatzgruppen and the Invention of the Holocaust* (New York: Vintage, 2002), 218–222.

29. Rudolph [Rudolf] Höss, *Death Dealer: The Memoirs of the SS Kommandant at Auschwitz*, ed. Steven Paskuly (New York: Da Capo, 1996), 153.

30. Raul Hilberg, *Destruction of the European Jews*, 3rd ed., 3 vols. (New Haven, CT: Yale University Press, 2003), 1:343–344.

31. Michael Wildt observes that the men who led the Reich Security Main Office (RSHA) adhered to a "particular form of political thought. Politics always aimed at the unconditional or the whole and was never to be subordinated to a regulating norm or moral law of any kind." Michael Wildt, *An Uncompromising Generation: The Nazi Leadership of the Reich Security Main Office*, trans. Tom Lampert (Madison: University of Wisconsin Press, 2009), 432. As Wildt notes, in Poland and in the German-occupied territories of the Soviet Union, this "dissolution of boundaries and regulations" was complete. Ibid., 433.

32. Quoted in Kershaw, *Hitler*, 1:529. *On the phenomenon of "working towards the Führer":* see, generally, ibid., 529–591.

33. Forster had been *Gauleiter* (head of the party regional district) of Danzig, Greiser the president of the Danzig Senate. Ibid., 2:239, 250–252.

34. Ibid., 484–485; for other examples of subordinates radicalizing policy on the ground without instructions from Berlin, see Christopher R. Browning, *The Origins of the Final Solution: The Evolution of Nazi Jewish Policy, September 1939–March 1942*, with contributions by Jürgen Matthäus (Lincoln: University of Nebraska Press, 2004), 330–352. *On Chelmno:* ibid., 418.

35. *On Hitler's role:* Browning, *Origins of the Final Solution*, 320–321, 424–428; Ian Kershaw, "Hitler's Role in the Final Solution," in *Hitler, the Germans, and the Final Solution* (New Haven, CT: Yale University Press, 2008), esp. 107–111. The idea that Hitler's subordinates radicalized his thinking is speculation on my part, but seems justified by Hitler's close working relationship with Himmler in making decisions about Jewish policy in 1940–1941, and by Himmler's repeated efforts to expand his own power by pushing forward the radicalization of anti-Jewish measures, as thoroughly documented by Longerich in *Heinrich Himmler*.

CHAPTER 9

1. Adolf Hitler, *Mein Kampf* (Munich: Franz Eher Nachfolger, 1943), 772.

2. Jeffrey Herf, *The Jewish Enemy: Nazi Propaganda During World War II and the Holocaust* (Cambridge, MA: Harvard University Press, 2006).

3. Declaration on the Relation of the Church to Non-Christian Religions, *Nostra Aetate*, proclaimed by Pope Paul VI on October 28, 1965. *On this accusation*

in Catholic devotional literature in Germany: see Olaf Blaschke, *Victims or Offenders? German Jews and the Causes of Modern Catholic Antisemitism* (Lincoln: University of Nebraska Press, 2009), 34–35; Walter Laqueur, *The Changing Face of Anti-Semitism: From Ancient Times to the Present Day* (New York: Oxford University Press, 2006), 55–56.

4. *On conspiracy theories:* Laqueur, *Changing Face of Anti-Semitism*, 82. *On hostility to Christianity by Hess, Heydrich, Himmler, and Rosenberg:* see Peter Longerich, *Heinrich Himmler*, trans. Jeremy Noakes and Lesley Sharpe (New York: Oxford University Press, 2012), 218–221. According to Wolfgang Dierker, with Hitler's "silent agreement," Nazi Party radicals, including Bormann, Himmler, Heydrich, Rosenberg, and Goebbels, wanted to "completely eliminate the activity of the Christian religion among the German people in the long term." Wolfgang Dierker, *Himmlers Glaubenskrieger: Der Sicherheitsdienst der SS und seine Religionspolitik, 1933–1941* (Paderborn: Schöningh, 2002), 535. However, while attributing to Heydrich a "particular hatred" toward the Catholic Church during the 1930s, Heydrich's biographer, Robert Gerwarth, notes that Heydrich claimed to be opposed not to spirituality, but rather to the church's political influence. Robert Gerwarth, *Hitler's Hangman: The Life of Heydrich* (New Haven, CT: Yale University Press, 2011), 101–102. Joseph Goebbels's diaries also offer considerable evidence of his own intense hostility to Christianity and that of other leaders of the regime. *Die Tagebücher von Joseph Goebbels*, ed. Elke Fröhlich, *Teil II: Diktate, 1941–1945* (Munich: K. G. Saur, 1996), on Bormann, v. 1 (July-September 1941), 254 (August 18) and 372 (September 7); on Goebbels, v. 2 (October-December 1941), 500 (December 13), 504, 506–507 (December 14). See also Saul Friedländer's discussion of "redemptive anti-Semitism" in his *Nazi Germany and the Jews, 1933–1945*, vol. 1, *The Years of Persecution* (New York: HarperCollins, 1997), 73–112.

5. Jeremy Noakes and Geoffrey Pridham, eds., *Nazism 1919–1945: A Documentary Reader*, vol. 2, *State, Economy and Society, 1933–1939* (Exeter: University of Exeter Press, 1984), 522–523; Raul Hilberg, *Perpetrators Victims Bystanders: The Jewish Catastrophe, 1933–1945* (New York: HarperCollins, 1992), 120–121.

6. *On envy:* Götz Aly has presented a wealth of evidence in his *Warum die Deutschen? Warum die Juden? Gleichheit, Neid und Rassenhass, 1800–1933* (Frankfurt: Fischer Taschenbuch, 2011). *On Jews in German art during the 1920s:* see Friedländer, *Years of Persecution*, 108. *On the roots of Hitler's fury toward Jews in his own failures:* see Ian Kershaw, *Hitler*, vol. 1, *1889–1936: Hubris* (New York: W. W. Norton, 1999), 65–67.

7. Friedländer, *Years of Persecution*, 79.

8. Daniel Frymann [Heinrich Claß], *Wenn ich der Kaiser wär': Politische Wahrheiten und Notwendigkeiten* (Leipzig: Dieterich, 1912), 33, 36–38 ("Class 1912" hereafter, to distinguish this edition from the 1914 edition, also published in Leipzig by Dieterich ["Class 1914"]).

9. Friedländer, *Years of Persecution*, 93; Shulamit Volkov, *Germans, Jews, and Antisemites: Trials in Emancipation* (New York: Cambridge University Press, 2006), 121; Laqueur, *Changing Face of Anti-Semitism*, 105.

10. Class 1914, 253–254; this newspaper was the so-called *Kreuzzeitung. On the election:* Hans-Ulrich Wehler, *Deutsche Gesellschaftsgeschichte*, vol. 3, *1849–1914* (Munich: C. H. Beck, 1995), 1062, 1065–1066.

11. Laqueur, *Changing Face of Anti-Semitism*, 29, 85, 96ff. *On the importance of this document:* see also Jerome A. Chanes, *Antisemitism: A Reference Handbook* (Santa Barbara, CA: ABC-CLIO, 2004), 59.

12. Laqueur, *Changing Face of Anti-Semitism*, 99.

13. *On the decisive role of World War I:* see, for example, Laqueur, *Changing Face of Anti-Semitism*, 29–30; for Germany, Friedländer, *Years of Persecution*, 81. *On the limited appeal of conspiracy theories before World War I:* see, for example, Laqueur, *Changing Face of Anti-Semitism*, 101; Hitler, *Mein Kampf*, 337. *On the limited impact of racist anti-Semitism before World War I:* see Laqueur, *Changing Face of Anti-Semitism*, 94–95; Volkov, *Germans, Jews, and Antisemites*, 76–79.

14. Kershaw, *Hitler*, 1:101. Class was quoting Heinrich von Kleist in a nationalist screed attacking the French.

15. The revolution fell in October on the calendar then in use in Russia, but in November by the calendar used in Germany and the rest of Western Europe. Mann is quoted in Friedländer, *Years of Persecution*, 91.

16. Daniel Jonah Goldhagen, *Hitler's Willing Executioners: Ordinary Germans and the Holocaust* (New York: Knopf, 1996). The names of Goldhagen's critics are legion. Yehuda Bauer observes that professional historians, and especially specialists on the Holocaust, "have been overwhelmingly critical of the book" and comments on "the anti-German bias of the book, almost a racist bias." Bauer finds some merit in Goldhagen's book and characterizes him as "a gifted scholar," but his critique is fundamentally devastating to Goldhagen's argument. Yehuda Bauer, *Rethinking the Holocaust* (New Haven, CT: Yale University Press, 2001), 93–111, esp. 108, 111. Another thorough critique, which accuses Goldhagen of tendentious and selective use of evidence, among other failings, comes from Christopher R. Browning, one of Goldhagen's leading antagonists in the debate over his work, in his *Ordinary Men: Reserve Police Battalion 101 and the Final Solution in Poland*, rev. ed. (New York: HarperCollins, 1998), 191–223, esp. 211–217. In a more recent comment, Alon Confino observes of Goldhagen: "His attitude is profoundly anti-empirical: he presupposes the very motivations he intends to explore." Alon Confino, *Foundational Pasts: The Holocaust as Historical Understanding* (New York: Cambridge University Press, 2012), 69.

On the pervasiveness of this "eliminationist" anti-Semitism: see Goldhagen, *Willing Executioners*, 56 (on anti-Semitism generally in Germany), 59ff (on German society being "axiomatically antisemitic" throughout the nineteenth century), and the discussion at 74–77. Although he concedes that we cannot say "precisely how many Germans subscribed to it in 1900, 1920, 1933, or 1941" (75), he also finds it to have been "ubiquitous" since the early nineteenth century and to have constituted the "common sense" of German society (77). At 419 he asserts that German anti-Semitism was *"sui generis"* and "unmatched" in any other nation in many distinctive qualities; at 408–409 he limits transnational comparison to the observation that Danes and Italians resisted Nazi extermination policies, while Lithuanians, Latvians, and Ukrainians frequently assisted the Germans in the capture and murder of Jews. At 63 he briefly contends that in Germany, unlike in any other Western country, "groups with broad popular support" repeatedly advocated reversing Jewish emancipation. Goldhagen also contends, at 419, that the fact that "it was only in Germany that a rabidly antisemitic movement came to power—indeed was elected to power—that was bent on turning antisemitic fantasy into state-organized genocidal slaughter . . . substantiates the *Sonderweg* thesis: that Germany developed along a singular path, setting it apart from other Western countries." However, the Nazi Party was not "elected to power," having received only one-third of the vote in the last free elections, and was certainly not, at the time of taking power in 1933, "bent on" perpetrating genocide; by the time Goldhagen published his book, specialists in German history had largely discarded the *Sonderweg* thesis, as discussed above in Chapter 3.

17. Niall Ferguson, *War of the World* (New York: Penguin, 2006), 64–68; Laqueur, *Changing Face of Anti-Semitism*, 104, 109.

18. Dirk Walter, *Antisemitische Kriminalität und Gewalt: Judenfeindschaft in der Weimarer Republik* (Bonn: Dietz, 1999).

19. The figure of half a million elites is a somewhat arbitrary compromise between minimum and maximum estimates of the percentage of the German population made up by the society's elite in 1914, drawing on figures given by Hans-Ulrich Wehler, and applied to Germany's population of about 80 million on the eve of World War II (which had been expanded by the annexation of Austria and the Sudetenland). The maximum estimate is 5 percent of the population in 1914, of whom one in five would have been an adult male, producing an estimate of 800,000 men and a few thousand women in 1939. The minimum estimate limits the definition of "elite" to the elites of education (0.75 percent of the population at the lower range of estimates), titled aristocracy (0.3 percent, conservatively estimated), and the upper ranks of business owners and managers (0.5 percent), again assuming that one in five of these was an adult male, producing an estimate of 250,000 men and at most a few thousand women in 1939. Wehler, *Deutsche Gesellschaftsgeschichte*, 3:845–846; B. R. Mitchell, *European Historical Statistics* (New York: Columbia University Press, 1978), 3–4.

Organizations excluding Jews included the veteran's organization Stahlhelm (400,000 members), the Jungdeutscher Orden (200,000), the Deutschnationaler Handlungsgehilfenverband (400,000), the agricultural interest group Reichslandbund (1 million), and almost all student fraternities. Ulrich Herbert, "Extermination Policy: New Answers and Questions About the History of the 'Holocaust' in German Historiography," in *National Socialist Extermination Policies:*

Contemporary German Perspectives and Controversies (New York: Berghahn Books, 2000), 20. *On fraternities:* Michael Wildt, *An Uncompromising Generation: The Nazi Leadership of the Reich Security Main Office*, trans. Tom Lampert (Madison: University of Wisconsin Press, 2009), 45.

On attitudes in the population: Herbert, "Extermination Policy," 20; Friedländer, *Years of Persecution*, 110, quoting Donald L. Niewyk, *The Jews in Weimar Germany* (Baton Rouge: Louisiana State University Press, 1980), 80. *On anti-Semitism during the Third Reich:* Christopher R. Browning finds an "impressive" degree of consensus among scholars to the effect that anti-Semitism was "not a major factor in attracting support for Hitler and the Nazis," and that few Germans shared the "fanatical" anti-Semitism displayed by a minority of Nazi Party activists. Christopher R. Browning, "Ordinary Germans or Ordinary Men? A Reply to the Critics," in Michael Berenbaum and Abraham J. Peck, eds., *The Holocaust and History: The Known, the Unknown, the Disputed, and the Reexamined* (Bloomington: Indiana University Press, 1998), 253–255.

20. Herf, *Jewish Enemy*, 80–82; Katharine Graham, *Personal History* (New York: Vintage, 1997), 123; William D. Rubinstein, "Antisemitism in the English-Speaking World," in Albert S. Lindemann and Richard S. Levy, eds., *Antisemitism: A History* (New York: Oxford University Press, 2010), 150.

21. *On France:* a useful summary is Richard J. Golsan, "Antisemitism in Modern France: Dreyfus, Vichy, and Beyond," in Albert S. Lindemann and Richard S. Levy, eds., *Antisemitism: A History* (New York: Oxford University Press, 2010), 136–149. *On comparisons for the period before 1914:* Volkov, *Germans, Jews, and Antisemites*, 148–152. Thomas Nipperdey goes so far as to say that before 1914, the "classic countries of anti-Semitism" were France and Austria-Hungary, not Germany, while Russia differed from all three as a place of active governmental persecution. Saul Friedländer endorses the view that, compared to France, Austria, and Russia, Germany was "certainly not the most extreme." However, he does find two distinctive features of German anti-Semitism: the way anti-Semitism permeated all manner of civic organizations and economic and political pressure groups; and the development, if only among a small minority, of a full-blown anti-Semitic ideology. Thomas Nipperdey, *Deutsche Geschichte, 1866–1918*, vol. 2, *Machtstaat vor der Demokratie*, 3rd ed. (Munich: C. H. Beck, 1995), 289; Friedländer, *Years of Persecution*, 81, 87.

22. Hitler, *Mein Kampf*, 772.

23. *On Jews in the first Weimar cabinet:* Friedländer, *Years of Persecution*, 93–94.

24. Herbert, "Extermination Policy," 24; Ulrich Herbert, *Best: Biographische Studien über Radikalismus, Weltanschauung und Vernunft, 1903–1989* (Bonn: J. H. W. Dietz, 1996), 66–68; Wildt, *Uncompromising Generation*, 45.

25. Wildt, *Uncompromising Generation*, 44.

26. *On most Germans' anti-Semitism not causing the Holocaust:* Herbert, "Extermination Policy," 42.

CHAPTER 10

1. Quoted in Henry Friedlander, *Origins of Nazi Genocide: From Euthanasia to the Final Solution* (Chapel Hill: University of North Carolina Press, 1995), 1.

2. Ivan Hannaford, *Race: The History of an Idea in the West* (Baltimore: Johns Hopkins University Press, 1996), 326; Omer Bartov, "The Holocaust as Leitmotif of the Twentieth Century," in *Lessons and Legacies*, vol. 6, *The Holocaust in International Perspective*, ed. Dagmar Herzog (Evanston, IL: Northwestern University Press, 2006), 9–10; Detlev J. K. Peukert, "The Genesis of the 'Final Solution' from the Spirit of Science," in Thomas Childers and Jane Caplan, eds., *Reevaluating the Third Reich* (New York: Holmes and Meier, 1993), 236–237.

3. A good overview of Social Darwinism's impact is Mike Hawkins, *Social Darwinism in European and American Thought, 1860–1945: Nature as Model and Nature as Threat* (New York: Cambridge University Press, 1997).

See Alfred Kelly's devastating critique of several scholars' attempts to turn some leading pre–World War I popularizers of Darwin into obvious precursors of Nazism. However, Kelly largely misses the point: although Hitler or Himmler probably never read any books about Darwin, they thought in unmistakably Darwinian categories, using themes and language that had been the stock in trade of the German Right for decades. Alfred Kelly, *The Descent of Darwin: The Popularization of Darwinism in Germany, 1860–1914* (Chapel Hill: University of North Carolina Press, 1981), 119–122. For a trenchant summary of the role of Social Darwinism in Nazism, with the focus on Hitler's thinking, see Hawkins, *Social Darwinism*, 272–284.

On reasons for the popularity of Social Darwinism in Germany: Kelly, *Descent of Darwin*, 5. Kelly describes Darwin as "a popularizer's dream," because the ideas are simple and because Darwin wrote with an engaging "personalized, anecdotal technique." Moreover, Darwin's theory had "enormous philosophical, religious, political, and even emotional implications." Ibid., 4–5. In contrast, mystical racist thinkers such as Julius Langbehn and Houston Stewart Chamberlain, although very influential among elites, trafficked in murky notions of "spiritual substance" and "national souls" that would have taxed the patience of many readers. See the discussion in George L. Mosse, *Toward the Final Solution: A History of European Racism* (Madison: University of Wisconsin Press, 1985), Chapter 7.

4. Darwin described a second important mechanism, "sexual selection," which favored the reproduction of those members of a species who were especially attractive to prospective mates. Members of a species who held attractive traits would more easily find mates, he explained, and pass on their attractive traits to the next generation. I have omitted sexual selection from our discussion for the sake of simplicity, and because it did not figure very prominently in Social Darwinist thought.

5. Kelly argues persuasively that most adherents of popularized Darwinian thought in pre–World War I Germany were on "the left half of the political, cultural, and social spectrum." Kelly, *Descent of Darwin*, 8, 100–103, 123–141.

Kelly also argues, but in my view unconvincingly, that popularized Darwinism had little appeal for conservative German elites. He proceeds by narrowing his focus to the small set of right-wing popularizers "who believed that Darwin alone held the key to understanding human society," while dismissing the importance of "those vast ranks of saber-rattlers, socialist-baiters, and self-righteous rich" who "occasionally appropriated a Darwinian phrase or two." Here Kelly ignores the probability that the pervasive acceptance of Darwinian thinking made it unnecessary for these elites to belabor their references to Darwin, because Darwinian "truths" were already assumed. Ibid., 100–103.

6. *On the United States:* see Richard Hofstadter, *Social Darwinism in American Thought*, rev. ed. (Boston: Beacon Press, 1955), 5–10. *On France:* see the discussion of Clemence Royer in Hawkins, *Social Darwinism*, 123–132.

7. See, for example, Hawkins, *Social Darwinism*, 203–215.

8. See the discussion of Darwin's *The Descent of Man* (1871) in Hans-Ulrich Wehler, *Deutsche Gesellschaftsgeschichte*, vol. 3, *1849–1914* (Munich: C. H. Beck, 1995), 1081–1082.

9. Friedlander, *Origins of Nazi Genocide*, 1–3.

10. Kelly, *Descent of Darwin*, 106–107; Daniel Frymann [Heinrich Claß], *Wenn ich der Kaiser wär': Politische Wahrheiten und Notwendigkeiten* (Leipzig, Dieterich, 1912), 34–38 (quotation at 38).

11. Roger Chickering, *We Men Who Feel Most German: A Cultural Study of the Pan-German League, 1890–1914* (Boston: Allen and Unwin, 1984), 240–243. The League's journal was the *Alldeutsche Blätter*. Sheila Faith Weiss, "The Race Hygiene Movement in Germany, 1904–1945," in *The Wellborn Science: Eugenics in Germany, France, Brazil and Russia* (New York: Oxford University Press, 1990), 27.

12. Friedrich von Bernhardi, *Deutschland und der nächste Krieg* (Berlin: J. G. Cotta, 1912); Wehler, *Deutsche Gesellschaftsgeschichte*, 3:1149–1150.

13. Bernhardi, *Deutschland und der nächste Krieg*, 11, 13–16. A few phrases are emphasized in the original.

14. Ibid., 110–111.

15. Speech excerpted in Raymond M. Hyser and J. Chris Arndt, eds., *Voices of the American Past: Documents in U.S. History*, 4th ed. (Boston: Cengage Learning, 2008), 1:372. *On Social Darwinism as justification for American racism and imperialism during those years:* see Hofstadter, *Social Darwinism in American Thought*, 170–200. Cecil is quoted in Sven Lindqvist, *"Exterminate All the Brutes": One Man's Odyssey into the Heart of Darkness and the Origins of European Genocide* (New York: New Press, 1997), 140. I am indebted to John Cox for this reference.

16. Garland E. Allen, "The Ideology of Elimination: American and German Eugenics, 1900–1945," in Francis R. Nicosia and Jonathan Huener, eds., *Medicine and Medical Ethics in Nazi Germany: Origins, Practices, Legacies* (New York: Berghahn Books, 2002), 16–17, 19–28; Friedlander, *Origins of Nazi*

Genocide, 5–9; Weiss, "Race Hygiene Movement"; Mosse, *Toward the Final Solution*, 73ff; Marius Turda and Paul J. Weindling, "Eugenics, Race and Nation in Central and Southeast Europe, 1900–1940: A Historiographic Overview," in Turda and Weindling, eds., *Blood and Homeland: Eugenics and Racial Nationalism in Central and Southeast Europe, 1900–1940* (New York: Central European University Press, 2007), 6.

17. Allen, "Ideology of Elimination," 22–23, 25, 28; Friedlander, *Origins of Nazi Genocide*, 5–6. *On the discrediting of eugenics:* see, for example, Daniel J. Kevles, *In the Name of Eugenics: Genetics and the Uses of Human Heredity* (New York: Knopf, 1985), esp. 251ff.

18. A good brief account of the sterilization program is in Michael Burleigh and Wolfgang Wippermann, *The Racial State: Germany, 1933–1945* (New York: Cambridge University Press, 1991), 136–140. The leading work on the euthanasia program is Friedlander, *Origins of Nazi Genocide*; see also Burleigh and Wippermann, *Racial State*, 142–167; Richard J. Evans, *The Third Reich at War* (New York: Penguin, 75–100). It has been argued that the protests played little role in curtailing the euthanasia program, because by August 1941 it had reached its initial "target" of 70,000 killings. However, this target was arbitrary in the first place; the program's planners adjusted it upward and downward depending on the obstacles they encountered and the degree of "success" they were having. In the fall of 1940 the target stood at 130,000 to 150,000. Peter Longerich, *Holocaust: The Nazi Persecution and Murder of the Jews* (New York: Oxford University Press), 140–141, 277–278. It is also worth noting that the regime decided not to punish the leader of the protests, Bishop August Count von Galen, fearing that doing so would alienate the population of Westphalia as well as other Catholics. This is another example of the regime giving way when confronted by widespread dissent.

19. Burleigh and Wippermann, *Racial State*, 166; Yitzhak Arad, *Belzec, Sobibor, Treblinka: The Operation Reinhard Death Camps* (Bloomington: Indiana University Press, 1987), 16–18.

20. Hans-Adolf Jacobsen, "Vom Wandel des Polenbildes in Deutschland," in *Von der Strategie der Gewalt zur Politik der Friedenssicherung: Beiträge zur deutschen Geschichte im 20. Jahrhundert* (Düsseldorf: Droste, 1977), 302–331; Wilhelm Deist, Manfred Messerschmidt, Hans-Erich Volkmann, and Wolfram Wette, *Ursachen und Voraussetzungen der deutschen Kriegspolitik* (Stuttgart: Deutsche Verlags-Anstalt, 1979), 41–42, 44–45.

21. Adolf Hitler, *Mein Kampf* (Munich: Franz Eher Nachfolger, 1943), 314–317, 732, 742. The phrases "perishing from the Earth" and "slave people" are italicized in the original.

22. Ibid., 334, 742–743.

23. Ibid., 751.

24. Horst Boog, Jürgen Förster, and Joachim Hoffmann, *Der Angriff auf die Sowjetunion* (Stuttgart: Deutsche Verlags-Anstalt, 1983), 416–417, 444–446.

25. Ibid., 442–443. "Bulletin for the Troops" translates *Mitteilungen für die Truppe.*

26. *On the attitudes of civil servants:* see, especially, Raul Hilberg, *The Destruction of the European Jews*, 3rd ed., 3 vols. (New Haven, CT: Yale University Press, 2003), 3:1084–1104.

CHAPTER 11

1. Quoted in Christopher R. Browning, *Ordinary Men: Reserve Police Battalion 101 and the Final Solution in Poland*, rev. ed. (New York: HarperCollins, 1998), 72.

2. Michael Bilton and Kevin Sim, *Four Hours in My Lai* (New York: Penguin, 1993), 92–93.

3. Browning, *Ordinary Men*; Daniel Jonah Goldhagen, *Hitler's Willing Executioners: Ordinary Germans and the Holocaust* (New York: Knopf, 1996), 181–282 and *passim.*

4. Browning, *Ordinary Men*, 1. Browning formulates his conclusions as to their political background more cautiously, and with some reason, given that about 25 percent of the rank and file had joined the Nazi Party by 1942. Ibid., 47–48. However, many of the people who joined the party after Hitler took power in January 1933 may have done so out of opportunism, to further their careers, rather than out of commitment to Nazi ideology.

5. Edward B. Westermann, *Hitler's Police Battalions: Enforcing Racial Policy in the East* (Lawrence: University of Kansas Press, 2005), 15–16, 90. Of the 23 police battalions that went into the Soviet Union in the initial assault, 7 "were made up of older police reservists with no prior service." Peter Longerich, *Holocaust: The Nazi Persecution and Murder of the Jews* (New York: Oxford University Press, 2010), 186. The battalions averaged 540 men in size; subtracting commissioned and noncommissioned officers, that means at least 500 men per battalion, and 3,500 going into Russia who resembled the men of Battalion 101 in Poland.

6. Browning, *Ordinary Men*, 53–54.

7. Ibid., 2, 55–56.

8. Ibid., 2, 57.

9. Ibid., 121–132, 138–142.

10. Browning, *Ordinary Men*, 2, 170–171. Goldhagen has identified seven other police battalions and another armed unit in which officers informed men that they would not be punished for refusing to kill. Goldhagen, *Hitler's Willing Executioners*, 278. Edward Westermann challenges the applicability of Milgram's results to the police battalions, but his objections do not apply as well to the middle-aged conscripts as they do to the larger number of volunteers, and deference to authority figures need not supply a complete explanation for the killers' actions, since several other factors—anti-Semitism, the polarizing wartime context, conformity to a peer group, and adaptation to a role—were also at work. Westermann, *Hitler's Police Battalions*, 234–235.

11. Stanley Milgram, *Obedience to Authority: An Experimental View* (New York: Harper and Row, 1974).

12. Browning, *Ordinary Men*, 171–176.

13. Bilton and Sim, *Four Hours*, 74–85, 92–93. *On the American combat experience in Vietnam:* see Christian G. Appy, *Working-Class War: American Combat Soldiers and Vietnam* (Chapel Hill: University of North Carolina Press, 1993), 145–190.

14. Bilton and Sim, *Four Hours*, 92.

15. The US military's indiscriminate use of artillery strikes and aerial bombardment is believed to have cost the lives of between 400,000 and 550,000 Vietnamese civilians during the years 1965 to 1974. Appy, *Working-Class War*, 202–204; Bilton and Sim, *Four Hours*, 98–101.

16. Herbert C. Kelman and V. Lee Hamilton, *Crimes of Obedience: Toward a Social Psychology of Authority and Responsibility* (New Haven, CT: Yale University Press, 1989), 169–173.

17. Kelman and Hamilton formulate their conclusions somewhat more cautiously: "a large proportion of the U.S. population at the time viewed the killing of civilians under orders to be an appropriate and normatively expected response." Ibid., 174. A full 90 percent of respondents had heard of Calley's trial. Ibid., 172.

18. Rüdiger Overmans, *Deutsche militärische Verluste im Zweiten Weltkrieg* (Munich: R. Oldenbourg, 1999).

19. Kelman and Hamilton, *Crimes of Obedience*, 91, 104–107; Browning, *Ordinary Men*, 66, 72, 185, 215–216. Browning also found that a group of Silesian policemen, who could live at home during the time in which they were rounding up Jews and deporting them to Auschwitz, became brutalized much more slowly than men in units that operated far from home. Christopher R. Browning, *Nazi Policy, Jewish Workers, German Killers* (New York: Cambridge University Press, 2000), 149–150.

On men's motivation in combat: James M. McPherson, *For Cause and Comrades: Why Men Fought in the Civil War* (New York: Oxford University Press, 1997), esp. 77–89; Edward Shils and Morris Janowitz, "Cohesion and Disintegration in the Wehrmacht in World War II," *Public Opinion Quarterly* 12 (1948): 280–315.

20. Bilton and Sim, *Four Hours*, 18–19.

21. For a full-length discussion, see Philip Zimbardo, *The Lucifer Effect: Understanding How Good People Turn Evil* (New York: Random House, 2007); Browning, *Ordinary Men*, 167; Craig Haney, Curtis Banks, and Philip Zimbardo, "Interpersonal Dynamics in a Simulated Prison," *International Journal of Criminology and Penology* 1 (1983): 69–97.

22. Zimbardo, quoted in Browning, *Ordinary Men*, 168.

23. Browning, *Ordinary Men*, 168, 215–216. Other examples of Germans who were troubled by the murder of Jews in which they participated are presented in Browning, "Ordinary Germans or Ordinary Men? A Reply to the Critics,"

in Michael Berenbaum and Abraham J. Peck, eds., *The Holocaust and History: The Known, the Unknown, the Disputed, and the Reexamined* (Bloomington: Indiana University Press, 1998), 260–261. Browning found a similar tripartite division, in roughly the same percentages, in two other small groups of perpetrators he has studied. Browning, *Nazi Policy, Jewish Workers, German Killers*, 166–167. *On Höss:* Rudolph [Rudolf] Höss, *Death Dealer: The Memoirs of the SS Kommandant in Auschwitz*, ed. Steven Paskuly, fwd. Primo Levi, trans. Andrew Pollinger (New York: Da Capo Press, 1996), 88–89.

24. Browning, *Ordinary Men*, 176–184.

CHAPTER 12

1. Quoted in Peter Longerich, *"Davon haben wir nichts gewusst!" Die Deutschen und die Judenverfolgung, 1933–1945* (Munich: Siedler, 2006), 269.

2. The most thorough treatment of the Germans' knowledge is Bernward Dörner, *Die Deutschen und der Holocaust: Was niemand wissen wollte, aber jeder wissen konnte* (Berlin: Propyläen, 2007). At 608 he summarizes his claim for the extent of Germans' knowledge: "No later than the summer of 1943, the murder of the Jews had become a fact for almost all Germans." In contrast, Peter Fritzsche offers the interesting thesis that news of the shootings in the East "contained" knowledge of the Holocaust, leading Germans to see the persecution of the Jews as a set of isolated pogroms, rather than as a program of systematic extermination. However, he does not take the postwar surveys (see below) into account, nor does he cite Dörner, which may have appeared only after Fritzsche's work was in press. In particular, Fritzsche does not consider the effect of the regime's frequent declarations (discussed below) that it was "annihilating" or "exterminating" the Jewish people. Peter Fritzsche, *Life and Death in Nazi Germany* (Cambridge, MA: Harvard University Press, 2008), 264.

3. Bernward Dörner, *Die Deutschen und der Holocaust*, 93–94, 99–100, 102–103. Rüdiger Overmans puts the total number of men in all branches of service at 18.2 million, in his *Deutsche militärische Verluste im Zweiten Weltkrieg* (Munich: R. Oldenbourg, 1999).

In early October 1941 the commander of the 707th Infantry Division decided on his own initiative to murder Jews in the division's area of operations in Belorussia. In short order his men shot 19,000 people. Saul Friedländer, "The Wehrmacht, German Society, and the Knowledge of the Mass Extermination of the Jews," in Omer Bartov, Atina Grossmann, and Mary Nolan, eds., *Crimes of War: Guilt and Denial in the Twentieth Century* (New York: New Press, 2002), 20.

On "execution tourism": Ernst Klee, Willi Dressen, and Volker Riess, eds., *"The Good Old Days": The Holocaust as Seen by Its Perpetrators and Bystanders*, trans. Deborah Burnstone (Old Saybrook, CT: Konecky and Konecky, 1991), 126; order of September 24, 1941, by General von Rundstedt, Army Group South, in Yitzhak Arad, Israel Gutman, and Abraham Margaliot, eds., *Documents on the Holocaust*, 8th ed. (Lincoln: University of Nebraska Press, 1999), 388; Ulrich

Herbert, "Extermination Policy: New Answers and Questions About the History of the 'Holocaust' in German Historiography," in *National Socialist Extermination Policies: Contemporary German Perspectives and Controversies* (New York: Berghahn Books, 2000), 36.

4. *On numbers of soldiers participating:* Friedländer, "Wehrmacht, German Society, and Knowledge," 26. Bernward Dörner argues persuasively that "no later than the summer of 1943, it was clear to *every* soldier that hundreds of thousands of Jews must already have been murdered." Dörner, *Die Deutschen und der Holocaust,* 112 (emphasis added). Sönke Neitzel and Harald Welzer reach a similar conclusion in *Soldaten: On Fighting, Killing, and Dying. The Secret Transcripts of German POWs,* trans. Jefferson Chase (New York: Knopf, 2012), 99–119. *On the High Command acknowledging the killing:* Dörner, *Die Deutschen und der Holocaust,* 106–107, 108–109, using the term *Ausrottung.*

5. *On letters:* Longerich, *"Davon haben wir nichts gewusst!"* 224–225. *On soldiers who talked of the killings while on leave:* Dörner, *Die Deutschen und der Holocaust,* 93–114; Neitzel and Welzer, *Soldaten,* 101, 346–347.

6. Estimates of how many Germans listened to the BBC range between 1 million and 10 million, although, as Dörner points out, the latter figure is surely too high, given that there were only about 15 million radio sets in Germany. Dörner settles on an estimate of 3 million. Dörner, *Die Deutschen und der Holocaust,* 197, n. 414. Postwar surveys indicated that about half the population listened to enemy broadcasts at least once during the war, but the number who listened regularly must have been much smaller. Longerich, *"Davon haben wir nichts gewusst!"* 240 n. 152. The BBC enjoyed a reputation for "especial reliability" among Germans. Dörner, *Die Deutschen und der Holocaust,* 194. *On specificity of information in the broadcasts:* ibid., 202–209; Eric A. Johnson, *Nazi Terror: The Gestapo, Jews, and Ordinary Germans* (New York: Basic Books, 1999), 441–450.

7. Dörner, *Die Deutschen und der Holocaust,* 235–242; Longerich, *"Davon haben wir nichts gewusst!"* 303.

8. Dörner, *Die Deutschen und der Holocaust,* 242, 244.

9. Ibid., 243–244.

10. Wolf Gruner, "Von der Kollektivausweisung zur Deportation der Juden aus Deutschland (1938–1945): Neue Perspektiven und Dokumente," in Birthe Kundrus and Beate Meyer, eds., *Die Deportation der Juden aus Deutschland: Pläne, Praxis, Reaktionen, 1938–1945* (Göttingen: Wallstein, 2004), 21–62, esp. 51, 57–58. On January 15, 1945, Himmler decreed that all Jews in mixed marriages should be deported, but many, including the celebrated diarist Victor Klemperer, escaped amid the chaotic conditions in the last months of the war.

11. Longerich, *"Davon haben wir nichts gewusst!"* 184–185, 202–204. David Bankier reports that some newspapers, in late 1941, announced that the Jews would be gone from Germany by April 1942. However, he does not name the newspapers, citing only the Jewish Telegraph Agency and a file in the British

Public Records Office. David Bankier, *The Germans and the Final Solution: Public Opinion Under Nazism* (Cambridge, MA: Blackwell, 1992), 131.

On the scramble for Jews' possessions and apartments: Frank Bajohr, "Über die Entwicklung eines schlechten Gewissens: Die deutsche Bevölkerung und die Deportationen, 1941–1945," in Birthe Kundrus and Beate Meyer, eds., *Deportation der Juden aus Deutschland: Pläne, Praxis, Reaktionen, 1938–1945* (Göttingen: Wallstein, 2004), 183, 189; Herbert, "Extermination Policy," 28; Friedländer, "Wehrmacht, German Society, and Knowledge," 27–28; Longerich, *"Davon haben wir nichts gewusst!"* 199, citing Frank Bajohr, *Die "Arisierung" in Hamburg: Die Verdrängung der jüdischen Unternehmer, 1933–1945* (Hamburg: Christians, 1997), 334.

12. Longerich, *"Davon haben wir nichts gewusst!"* 177, 199–200; Saul Friedländer, *Nazi Germany and the Jews, 1933–1945*, vol. 2, *The Years of Extermination* (New York: HarperCollins, 2007), 261–262, 267. One thousand Berlin Jews who arrived at Riga on November 30, 1941, were also shot that day.

13. Christian Goeschel, "Suicides of Jews in the Third Reich," *German History* 25, no. 1 (2007): 34, citing Konrad Kwiet and Helmut Eschwege, *Selbstbehauptung und Widerstand: Deutsche Juden im Kampf um Existenz und Menschenwürde, 1933–1945* (Hamburg: Christians, 1984), 199; Jeremy Noakes and Geoffrey Pridham, eds., *Nazism 1919–1945: A Documentary Reader*, vol. 2, *State, Economy and Society, 1933–1939* (Exeter: University of Exeter Press, 1984), 549; World Health Organization, "Suicide Rates (per 100,000), by Gender, USA, 1950–2005," "Suicide Rates (per 100,000), by Gender and Age, USA, 2005," and "Number of Suicides by Age Group and Gender, United States of America, 2005," www.who.int/mental_health/media/unitstates.pdf, accessed October 21, 2013. The rate for American males in 2005 was 17.7 per year per 100,000 males. The rate for American females, keeping with a pattern consistent across many cultures, was much lower, 4.5 per 100,000.

14. Beate Kosmala, "Zwischen Ahnen und Wissen: Flucht vor der Deportation (1941–1943)," in Birthe Kundrus and Beate Meyer, eds., *Deportation der Juden aus Deutschland: Pläne, Praxis, Reaktionen, 1938–1945* (Göttingen: Wallstein, 2004), 141–142; Friedländer, *Years of Extermination*, 308.

15. For example, Inge Deutschkron, cited in Kershaw, *Hitler, the Germans, and the Final Solution* (New Haven, CT: Yale University Press, 2008), 224. Especially notable is Victor Klemperer's diary, published as *I Will Bear Witness: A Diary of the Nazi Years*, trans. Martin Chalmers, 2 vols. (New York: Random House, 1998–1999).

16. Fritzsche, *Life and Death in Nazi Germany*, 264. "Open secret" is a formulation I take from Frank Bajohr and Dieter Pohl, *Der Holocaust als offenes Geheimnis: Die Deutschen, die NS-Führung und die Alliierten* (Munich: Beck, 2006), and Longerich, *"Davon haben wir nichts gewusst!,"* esp. 201–262.

17. Dörner, *Die Deutschen und der Holocaust*, 135–193, esp. 137–141; Ian Kershaw, *Hitler*, vol. 2, *1936–1945: Nemesis* (New York: W. W. Norton, 2000),

153. "Exterminating" and "annihilating" translate *ausrotten* and *vernichten*, respectively. The apt characterization of these statements as "death threats" is Dörner's.

18. Saul Friedländer even argues that once the United States entered the war in December 1941, making it truly a world war, Hitler needed to fulfill his prophecy by ordering the murder of all Jews in Europe. Friedländer, *Years of Extermination*, 287; Dörner, *Die Deutschen und der Holocaust*, 159–160. The BBC's German Service actually claimed that the Nazi regime had murdered the Jews in order to create this shared fear of retribution. Johnson, *Nazi Terror*, 447. In November 1943, Goebbels wrote, in *Das Reich* (circulation 1.4 million): "As for us, we've burned our bridges behind us. We can't go back, and we don't want to anymore. We will either go down in history as the greatest statesmen or the greatest criminals." Fritzsche, *Life and Death in Nazi Germany*, 286. The regime's propaganda, especially after Stalingrad, frequently stoked fears of the "Jewish revenge" that would follow a defeat. Longerich, *"Davon haben wir nichts gewusst!"* 263–296, 326.

19. Dörner, *Die Deutschen und der Holocaust*, 423–424.

20. Longerich, *"Davon haben wir nichts gewusst!"* 160–161. The most thorough treatment of this topic is Jeffrey Herf, *The Jewish Enemy: Nazi Propaganda During World War II and the Holocaust* (Cambridge, MA: Harvard University Press, 2006).

21. Herf, *Jewish Enemy*, 8–15, 267, 274.

22. Ibid., 113; Dörner, *Die Deutschen und der Holocaust*, 426–427; Longerich, *"Davon haben wir nichts gewusst!"* 168–169, 267–281.

23. Herf, *Jewish Enemy*, 143–144. It is unclear whether the emphasis is Herf's or was present in the written text of Hitler's speech. Longerich, *"Davon haben wir nichts gewusst!"* 267–281.

24. Kershaw, *Hitler, the Germans, and the Final Solution*, 142–144, 224–225.

25. See the interesting discussion of repression in Dörner, *Die Deutschen und der Holocaust*, 458. On Kardorff: Bankier, *Germans and the Final Solution*, 103; Longerich, *"Davon haben wir nichts gewusst!"* 229.

26. Longerich, *"Davon haben wir nichts gewusst!"* 230–232; David Bankier concludes that few Germans could imagine the magnitude of the murder program, which was "inconceivable." Bankier, *Germans and the Final Solution*, 115.

27. Longerich, *"Davon haben wir nichts gewusst!"* 325.

28. The 1961 and 1988 surveys were conducted in West Germany, and the 1991 survey only of people living on the territory of the former West Germany (East and West Germany were united in 1990). The 1995 and 1996 surveys, telephone polls of a sample taken from all parts of united Germany, suffer from some problems of representativeness, since many inhabitants of the former East Germany did not have telephones. Karl-Heinz Reuband, "Gerüchte und Kenntnisse vom Holocaust in der deutschen Gesellschaft vor Ende des Krieges: Eine Bestandsaufnahme auf der Basis von Bevölkerungsumfragen," *Jahrbuch für Antisemitismusforschung* 9 (2000): 196–233, esp. 222.

29. The original questions in German were as follows: "Wann haben Sie zum allerersten Mal etwas von der Massenvernichtung gehört? Ich meine nicht Einzelheiten, sondern ganz allgemein: daß es überhaupt vorkam?" "Wann haben Sie von den Verbrechen der Nazis erfahren?" "Haben Sie selbst etwas mitbekommen, haben Sie damals von anderen etwas darüber gehört oder haben Sie erst nach dem Krieg davon erfahren?" Ibid., 205.

30. Ibid., 222; Eric A. Johnson and Karl-Heinz Reuband, *What We Knew: Terror, Mass Murder, and Everyday Life in Nazi Germany. An Oral History* (New York: Basic Books, 2005), 328, 369–372.

Only the 1991 poll gave a result outside of this narrow range—40 percent—but this may only reflect an error in the way the poll was conducted. Reuband, "Gerüchte und Kenntnisse vom Holocaust," 207. This remarkable consistency across six polls between 1961 and 2000 provides considerable assurance that the Germans who were surveyed did not project their postwar knowledge of the Holocaust back into the wartime years. If they had a tendency to do so, the percentage of those who answered yes would surely have risen from one poll to the next. Ibid.

Because the survey questions were broadly formulated, some respondents might have been thinking of the prewar persecution of German Jews, or of the confinement of political prisoners in concentration camps, when they admitted to knowing about mass murder, which could indicate that the percentage who actually knew was somewhat less than one-third of the population. Ibid., 220. However, this fraction (of a bit less than a third) must stand as only a *minimum* estimate of the percentage of Germans who knew, because many survey respondents surely lied when they said they had not known, while others may have forgotten, since the first survey was taken sixteen years after the war ended.

Various studies show mixed results on the quality of long-term memory. Roger Tourangeau, Lance J. Rips, and Kenneth Rasinski, eds., *The Psychology of Survey Response* (New York: Cambridge University Press, 2000), shows a clear deterioration in memory over time, but surprisingly good memory in some categories (for example, for names of school classmates, at 83–85). A longitudinal study of political studies among women who had attended Bennington College found a high degree of agreement between earlier political attitudes and the way they were recalled, but with notable exceptions, especially that 45 percent of the women who had described themselves as Republicans in 1960 recalled having been Democrats at that time, when questioned in 1984. Duane F. Alwin, Ronald L. Cohen, and Theodore Newcomb, *Political Attitudes Over the Life Span: The Bennington Women After Fifty Years* (Madison: University of Wisconsin Press, 1991), 128–131.

31. *On lying:* Tourangeau et al., eds., *Psychology of Survey Response*, 269–275. *On honesty about Nazi affiliation or sympathies:* Reuband, "Gerüchte und Kenntnisse vom Holocaust," 203, based on surveys conducted by the US Strategic Bombing Survey in 1945, as cited in Helen Peck, *Psychological Monographs* 6 (1945), 37ff. Reuband aptly comments that past membership in the Nazi Party

was "very much taboo" (*stark tabuisiert*) in Germany at that time. Karl-Heinz Reuband, "Das NS-Regime zwischen Akzeptanz und Ablehnung: Eine retrospektive Analyse von Bevölkerungseinstellungen im Dritten Reich auf der Basis von Umfragedaten," *Geschichte und Gesellschaft* 32, no. 3 (2006): 315–343.

The more interested in politics the respondents declared themselves to have been, the less likely they were to report having known of the murders. Of respondents with a primary school education (to age fourteen), 30 percent of the "politically interested" admitted knowing, while 35 percent of the "politically uninterested" reported knowledge; similarly, among those whose education went beyond primary school, 39 percent of the "politically interested" reported knowledge, while 44 percent of the "politically uninterested" said they knew. This pattern is the exact opposite of what one would normally expect: those who were more interested in politics should have been paying closer attention to what the government was doing. Reuband speculates that those who were politically engaged felt more responsibility for the government's actions, hence more shame over their own knowledge of the Holocaust, and a greater need to conceal their knowledge from the interviewers conducting the survey. Reuband, "Gerüchte und Kenntnisse vom Holocaust," 212–213.

32. Kershaw, *Hitler, the Germans, and the Final Solution*, 229. Otto Dov Kulka, who has edited a collection of opinion reports, finds that during the war years, "the dominant line is almost total silence regarding the Jews." Otto Dov Kulka, "The German Population and the Jews: State of Research and New Perspectives," in David Bankier, ed., *Probing the Depths of German Antisemitism: German Society and the Persecution of the Jews, 1933–1941* (New York: Berghahn Books, 2000), 274; Otto Dov Kulka and Eberhard Jäckel, eds., *Die Juden in den geheimen NS-Stimmungsberichten, 1933–1945* (Düsseldorf: Droste, 2004).

33. *On fear of the Gestapo generally*: Robert Gellately, *The Gestapo and German Society: Enforcing Racial Policy, 1933–1945* (New York: Oxford University Press), 129; Johnson and Reuband, *What We Knew*, 348–349. Johnson and Reuband draw the opposite conclusion: they are more impressed by the fact that most respondents did not recall knowing anyone personally who had had an encounter with the Gestapo.

In Würzburg and Lower Franconia, the Gestapo investigated people for shaking the hands of longtime Jewish friends on the street, for stating a wish to continue using a Jewish family doctor, for saying that Jewish businesses sold goods at better prices, and for other equally innocuous "offenses." Gellately, *Gestapo and German Society*, 160, 174–175, 207–210.

On the level of criticism of government policy: Kulka, "German Population and the Jews," 274; Ian Kershaw, *Popular Opinion and Political Dissent in the Third Reich: Bavaria, 1933–1945* (New York: Oxford University Press, 1983), 283–303.

34. Kershaw, *Hitler, the Germans, and the Final Solution*, 226–227; Michael Müller-Claudius, *Der Antisemitismus und das deutsche Verhängnis* (Frankfurt:

J. Knecht, 1948), 166ff. Cf. Longerich, *"Davon haben wir nichts gewusst!"* 234–235. Some historians argue that Germans said so little about the Holocaust because they supported the regime's murderous policy (e.g., Kulka, "German Population and the Jews," 277). The only documentary evidence offered in support of this conclusion comes in the form of an opinion poll conducted in Germany in October 1945 (ibid., 279). However, as Sarah Gordon has pointed out, these surveys conducted by the American occupying forces are fraught with methodological problems. One survey suggests that less than 1 percent of the population approved of Nazi policy toward the Jews. Sarah Gordon, *Hitler, Germans, and the "Jewish Question"* (Princeton, NJ: Princeton University Press, 1984), 197–206. Another problem with Kulka's thesis is that if Germans really supported the regime's policy, they probably would have frequently blamed Jews for their own wartime suffering, as the government encouraged them to do. There are a few examples of such comments in Kulka and Eberhard Jäckel's exhaustive compilation of opinion reports concerning the Jews, but the number of these is insignificant measured against the total volume of the regime's reports on the public mood. Here is a near-complete list of reports containing such comments blaming Jews for the war and its consequences: Kulka and Jäckel, eds., *Die Juden in den geheimen NS-Stimmungsberichten*, documents numbered 3277, 3279, 3299, 3361, 3401, 3437, 3439, 3444, 3482, 3509, 3581, 3582, 3587, 3588, 3610, 3627, 3628, 3634, 3708, 3718, 3724, 3726. Many of these documents appear only on the CD-ROM that accompanies the book, and not in the printed volume. Müller-Claudius's survey also tends to disprove Kulka's thesis. If only three out of sixty-one committed Nazis expressed approval of the murders, it is difficult to see how the general population, most of whom were not party members, could have supported the regime's policy.

In contrast, Peter Longerich contends that most Germans felt "indignation" (*Unwille*) at the regime's murder of Jews, but there is scant evidence for this conclusion beyond the unpersuasive argument that if Germans had not strongly objected to the genocide, the government would not have mounted such a massive anti-Semitic propaganda campaign. Longerich, *"Davon haben wir nichts gewusst!"* 52–53, 320. The only solid evidence supporting Longerich's position is the strongly negative reaction Germans displayed toward the introduction of the yellow star in September 1941. David Bankier argues that Germans, while accepting anti-Jewish policy in the abstract, for a brief period reacted negatively to this tangible act of cruelty toward concrete, living individuals. Bankier, *Germans and the Final Solution*, 128–129. Longerich also argues, even more implausibly, that the regime's internal reports were not intended to give the government an accurate picture of public opinion, but rather to "artificially create a homogeneous public mood" and document the public's support of the regime. Leaving aside the problem of how confidential reports could "create" a "public mood," Kershaw's research defeats this argument by showing how much dissent, from a socioeconomically fractured public that was clearly not "homogeneous," was reflected in the official reports. See Longerich, *"Davon haben wir nichts gewusst!"* 42–46, and Kershaw, *Popular Opinion and Political Dissent*, 281–330, 372–373.

35. *On new research on dissent:* Nathan Stoltzfus, *Coercion and Compromise*, forthcoming, cited with the author's permission. *On intermarried Jews:* Stoltzfus, *Resistance of the Heart: Intermarriage and the Rosenstrasse Protest in Nazi Germany* (New York: W. W. Norton, 1996).

36. Samantha Power, *"A Problem from Hell": America and the Age of Genocide* (New York: Basic Books, 2002), 329–389, esp. 366, 378ff.

37. Müller-Claudius, *Der Antisemitismus und das deutsche Verhängnis*, 167–168. "I want [to live in] normal conditions" translates "Ich will geordnete Verhältnisse." "An all-powerful government" translates "einen totalen Staat."

38. Erwin Staub, *The Roots of Evil: The Origins of Genocide and Other Group Violence* (New York: Cambridge University Press, 1989), 87; Zygmunt Bauman, *Modernity and the Holocaust* (Ithaca, NY: Cornell University Press, 1989), 155.

39. Helen Fein defines the universe of obligation as "the circle of people with reciprocal obligations to protect each other whose bonds arise from their relation to a deity or sacred source of authority." Helen Fein, *Accounting for Genocide: National Responses and Jewish Victimization During the Holocaust* (Chicago: University of Chicago Press, 1984), 4, quoted in Staub, *Roots of Evil*, 26.

CONCLUSION

1. In addition to the examples adduced above, Olaf Blaschke argues that conflict between Protestants and Catholics was "certainly one of the most prominent causes of the escalation of antisemitism," because unity of Christians against Jews, like appeals to racism, offered a way to ease or surmount confessional tensions. Olaf Blaschke, *Victims or Offenders? German Jews and the Causes of Modern Catholic Antisemitism* (Lincoln: University of Nebraska Press, 2009), 41–51.

2. *On the use of anti-Semitism and the exclusion of Jews to define and strengthen the Nazis' idealized harmonious "racial community" (Volksgemeinschaft):* see, for example, Peter Longerich, *Holocaust: The Nazi Persecution and Murder of the Jews* (New York: Oxford University Press, 2010), 76–80. See also the fascinating and innovative arguments in Thomas Kühne, *Belonging and Genocide: Hitler's Community, 1918–1945* (New Haven, CT: Yale University Press, 2010).

3. For an overview of the institutions participating in the extermination program, see Raul Hilberg, *The Destruction of the European Jews*, 3rd ed., 3 vols. (New Haven, CT: Yale University Press, 2003), 1:49–59.

On the military: Jürgen Förster, "Complicity or Entanglement? Wehrmacht, War and Holocaust," in Michael Berenbaum and Abraham J. Peck, eds., *The Holocaust and History: The Known, the Unknown, the Disputed, and the Reexamined* (Bloomington: Indiana University Press, 1998), 266–283; Longerich, *Holocaust*, 246–247; Sönke Neitzel and Harald Welzer, *Soldaten: On Fighting,*

Killing, and Dying. The Secret WWII Transcripts of German POWs, trans. Jefferson Chase (New York: Knopf, 2012), 99–119.

On the civil service: Mary Fulbrook, *A Small Town Near Auschwitz: Ordinary Nazis and the Holocaust* (New York: Oxford University Press, 2012), esp. 9, 66–67, 343–356; Hilberg, *Destruction of the European Jews*, 3:1084–1104; Hans Mommsen, "The Civil Service and the Implementation of the Holocaust: From Passive to Active Complicity," in Michael Berenbaum and Abraham J. Peck, eds., *The Holocaust and History: The Known, the Unknown, the Disputed, and the Reexamined* (Bloomington: Indiana University Press, 1998), 219–227.

On big business: see especially the thematically rich essay by Peter Hayes, "State Policy and Corporate Involvement in the Holocaust," in Michael Berenbaum and Abraham J. Peck, eds., *The Holocaust and History: The Known, the Unknown, the Disputed, and the Reexamined* (Bloomington: Indiana University Press, 1998), 197–218; Peter Hayes, *Industry and Ideology: IG Farben in the Nazi Era* (New York: Cambridge University Press, 1987), esp. 325–376.

4. *On the interchangeability of perpetrators with those who were not chosen to participate:* Hilberg, *Destruction of the European Jews*, 1084–1085. The polls suggest that roughly 40 percent of Germans with higher education (as compared to around a third of those with schooling only to the age of fourteen) had some knowledge of the Holocaust. Karl-Heinz Reuband, "Gerüchte und Kenntnisse vom Holocaust in der deutschen Gesellschaft vor Ende des Krieges: Eine Bestandsaufnahme auf der Basis von Bevölkerungsumfragen," in *Jahrbuch für Antisemitismusforschung* 9 (2000): 212–223, 218.

5. *On anti-Semitism in Nazi campaign propaganda:* Ian Kershaw, *Hitler*, vol. 1, *1889–1936: Hubris* (New York: W. W. Norton, 1999), 410. More generally, Christopher R. Browning finds an "impressive" degree of consensus among leading scholars that anti-Semitism was "not a major factor in attracting support for Hitler and the Nazis." Christopher R. Browning, "Ordinary Germans or Ordinary Men? A Reply to the Critics," in Michael Berenbaum and Abraham J. Peck, eds., *The Holocaust and History: The Known, the Unknown, the Disputed, and the Reexamined* (Bloomington: Indiana University Press, 1998), 253.

INDEX

263